# SCHOOL
# ENVIRONMENT
## IN AFRICA
## AND ASIA PACIFIC

authorHOUSE®

AuthorHouse™
1663 Liberty Drive
Bloomington, IN 47403
www.authorhouse.com
Phone: 1 (800) 839-8640

Published by AuthorHouse  09/07/2018

ISBN: 978-1-5462-5799-8 (sc)
ISBN: 978-1-5462-5798-1 (e)

Library of Congress Control Number: 2018910358

Print information available on the last page.

Any people depicted in stock imagery provided by Getty Images are models,
and such images are being used for illustrative purposes only.
Certain stock imagery © Getty Images.

This book is printed on acid-free paper.

# ABOUT THE EDITORS

**Dr. Princewill I. Egwuasi** NCE, BA Ed. (English), M.Ed, Ph.D (Educational Management and Planning), is of the University of Uyo, Uyo, Nigeria. He is currently the Business Editor of three reputable journals, an international reviewer to several global online and print journals. His areas of specialization are English Education and Educational Management and Planning. A recipient of the Nigerian Merit Gold Award for Productivity 2011 and Nigerian Hall of Fame Awards 2013, Dr. Egwuasi has over 40 publications in both national and international journals. He is the initiator of the book on School Environment in Nigeria and the Philippines, published in 2015 and the 2nd edition, School Environment in Nigeria, Ghana and the Philippines published in 2017. Dr. Egwuasi belongs to several academic professional bodies and is currently serving as the Vice Chairman, World Educators Forum.

**Dr. Jake M. Laguador** is currently the director, Research and Statistics Center, Lyceum of the Philippines University, Batangas City, Philippines and *Research Journal Editor,* Lyceum Engineering Research Journal, Lyceum of the Philippines University. He is also the Associate Editor of Asia Pacific Journal of Education, Arts and Science. He has published several papers in reputable international journals.

**Dr. Ngozika A. Oleforo** is currently a Senior Lecturer in the Department of Curriculum Studies, Educational Management and Planning, University of Uyo. An astute scholar who has published several journal articles in referred journals, both in Nigeria and the Overseas. She has received several awards due to her contribution in human resources development.

**Dr. Stella Nwosu** is a renowned scholar with the Institute of Education and Professional Development, University of Uyo, Uyo, Nigeria. She is widely published and has attended several international and national conferences where she has presented topical issues bothering the field of education.

**Dr. Rania Khalil** is the Research Coordinator for the Faculty of Arts and Humanities, British University, Egypt. She has also served as International Office University Consultant and Quality Assurance Coordinator. Dr. Khalil was one time Online Courses University Coordinator (5 faculties). She is an Assistant Professor of English Literature and Language.

**Sudhanshu Kumar Sultania** is a Senior Research Fellow in the Discipline of Sociology, School of Social Sciences, Indira Gandhi National Open University (IGNOU), New Delhi.

# PREFACE

This publication on *School Environment in Africa and Asia Pacific* is a continuation of our maiden and second publications on *School Environment in Nigeria and the Philippines*, published in February, 2015 and *School Environment in Nigeria, Ghana and the Philippines* published in March, 2017. The philosophy being that since there is a shift from globalization to internationalization and to cross-border education, there is the urgent need to revisit some topical issues in our school environment towards the realization of an internationalized, qualitative and cross-border teaching and learning, using Information and Communication Technology. It is therefore, based on this, that the Dakar framework for action (UNESCO, 2000) stipulates the use of ICT as one of the major strategies to attain Education For All (EFA) goals. The focus on Africa and Asia Pacific in this edition is a conviction of the strategic positions of the continents' drive for a technologically induced education, not only as fast and dynamic developing economies in the world, but ones with enviable and transformational education cultures. In this edition, all the articles are theoretically, conceptually and/or empirically assembled to address diverse but all-important facets of the school environment in Africa and Asia Pacific, with a view of proffering solutions, suggestions and recommendations to several questions that may have arisen over time, not to ignore the contributions to existing knowledge and literature of the academia. The articles were also subjected to international peer reviews and went through insightful scrutiny for standardization. It is the utmost belief of the editors, that this book would become a springboard to other continents of the world that sincerely require the best in their educational system, hence, the editors welcome more collaborations, especially from Australia and South America continents.

***Editors***

# ACKNOWLEDGMENT

The production of this academic project would not have been possible without the benevolence of the Almighty God, through whose grace, wisdom was bestowed on the initiator of the project, Dr. Princewill I. Egwuasi, of the Department of Curriculum Studies, Educational Management and Planning, University of Uyo, Nigeria, to visualize this work. From the maiden edition to the present, several individuals and institutions shall be continually acknowledged for their roles in making the book a reality. The Lyceum of the Philippines University, Batangas-City, Philippines, South Asia, is worthy of recognition. Through its Dean, Postgraduate School, Dr. Jake M. Laguador, the university has continued to support this vision. We are also indebted to Dr. Rania Khalil of British University, Egypt and Sudhanshu Kumar Sultania of Indira Gandhi National Open University (IGNOU), New Delhi for accepting to collaborate with us and being part of the editors. To Dr. Ngozika A. Oleforo and Dr. Stella Nwosu of the University of Uyo, Uyo, Nigeria, we say thank you for contributing to the realization of this third edition. Finally, the Book Coordinator is appreciative of all the efforts of the chapter contributors to this publication and wishes to thank them immensely for believing in our commitment and genuine dedication to this course. Not forgetting the unquantifiable expertise of Princess Joan I. Egwuasi, CNA, who designed the book. At this point, we state categorically that the views and findings as expressed in this book are strictly those of the authors.

**Princewill I. Egwuasi** *Ph.D*
***Book Coordinator***

# LIST OF CONTRIBUTORS

**Princewill. I. Egwuasi,** *Ph.D*
Department of Curriculum Studies,
Educational Management and Planning
University of Uyo, Uyo, Nigeria

**Gertrude Archibong** *Ph.D*
Department of Educational Foundations, Guidance and Counseling
University of Uyo,Uyo
Nigeria

**Mercy U. Etteh**
Department of Curriculum Studies,
Educational Management and Planning
University of Uyo, Uyo, Nigeria
Nigeria

**Rania R. Khalil** *Ph.D*
Research Coordinator
Faculty of Arts and Humanities, The British University in Egypt (BUE)
El Sherouk City, Suez Desert Road, Cairo 11837, Egypt

**Sa'adatu M. Abubakar**
Department of Science Education
Faculty of Technology Education
Abubakar Tafawa Balewa University, Bauchi
Nigeria

**Ekaette E. Iroegbu**
Department of Curriculum Studies,
Educational Management and Planning,
Faculty of Education
University of Uyo, Uyo
Nigeria

**Maria E. Maxwell**
Department of Curriculum Studies,
Educational Management and Planning
Faculty of Education
University of Uyo, Uyo
Nigeria

**Inimbom I. Edet**
Department of Curriculum Studies,
Educational Management and Planning
Faculty of Education
University of Uyo, Uyo
Nigeria

**Umar A. Abubakar**
Department of Library and Information Science,
Abubakar Tafawa Balewa University, Bauchi,
Nigeria

**Professor Victor N. Nwachukwu**
Department of Library and Information Science
University of Nigeria, Nsukka
Nigeria

**Jake M. Laguador** *PhD*
Lyceum of the Philippines University,
Batangas City,
Philippines

**Agbegbedia O. Anthony** *Ph.D*
Achievers University, Owo
Nigeria.

**Joy O. Omaga**
Department of Science Education,
Abubakar Tafawa Balewa University, Bauchi
Nigeria

**Mangut Mankilik**
Department of Science and Technology Education,
University of Jos, Jos
Nigeria

**Bala S. Musa**
Department of Science Education,
Abubakar Tafawa Balewa University, Bauchi.

**Binta Sani** *Ph.D*
School of Technology
Kano State Polytechnic, Kano
Nigeria

**Ngozika. A. Oleforo,** *PhD*
Department of Curriculum Studies,
Educational Management and Planning
University of Uyo, Uyo
Nigeria

**Anietie K. Onyenso**
Department of Curriculum Studies,
Educational Management and Planning,
Faculty of Education
University of Uyo, Uyo,
Nigeria

**Augustine A. Agbaje** *PhD*
Department of Educational Foundations
Guidance and Counselling
University of Uyo, Uyo
Akwa Ibom State
Nigeria

**Sudhanshu K. Sultania,**
Ph.D. Research Scholar & Senior Research Fellow,
Discipline of Sociology, School of Social Sciences
Indira Gandhi National Open University (IGNOU), New Delhi,
India

**Ima M. P. Usoro** *Ph.D*
The Main Library
University of Uyo, Uyo
Nigeria

**Eboro Umoren** *Ph.D*
Department of Educational Technology and Library Science
University of Uyo, Uyo
Nigeria

**Nse Akwang** *Ph.D*
Akwa Ibom State University Library
Ikot Akpaden
Nigeria

**Stella N. Nwosu,** *Ph.D*
Institute of Education and Professional Development
University of Uyo, Uyo
Nigeria

**Utibe-Abasi I. Ekpe**
Institute of Education and Professional Development
University of Uyo, Uyo
Nigeria

**Thelma Ekukinam** *Ph.D*
Department of Educational Technology,
Library and Information Science
University of Uyo, Uyo, Nigeria

# GUIDELINES FOR AUTHORS

The Project Co-ordinator and Board of Editors welcome scholarly articles on *Contemporary Issues in School System of Africa, Asia, Australia and South America* for publication in its 4th edition of a book titled, **"SCHOOL ENVIRONMENT IN FOUR CONTINENTS: AFRICA, ASIA, AUSTRALIA AND SOUTH AMERICA"**. It is an international book with editors from Universities in the four continents, which aims at showcasing their educational systems. Interested contributors are to abide by the following instructions;

- Submit an online copy of manuscript(s), including abstract and references, in MS Word format to dr.princewilluniuyoedu@gmail.com
- The title page of the article should carry the authors' names, status/rank and address, place of work and affiliations.
- Abstract of not more than 250 words.
- Manuscripts are received on the understanding that they are original and unpublished works of the author(s) not considered for publication elsewhere.
- Current APA style of referencing should be maintained.
- Author(s) e-mail addresses and phone numbers should accompany the paper.
- Figures, tables, charts and drawings should be clearly drawn and the position marked in the text.
- Pay a publication fee of $200.00 only.
- All manuscripts should reach the Project Co-ordinator on or before 31st March, 2019.

**Dr. Princewill I. Egwuasi**
**Department of Curriculum Studies**
**Educational Management and Planning**
**University of Uyo, Uyo**
**Akwa Ibom State**
**Nigeria**
**princewilliegwuasi@uniuyo.edu.ng**
**+2348038955075, +2348094454419**

# CONTENTS

## INFORMATION AND COMMUNICATION TECHNOLOGY ISSUES

## QUALITY ASSURANCE ISSUES

## MANAGEMENT ISSUES

ENVIRONMENTAL ISSUES

# INFORMATION AND
# COMMUNICATION
# TECHNOLOGY ISSUES

# 1

# Sustaining E-learning Resources for Entrepreneurial Skills Development: A Counselling Approach

Princewill. I. Egwuasi, Ph.D, Gertrude
Archibong Ph.D & Mercy U. Etteh

## Abstract

*T his paper discusses how to sustain e-learning resources for entrepreneurial skills development using counselling approach. To further drive this stance, the paper looked at the meaning of e-learning resources, entrepreneurship education and made a nexus for better output of the two concepts. The paper also examined the concept of counselling and the benefits that abound in applying counselling techniques in the teaching of entrepreneurship education using the e-learning resources. The recommendation, among others, is that all teachers involved in the use of e-learning resources in the teaching of entrepreneurship courses must be re-trained in order to acquire basic counselling techniques.*

**Keywords:** E-learning Resources, Entrepreneurship, Counselling Approach

## Introduction

One of the major quandaries facing Nigeria is the inability of successive governments to take clear decisions in every difficult situation that has befallen us. It could also be further argued that even when lofty decisions are finally arrived at, it is suicidal to attempt the full implementation of such decisions. From the pre-colonial era to the post-independence, the military to the civilian rule, it is business as usual when it comes to the judicious execution of programmes and policies.

The education sector is the worst hit. This is evident in the fact that the educational system of the Nigerian society has often been ridiculed by programmes and policies that never stand the test of time, irrelevant to the needs of the Nigerian child and inadaptable to the fast changing global trends. However, it is with all fairness that the present researchers observe that one of the few valuable and meaningful programmes introduced to Nigeria's educational curriculum in recent times is the entrepreneurial or entrepreneurship education.

To this end, Suleiman (2006) sees entrepreneurship education as the willingness and ability of an individual to seek for investment opportunities, to establish and run an enterprise successfully. Gibson (2011), in agreement with Suleiman (2006), remarks that it is a process of using private initiatives to transform a business concept into a new venture or to grow and diversify an existing venture and enterprise with high potential. It is based on this philosophy that in 2006, the Federal Government of Nigeria under the leadership of the then president, Chief Olusegun Obasanjo, directed all Nigerian higher education institutions to include Entrepreneurship Education (EED) as a compulsory course for all students with effect from the 2007/2008 academic session, with the main goals to:

- Identify and solve problems using critical and creative thinking;
- Work effectively with others as a proactive team member and cultivate the ability to resolve conflict;
- Organize and manage one's self and one's activities;
- Collect, analyse, organize and critically evaluate information (to make decisions that must be thorough);
- Communicate and negotiate effectively;
- Reflect on experience and explore various strategies for effective learning… learning to learn at all times;
- Become curious leading to readiness to experiment and innovate (being never satisfied with the status quo);
- Consider self-employment as a viable option upon graduation from their institution.

In another development, Odjegba (2005) observes that entrepreneurship is built on vision, focus and determination. It is built on standards management, practices, enabling environment, access to funds, among other things. Odjegba also posits that the challenges of entrepreneurship education in Nigeria which hinders its development include the following:

- Finance;
- Inadequate equipment and technology;
- Economic pressure from parents;
- Entrepreneurship education demands a talented workforce;

- Entrepreneurial attitude;
- Data;
- Research and linkages; and
- Inadequate infrastructural facilities due to inadequacy of facilities,

From the aforementioned, the researchers consider the issue of inadequate infrastructural facilities as very high integral aspect in the proper implementation of the entrepreneurship education process in our educational system.

## Infrastructural Facilities and Entrepreneurship Education

Infrastructural facilities are those physical and non-physical materials and human resources employed in the teaching and learning environments. Olutola (1998) averred that these facilities are the physical resource inputs that make the implementation of school curriculum easy or simple. In fact, these facilities have been found to enhance the achievement of school goals in the long run. Olutola further stated that these facilities could be consumable or non-consumable, while Adeboyeje (1999) grouped them to include:

- the school site
- classrooms
- libraries
- toilets
- cafeteria
- stores
- gardens
- sport fields
- tools
- instructional facilities
- staff and pupils furniture
- teachers and pupils textbooks
- utilities, among others.

It is regrettable though, to observe that little or no proper attention is given to the e-learning resources/materials. Literature upon literature show the negligence of the use of e-learning resource materials in the teaching and learning process in most public schools in Nigeria, especially as it relates to entrepreneurship education. It is more alarming in the tertiary institutions, in that, observations also reveal that factors such as lack of constant power supply, over population in students' enrollment, skilled manpower and maintenance culture, among others, militate against the use of e-learning resources.

Scholars such as Akpa (2007), Suleiman (2006) and Ocho (2005) posit that as a way forward towards the realization of full-blown entrepreneurship education and effective practice of entrepreneurship by youth in tertiary institutions in Nigeria, the youths should be exposed to training in technology (especially new discoveries) from time to time. This would keep them in tune with the trends of the technological world and thus avoid drudgery in their endeavours. They also argue that entrepreneurial teachings have to go beyond the traditional teachings in the classroom. This implies therefore that there should be the usage and more availability of e-learning resources in our institutions of higher learning for the teaching and learning of entrepreneurship education.

## E-learning Resources and Entrepreneurship Education

E-learning denotes the use of Information and Communication Technology (ICT) by both teachers and students. Fry (2000) and Wild, Griggs and Downing (2002), describe e-learning as the delivery of training and education via networked interactivity and distribution technologies. Khan (2005) points out that e-learning has been described in various ways as learning using a number of different technologies and methods for delivery, such as Computer-Based Training (CBT), Internet-Based Training (IBT), Web-Based Instruction (WBI), Advanced Distribution Learning (ADL), Distribution Learning (DL), mobile learning (or m-learning) or remote learning and Learning Management System (LMS). All these are considered as e-learning resources.

According to UK.Essays (2015), the basic e-learning resources include e-textbooks, power point presentations of lectures and electronic notice boards. Al-Ammari and Hamad (2008), lay their stance as they confirm that as students learning in the e-learning system, they interact every time from wherever with different instructional materials which include text, sound, pictures, video, among other things. In addition, the authors also add that learners can also communicate with their teachers and classmates both individually and as a group with the use of message boards, instant message exchanges and video conferencing.

On this premise, Khan (2005) considers that the e-learning system with its resources when analysed can be an inventive approach for delivering learner-centred, interactive and well facilitating learning environment to any place, anyone, anytime, by utilizing the lectures and resources of different digital technologies among other types of learning materials suited for an open, distributed and flexible learning environment. Ubah (2011) states that with the introduction of Information and Communication Technology (ICT) (or e-learning resources) in tertiary entrepreneurship education, emphases are placed on practicable teaching methods that are more useful in vocational and technical training and the experiencing of realities in the course of learning. All these are directed towards the preparation and participation in the occupation of vocational and technical values which is designed to develop understanding, comprehension, attitudes, abilities, skills and work habits, among others. Ubah then outlines the benefits of e-learning resources to entrepreneurship education to include:

- to provide tools to increase students' productivity;
- to engage learners through motivation and challenges;
- to provide opportunities to investigate and build knowledge;
- to promote and encourage active learning and authentic assessment;
- to increase learners' independence;
- to promote collaborative and cooperative learning;
- to tailor learning to the learner; and
- to provide platform to support higher level thinking.

Having all these in mind, Onu (2013) concludes that to effectively teach entrepreneurship education in educational institutions in Nigeria, teachers' competence must be carefully assessed. Teachers, as important role models, must possess requisite knowledge of entrepreneurship to be able to motivate students in developing a positive attitude towards entrepreneurship, focusing on the use of the different e-learning resources (ICT). The question now arises, how can these e-learning resources be sustained in the teaching and learning of entrepreneurship education in Nigeria, now and beyond and to further facilitate the achievement of the Sustainable Development Goals of Nigeria from 2016?

## Sustaining E-learning Resources for Entrepreneurship Education

The concept of sustenance is widely viewed from different facets of human endeavours. To the educationists, sustenance or sustainability could be to simply maintain the existence of a process, idea, philosophy, concepts, programmes and policies, among other things. To this end, Bates (2001) states that the policy issue with respect to e-learning (and its resources) for all countries, rich or poor, is not one of direction but of readiness and scale, in that, e-learning is heavily dependent on appropriate technological infrastructure already being in place for commercial or government reasons. Bates also argues that there is the need for a skilled workforce to support e-learning. Even if the infrastructure is in place, there must be a capacity to supply the necessary trained people to support and sustain e-learning, as well as technically trained people who can install, manage and maintain the necessary infrastructure. Most importantly, the present researchers are of the assertion that teachers and all those who, in one way or the other, use the e-learning and its resources must have basic counselling skills and techniques to be able to utilize, manage and explore the full potentials of e-learning resources for the proper sustenance in the teaching and learning of entrepreneurship education in our institution of higher learning.

## Benefits of the Counselling Approach

Counselling is a help or assistance given by a professionally-trained personnel called the counsellor to an individual or group of people who have challenges, to help them understand themselves and their environment with a view to solving their problems, making necessary adjustments, bringing about right decisions and finally living a satisfactory and productive life now and in the future (Anyamene and Associates, 2009). The later part of this definition, "…productive life…", gives the precedence for the present researchers' call for the inclusion of counselling approach in the sustenance of e-learning resources in the teaching and learning of entrepreneurship education in Nigeria. Thus, the benefits of such inclusion include that:

- Counselling knowledge will equip both the teachers and students with sound management skills of which will facilitate learning of entrepreneurship education through the use of the e-learning resources.
- Counselling knowledge will enable the teachers to examine the instructional resources needs of the learners in the bid to suggesting the right choice for proper understanding of concepts during learning.
- Counselling knowledge will enable the teachers to use the e-learning resources in producing graduates with entrepreneurial skills.
- Counselling knowledge will enable the teachers to develop the spirit of supervision and follow-up on the learners, during and after learning had taken place.

## Conclusions

The world today is shifting from a traditional to a technologically-driven society, where every aspect of life is digitalized. Hence, it is only an economy that is based on this philosophy that would be assured of a future. Therefore, with the introduction of entrepreneurship education into the Nigerian education system, we are in the right direction. But more importantly, this programme must be sustained and this would be achieved through several ways, among which is the application of counselling approach in the usage of e-learning resources in the teaching and learning of entrepreneurship education in all our institutions of higher learning.

## Recommendations

The researchers recommend as follows:

- All teachers involved in the use of e-learning resources in the teaching of entrepreneurship courses must be constantly re-trained in order to acquire basic counselling techniques.
- Institution managements must organize refresher courses for all teachers for the proper usage and management of e-learning resources.
- Government, in its sustainable development goals from 2016, must solve the issue of provision of sufficient funds to higher institutions, for the installation of e-learning resources in academic courses.
- Parents and guidance should encourage their children and wards about the proper utilization of electronic devices in their academic pursuit instead of indulging in otherwise.

## References

Adeboyeje, R. A. (1999). A practical approach to effective utilization and maintenance of physical facilities in secondary schools. In J. O. Fadipe and E. F. Oluchukwu (eds.). *Educational Planning and Administration in Nigeria in the 21st Century,* pp. 88-103.

Akpa, A. (2007). *Challenges of the Nigerian entrepreneur in the 21st century.* A Paper Presented at the Maiden Annual College of Management Sciences Seminar, University of Mkar.

Anyamene, A. N., Anyachebelu, F. E., Nwokolo, C. N., & Izuchi, M. N. (2009). Strategies for promoting entrepreneurship education among undergraduates: the perception of counsellors. *UNIZIK Orient Journal.* 3 (1), 87-9

Bates, T. (2001). Natural strategies for e-learning in post-secondary education and training. *International Institute for Educational Planning.* www.unesco.org/iiep. Retrieved on October 29, 2015.

Fry, K. (2000). *"Forum focus and overview".* Telcam Group, University of Technology, Sydney. https://pdfs.semanticscholar.org/36fe/6de18bbf6b001a9de14ae99f575b1431d7fb.pdf

Gibson, A. 2011). *Business development service: core principles and future challenges.* London: Small Enterprise Development.

Khan, B. (2005). *Managing e-learning strategies: design, delivery, implementation and training.* www.google.com. Retrieved on October 02, 2015.

Ocho, L. O. (2005). Basic resources needs for successful business management. In I. O. Nwangwu, R. C. Aguba, G. C. Ezike Mba, P. Eya (Eds.). *Education and Life Issues and Concerns.* Enugu: Institute for Development Studies.

Odjegba, E. (2005). "Building Nigeria's entrepreneurship: what stakeholders say about essential ingredients". Sunday Vanguard, July 3.

Olutola, A. D. (1988). Educational facilities and students' performance in WASC examination. *Journal of Educational Management.* 1 (1), 17-25.

Onu, A. J. C. (2013). Stimulating entrepreneurship in educational institutions in Nigeria. *European Scientific Journal.* 9 (25). www.google.com. Retrieved on October 03, 2015.

Suleiman, A. S. (2006). The business entrepreneur. *Entrepreneurial Development, Small and Medium Enterprise,* 2ⁿᵈ Edition. Kaduna: Entrepreneurship Academy Publishing.

Ubah, M. C. (2011). Towards achieving effective entrepreneurship education in social studies teaching interactive agenda through Information and Communication Technology (ICT). *Journal of Economics and Environmental Studies.* Vol. 1 (1). www.soslean.org. Retrieved on September 28, 2015.

Uk.Essays (2015). *Is e-learning the way forward?* www.ukessays.com. Retrieved on October 10, 2015.

Wild, R. H., Griggs, K. A., and Downing, T. (2002). "A framework for e-learning as a tool for knowledge management". *Industrial Management and Data Systems,* vol. 102, No. 7, pp. 371-380.

# 2

# Blended Librarianship Trends for Effective Service Delivery in Nigerian University Libraries

## Umar A. Abubakar & Professor Victor N. Nwachukwu

## Abstract

*T* *he role of the librarian in the attainment of academic success by the students and staff alike cannot be overstated. This study therefore investigated blended librarianship trends for effective service delivery in Nigerian university libraries. The paper identified who a blended librarian is, the functions and place in the 21ˢᵗ century librarianship. The relationship between the blended librarian and effective service delivery was established. In the end, the paper concluded that the university libraries and librarians first task is blended librarianship, which promotes self-directed teaching and learning among students. This requires them to become lifelong learners, monitors and assesses their learning progression.*

**Keywords:** Blended Librarianship, Service Delivery, University Libraries

## Introduction

Universities as communities of those who teach and those who learn must have the noble vision and mission of generating, expanding, and disseminating knowledge in all disciplines for the advancement of human civilization and production of highly skilled graduates with the capacity of life-long, critical, conceptual and reflective thinking. This is all achievable through active involvement and facilitation of information literacy initiatives by various stakeholders of the universities because of the continually evolving paradigm shift in technology that is turning librarians and university libraries as an integrated learning environment with the adaptation and utilization of different pedagogical approaches. The paradigm shift also increases the importance of the libraries physical spaces where new and emerging information technologies are combined with traditional knowledge resources in a user-focused, service-rich environment that supports today's social and educational patterns of learning, teaching, and research.

The imperatives of university libraries of becoming places for communities of people to visits together on levels and in ways that they might not in the other places have in a cursory look translating the university environments that combines scholars dedicated to the advancement of knowledge and for the establishment of proper intellectual integrity among the faculty, between the faculty and the students, and between the faculty and the national and international academic community. This intellectual integrity is fostered by the creation of an environment of personal interaction and mutual trust whereby its members are mindful of their responsibilities to maintain standards of competence, and a proper attitude of objectivity, industry, and cooperation with their associates within and without the university community.

Hence, the ideal goal of university education is among other things to strengthen teaching, learning and research process of students and faculty from the dictated curriculum. The value of library instruction in such a situation by students is mostly attainable when that instruction is valued by the faculty, and relevant to the work that students are expected to produce. Thus, the trend calls for librarians in the university settings and their roles in a changing technological and blended learning environments in order to remain relevant in the realm of a wider exchange of information and collaborate with other specialists from both academic and other category of staff to share expertise in technology and educational/instructional design.

The implication for such collaboration in library practice in the Nigerian universities is that ICT-Campus driven society is impacting on information needs and seeking behavior of both students and lecturers and turning them into savvy information users and it is therefore changing librarians' roles from the university libraries to blend their services and collaborate with faculty and instructional design expert to provide teaching and learning resources and services to target audience in a specific mix-mode approach. According to National Impact of Library Public Programs Assessment White Paper of December (2014), librarians have easily adapted to emerging needs of the century information practice. Rather than being threatened by the profound changes in how people access information through technology, librarians set up programs and facilities to teach people how to use technology more effectively.

The tandem of this trend is the librarians' long-term engagement and collaboration with many stakeholders outside the library, such as academic faculty, information technologists, instructional designers, students and other partners on campus would be visible in a blended situations and the shift would indicate an appreciable drive in the services of the Nigerian university libraries adopting world information provision and services based-practices. It should be noted that the concern here, is that the university libraries in the blended world arena have developed into a center of learning and collaboration that is truly becoming the heart of campuses within the university community.

## University Libraries

Universities are the communities of those who teach and those who learn with the noble vision and mission to generate, expand, and disseminate knowledge in all disciplines for the advancement of human civilization and to produce highly skilled graduates with a capacity for life-long, critical, conceptual and reflective thinking which is achievable through active involvement and facilitation of information literacy initiatives by various stakeholders of the universities (Abubakar, 2014). Hence, the teaching strategies realm of education and research in these universities is continually evolving because of the paradigm shift in technology, turning librarians and university libraries into an integrated learning environment with the adaptation and utilization of different pedagogical approaches. As such libraries are intellectual spaces where students can explore and create meaningful knowledge.

It is therefore an indication that keeping abreast of the trends and paradigms-shift in the operations of libraries which requires designing and delivering online information tools and services through design thinking process are needed for the 21st century librarians to remain relevant. Mullins (2014) state that effective library instructional programs reflect the current demands for flexible learning environments, technological advances, and the dynamic nature of information. Traditionally, librarians collaborated with instructional designers and other support resources to develop effective instruction. Due to recent declines in academic budgets, access to instructional design resources has decreased. In response to this trend, there has been an increase of library positions that integrate instructional design within the role of academic librarianship. It is apparent that the wants and needs of end users in the university community is turning to savvy one, that requires the librarians to transform and sought ways for redefining what the library building and librarians services mean to them in the flexible learning to learn environments.

Century students are not only savvy information users. According to Nyam and Akawe (2015), students are the first generation to be, largely, greater producers than consumers of content. They need a place to experiment with integrating this content into their learning to explore and exchange ideas with peers. Of course libraries are very important components of any educational enterprise. They form an integral part of any institutions such that without them, the quality, success and progress of education at any level are negatively affected.

Conversely, the Xlibris Project Team (2016) affirmed that the paradigm shift also increases the importance of the library as a physical space where new and emerging information technologies can be combined with traditional knowledge resources in a user-focused, service-rich environment that supports today's social and educational patterns of learning, teaching, and research. It becomes a place for the community where people come together on levels and in ways that they might not be in the other places. In such development, librarians need to consider how their actions reinforce perceptions of the librarian simply as a service provider. For example, more often than not, librarians adjust teaching strategies to faculty-outlined objectives and goals, which are typically bound up in research assignments (D'Angelo, Maid and Walker; 2016).

## Librarianship

Willingness by 21<sup>st</sup> century librarians to explore new areas and approaches to effective services delivery in the university, have resulted to the emergence of embedded librarianship, information commons, hybridization, information literacy initiatives and other areas essential for blended librarianship practices which is also turning the conventional role of librarians to teachers and instructional designers to partners with the faculty. Sinclair (2009) contends that librarianship is often traditionally framed as a science, librarians have always been designers: creators of tools and services (everything from indexes to curricula to) which connect people with information. Librarians have never really explicitly conceptualized their work as design work or viewed themselves as designers. Rather in the recent years, the practice have seen an upsurge of interest in applying design thinking to library work, but librarianship also aligns with design knowing—foundations of knowledge in design that differentiates it from science. This has been the view of Hill and Goldenson (2013) that librarianship in the era of technology emphases mainly on participatory culture. Because the libraries of the century are not only places to watch, read, and listen (in other words consume) passively but are now places where new social relationships are forged and knowledge is created, explored, and shared. It is a better space for real-time knowledge creation, design for experimentation and community-driven innovation.

## Blended Librarianship Practice and Concept

The paradigm-shift in technology and library practices are currently embracing teaching learning strategies as essential for addressing diverse needs of information users. As such the librarians are blending their services with innovative instructional approach through the utilization of ICT facilities and instructional design capabilities to offer the opportunities for students and teaching faculty to increase flexibility of access to learning resources and enhance self-directed learning at any time and pace. In testimony of the situation, Bell and Shank (2004) stated that librarianship and librarians in the university is turning into a critical professional juncture with a growing ambiguity about its professional role and where its future lies in the academic enterprise during this tumultuous period of change. Notwithstanding, as a profession they are struggling with ways to harness and weave new technologies into the currently existing fabric of high quality information service delivery.

Poignantly blended librarianship practice, utilizes design thinking techniques and technologies to integrate library system and services into the teaching and learning environments and has been the view of Gilbert (2007), that blended librarianship is building new efficiencies and new accomplishments upon a foundation of new synergies— taking advantage of the very paradox that is daunting to so many others whereas, Bell and Shank (2007) submitted that blended librarianship is largely a product of design thinking. It was developed quickly, primarily in order to create a workshop from rough ideas that were still going through the formative process. The early version of blended librarianship was a prototype, and through feedback from participants, it was continually modified as it grew. Abubakar and Nwachukwu (2017) contend that blended librarianship practice is all about the integration of new skill sets from instructional design and technology into one's practice and using those skills to better integrate the library into the teaching and learning process.

Essentially, Giesecke (2010) contends that higher education courses have been found to be increasingly combining a mix of face-to-face and online elements, becoming blended or hybrid courses. Therefore, blended librarians' knowledge in the use of web 2.0 tools and emerging communication technologies can be directly present in both environments to provide course related instruction, deliver library resources and tutorials, as well as answer reference questions. Moreover, by integrating fundamental instructional design skills and knowledge, blended librarians become partners with faculty and other academic professionals in designing courses and incorporating information literacy and research skills into academic programs to achieve student learning outcomes.

It appears that, the key to making an impact in this drive is clear that blended librarianship practice is an integral of the information service learning commons that revolve around the concept of information literacy initiatives. Which combines the use of ICT related infrastructures and facilities with traditional learning methods. Shank and Bell (2011) affirmed that the growing torrent of digital information will challenge educators' ability to teach the appropriate skills and knowledge that will allow students to become and stay knowledgeable. Blended librarianship can serve as a salient metaphor for the evolving educational role of the academic librarian in several ways. In this regard blended librarianship practice refers to the form of instruction that combines online instruction with traditional face-to–face instruction which is also known as hybrid, mixed-mode, and flexible learning; blended librarianship appears to be gaining in popularity. Thus, it is about integrating new skill sets from instructional design and technology into one's practice and using those skills to better integrate the library into the teaching and learning process.

## Who is a Blended Librarian?

Blended librarian is a librarian who combines the traditional skill set of librarianship with the information technologist's hardware/software skills, and the instructional or educational designer's ability to apply technology appropriately in the teaching-learning process. According to Bell (2003) a blended librarian is the academic professional who offers the best combination of skills and services to help faculty apply technology for enhanced teaching and learning. Thus, today, more than ever, a librarian needs to facilitate users' physical and intellectual access to the surfeit of sometimes overwhelming and complex information. Instruction has become a core function for most librarians, yet academic preparation of librarians does not always include the principles of instruction, especially that of instructional design (Farmer; 2004).

According to Merrill (2009), Instructional Design (ID) is the systematic process of planning and managing instruction to achieve effective learning. It is undertaken during the development of training and educational programs and resources. Design thinking issues for libraries is an approach for improving library operation through creative problem solving (Bell, 2016).

Because learning situations are dynamic, therefore instructional design is an interative process that is undertaken not once but repeatedly, for every learning situation, even when the materials to be used have themselves undergone an instructional design process (Thiagi; 2008). In reality, learning more about instructional design and technology would better equip librarians to communicate effectively with their institution's instructional designers and technologists. They can learn about instructional design from their institutional colleagues or enter into formal degree programs if they are to remain relevant and better enhance their ability to support the instructional needs of faculty and become fully blended.

Interestingly, Walter (2008) assert that in discussing issues of librarianship and teaching, most a times, librarians find themselves increasingly called upon to act (and to think of themselves) as teachers, but very few are provided with any training on how to teach as part of their professional education. The application of blended instruction has quickly increased because instructors believe that varied delivery methods can increase students' satisfaction from the learning experience as well as their learning outcomes (Lim., Morris and kupritz,; 2009).

While, Whitchurch (2008) posits that blended librarians in higher education are staff with mixed backgrounds and portfolios, dedicated to progressing activity within professional and academic cycle. It is evident that, Sinclair (2009) affirmed that blended librarians focused on course goals and learning objectives outside of the library and across the curriculum. Essentially they are versed in the utilization of both print and online tools and can help faculty meet course goals, regardless of the medium or technology. It is therefore a new call to outreach. The blended librarian seeks to build new collaborations with students, faculty, staff, and other information and instructional technology professionals both in and outside of the classroom—in physical spaces and virtual environments— in order to match learners and teachers with the information tools they need.

Effective librarianship cannot occur in a vacuum. Cordes (2007) reported that instructional technology librarian in Iowa State University, USA during the period, were found and reported to be working closely with the campus instructional technology, central computing, teaching faculty, and others critical to the best practice of technology in the learning process. Indeed it served as representative of the library in campus teaching and learning circle and the faculty senate IT committee and finally initiative and developed an educational technology event series that creates a common ground in the library for sharing and dialoguing about experiences related to technology in the teaching and learning process

This is how it is supposed to be because, blended librarians' work is not meanly on the students' immediate information need, but also with the broader learning objectives of the assignment and course. But it is also for instructors who seek to use new forms of multimedia— streaming video, podcasts, digitized images, 3-D animations, screen casts, etc.—to engage students and enhance the learning experience, the blended librarian is there to provide guidance and expertise as well. According to Bell (2015) what differentiates the blended librarian is his or her instructional design and learning skills, as well as their knowledge of utilizing educational technology to enhance learning. As higher education and librarianship increasingly move toward the digital, perhaps these skills are more routinely accepted as the nature of the work librarians do.

More importantly, the founders of blended librarianship believed that for librarians to remain relevant they must be open to adopting new skills, knowledge, and ideas. It complements several of the emerging ideas about academic libraries and librarians today. Blended librarianship is essential to creating the partnerships and collaboration necessary to develop an institution's information, learning, and knowledge commons successfully. Blended librarians complement both the Embedded Librarian and Librarian 2.0. BL does not seek to replace instructional designers and technologists. Rather, it seeks to strengthen the ties and relationship between these professional groups so that together effective cross-functional teams can be created to work with faculty to enhance student learning (Zabel, 2011).

In the emerging world of blended librarianship, librarians and instructional design specialists, faculty development professionals, and technology professionals are learning from one another's expertise and developing, together, new ways of enhancing and supporting undergraduate teaching, learning and even research. They are increasing the value of the education they help others provide (Gilbert, 2007). What matters is for the blended librarians to push the boundaries of faculty, staff, and student adoption of new educational technologies to improve learning as compassionate, disruptive innovators on their campuses.

## Concept of Effective Service Delivery

Attainment of effective service delivery in university libraries is determined by the level of professional practices and involvements of other stakeholders in the planning and implementation of product-oriented resources and services to satisfy the needs of user communities. Hence, the concept of service delivery in work environment is referring to different things and meanings to different researchers. For example, Nealer (2007) has defined service delivery as a provision for public activities, benefits or satisfaction while according to Mathibane (2010) service delivery is the implementation of exact policy objectives in the public sector with numerous grades of success.

Service delivery consists of a series of highly localized actions by agents in public agencies or private enterprises to provide needed goods and services to citizen beneficiaries in a way that meets their expectations (Kim 2012). It is apparent that according to World Meteorological Organization (WMO) (2014) for a service to be effective, it should possess these following attributes:

- Available and timely: at time and space scales that the user needs
- Dependable and reliable: delivered on time to the required user specification
- Usable: presented in user specific formats so that the client can fully understand
- Useful: to respond appropriately to user needs
- Credible: for the user to confidently apply to decision making
- Authentic: entitled to be accepted by stakeholders in the given decision contexts
- Responsive and flexible: to the evolving user needs
- Sustainable: affordable and consistent over time
- Expandable: tobe applicable to different kinds of services.

Notwithstanding, library effectiveness is determined from the range of technical efficiency measures to indistinct statements of goodness, but the paradigm is now focusing on goal achievement, efficiency, user satisfaction, personnel management, and ability of the organization to survive. As such, effective service in the library practice is denoting to library service effectiveness.

## Principles of Blended Librarianship

The proponents of blended librarianship highlighted the following six approaches as the fundamental principles of "blend- to- serve" which included:

1. Ability of librarians to take a leadership position as campus innovators and change agents which is critical to the success of delivering library services in today's information society,
2. Commitment to the development of campus-wide information literacy initiatives on our campuses in order to facilitate our ongoing involvement in the teaching and learning process,
3. Involvement in instructional design and educational programs and classes to assist patrons in using library services and learning information literacy that is absolutely essential to gaining the necessary skills (trade) and knowledge (profession) for lifelong success,
4. Collaboration and engaging in dialogue with instructional technologists and designers which is vital to the development of programs, services and resources needed to facilitate the instructional mission of academic libraries,
5. Implementation of adaptive, creative, proactive, and innovative change in library instruction that can be enhanced by communicating and collaborating with newly created instructional technology/design librarians and existing instructional designers and technologists and
6. Transformation of relationship with faculty that would emphasize librarians ability to assist them with integrating information technology and library resources into courses, but adding to that traditional role a new capacity to collaborate on enhancing student learning and outcome assessment in the area of information access, retrieval and integration (Bell and Shank; 2007,Pg 8)

The new teaching and learning platforms paradigm created by blended library practice is felt and recognized by most universities in the developing countries to re-conceptualize the roles and responsibilities of librarians that lead to the establishment of unit and new library job positions labelled: Instructional Design Librarian, System Design Librarian, Embedded Librarian, Hybrid Librarian or Blended Librarian amongst others. Details could be found from https://www.indeed.com/q-Instructional-Design-Librarian-jobs.html

From the forgoing it is crystal clear that, the information service delivery in the 21st century offered by university libraries and librarians has been transformed into blended librarianship through structured collaborative teaching and learning by librarians, faculty and instructional technologist. Therefore, successful blended librarianship practice requires an understanding of the pedagogical attributes and affordances of new and emerging learning technologies.

To achieve this in the Nigerian universities, it deemed necessary for librarians to embrace design thinking approach and other expert approach from and across faculties for the realization, utilization and prompting blended library facilities and services. Thus, lack of proper awareness of the role of blended librarianship practices in university setting particularly in Nigeria may pose a serious challenge of effective collaboration between librarians and faculty which will have negative effects on the acquisition of blended librarians skills by the librarians and utilization of its facilities which in turn would hamper teaching, learning and research capability of both faculty and students. Hence, librarians in the universities would remain irrelevant because the global best- practices demands for the application of blended librarianship practices in information services on the campuses of higher learning.

In furtherance of the justification and according to Bell and Shank (2004), in the academic library sector, the 'blended librarian' has been conceived as a professional combining the skill set of librarianship with information technology and educational design. Therefore, Shank (2006) in another separate analysis of advertisements for librarians found that the most common responsibilities of this position would be to create online resources such as; modules, tutorials and guides and to have skills or experience in the use of instructional technologies.

Abubakar (2012) reported that librarians in the university libraries teach and facilitate the acquisition of knowledge and skills for effective use of library to fresh undergraduate students. Notwithstanding, blended librarians paradigm-shift is booming as Fister (2006) reported that librarians are contributing to effective teaching and faculty research with others occupying positions in the management and operations of libraries which made it possible for them to interact with users from across devise discipline and professions to initiate access and retrieval forms and policy for information resources utilization within and outside the confines of a university environment.

## Conclusion

Libraries and librarians in the university settings are key components for leveraging support for desired achievement in teaching and learning across the university curricula. Meanwhile the teaching role of the librarian has been developing a broad spectrum throughout the university to collaborate with faculty and instructional technologists to meet emerging research needs of the user community, curricular content of the parent organization. The implication is that university libraries and librarians first task in blended librarianship era is to learn and understand the students need and ascertain their information gap in which the blended librarians from university libraries would play their prominent role to promote self-directed teaching and learning among students which require students to become independently life-long learners, monitors, and assess their learning progression.

## References

Abubakar, U. A. (2012). Digital-divide as a challenge to libraries and librarians in Nigerian universities: a case study of Abubakar Tafawa Balewa University, Bauchi State. *Journal of Research in Education and Society; 3, (2) p5-11 Retrieved from* www.icidr.org.

Abubakar, U. A. (2014). Library stakeholders' perception and involvement in Information Literacy Initiatives (ILI) in federal universities in North East, Nigeria. A Master's Thesis, Department of Library and Information Science, University of Nigeria Nsukka. Retrieved from http://repository.unn.edu.ng:8080/jspui/bitstream/123456789/1854/1/Umar%20Aliyu%20Abubakar.pdf on 25/08/16.

Bell, S. J., & Shank, J. D. (2004). The blended librarian: a blueprint for redefining the teaching and learning role of academic librarians. *College and Research Libraries News,65*(7), http://crln.acrl.org/content/65/7/372.full.pdf

Bell, J. S. and Shank, D. J. (2007). Academic librarianship by design: A blended librarian's guide to tools and techniques. Chicago. Retrieved from http://www.alastore.ala.org/detail.aspx?ID=39 on 20/02/2016.

Blended Librarian Blog (2016). Design technology librarianship. Retrieved from http://blendedlibrarian.learningtimes.net/blblog/#.V8_vv98rLdo

Bell, J. S. (2016). What do you know about instructional designers? From the Bell Tower, Blog. Retrieved from http://lj.libraryjournal.com/2016/01/opinion/steven-bell/new-opportunities-in-learning-experience-curation-from-the-bell-tower/#respond on 20/08/2016

Cordes, S. (2007). Where it all begins Blended Librarianship. In Bell, J.S and Shank, D.J (2007). Academic Librarianship by Design: A Blended Librarian's Guide to Tools and Techniques. Chicago. Retrieved from http://www.alastore.ala.org/detail.aspx?ID=39 on 20/02/2016.

D'Angelo, S. J, Maid, B and Walker R. J(2016). Information literacy: research and collaboration across disciplines in writing information literacy: a retrospective and a look ahead Edited by Barbara J. Colorado University Press of Coloradohttps://wac.colostate.edu/books/infolit/collection.pdf pg 18

Farmer, L. S. J. (2004). Instructional design for librarians and information professionals. New York London: Neal-Schuman Publishers

Fister, B. (2006). Fostering information literacy through faculty development. Library Issues Briefings for Faculty and Administrators, 29, (4) p1-3 Retrieved from ;http:// homepages.gac.edu/~fister/LIfacultydevelopment.pdf

Giesecke, J and McNeil, B (2010). *Fundamentals of Library Supervision*. United States of America: American Library Association. Retrieved from http://www.alastore.ala.org/ pdf/9780838910160_excerpt.pdf 06/01/1

Gilbert, W.S. (2007).Academic librarianship by design: a blended librarian's guide to tools and techniques. Chicago

Hill, N. & Goldenson, J. (2013). Making room for innovation. *Library Journal*. Retrieved from: http://lj.libraryjournal.com/2013/05/future-of-libraries/making-room-for-innovation/

Kim, J. K. (2012). Delivering on development: harnessing knowledge to build prosperity and end poverty. Keynote Address to World Knowledge Forum, Seoul, Republic of Korea, October 9, 2012. http://www.worldbank.org/en/news/speech/2012/10/08/ delivering-development-harnessingknowledge-build-prosperity-end-poverty

Lim, D. H., Morris, M. L., & kupritz, V. W. (2006). online vs. blended learning: differences in instructional outcomes and learner satisfaction. Retrieved from: http://eric.ed.gov

Mathibane, L. (2010) A Thesis on: Improving service delivery through partnerships between Local Government, Civil Society and the Private Sector: A case study of Imizamo Yethu, Stellenbosch: Stellenbosch University.

Mullins, K. (2014). Good IDEA: instructional design model for integrating information literacy. Post Library Faculty Publications. Retrieved from https://digitalcommons.liu. edu/cgi/viewcontent.cgi?article=1007&context=post_libfacpubs on 25/12/2017

National Impact of Library Public Programming Assessment White paper (2014). A project of the American Library Association t (NILPPA) funded by the ALA Cultural Communities Fund.

Nealer, E. (2007) Local government and service delivery. In Van der Waldt, G. (Ed). Municipal Management: Serving the people., Cape Town: Juta.

Nyam, S. S. and Akawe, M. N. (2015). History of libraries. In R. E. Ozioko (ed.), *Book of Readings* (pp. 39-65). Makurdi: Climax Graphics and Publishers Ltd.

Sinclair, B. (2009). The blended librarian in the leaning commons: new skills for the blended library. *College and Research Libraries News.*70 (9)

Thiagi. (2008). Rapid instructional design. learning activities that incorporate different content sources. *Thiagi Gameletter*, February 2008. Retrieved from http://www.thiagi. com/pfp/IE4H/february2008.html#RapidInstructionalDesign

Walter, S. (2008). Librarians as teachers: A qualitative inquiry into professional identity. *College & Research Libraries, 69*(1)

Whitchurch, C. (2009). The rise of the blended professional in higher education: a comparison between the United Kingdom, Australia and the United States', Higher Education, 58 (3),

World Meteorological Organization (WMO) (2014). Strategy for service delivery. Geneva, Switzerland. Retrieved from: http://www.wmo.int/pages/prog/amp/pwsp/documents/ WMO-SSD-1129_en.pdf

Zabel, D (2011). Blended librarianship:[Re] envisioning the role of librarians as educators in the digital age by Shank, J. D and Bell, J. S, Zabel, D edited Retrieved from https:// journals.ala.org/rusq/article/view/4025/4568 pdf on 03/3/2016

# 3

# ICT Proficiency in School Administration: A Case for Life Long Learning of Educational Administrators for Sustainable National Development

Stella N. Nwosu, Ph.D & Utibe-Abasi I. Ekpe

## Abstract

*T he study investigated the influence of area of specialisation and years of experience on school administrators' proficiency in the use of ICT tools in their job. A sample of 50 secondary school principals drawn for a population of seventy three principals in public and private schools in Calabar Municipality was used for the study. The expost facto research design was used to answer the two research questions and test the two hypotheses formulated to guide the study. Data on principals area of specialisation, years of experience and ICT proficiency was collected using a researcher produced 32 item, four point rating scale the "Principals' Variables and ICT Proficiency Questionnaire".The questionnaire's validity was established by three experts. A reliability coefficient of 0.78 was obtained for the instrument using the Cronbach Alpha test of internal consistency. The collected data was analysed using mean and standard deviation to answer the research questions and Analysis of Variance to test the hypotheses at .05 alpha levels. The results revealed that both area of specialisation and years of experience influenced the principals' proficiency in using ICT tools in their job. The study concluded that there was need for school administrators to continuously use ICT tools in their job and to update their skills. The study recommended, among others, the setting up of ICT centers for Continuous Professional Development (CPD) and capacity building of employees by State governments.*

**Keywords:** ICT proficiency, school administration, lifelong learning, sustainable development

## Introduction

Proficiency in ICT simply refers to a measure of one's competence in the use of information and communication technology (ICT) tools such as mobile devices, tablets, computers as well as the software programs that are run by these devices; thereby having the ability to access, manage and share information in an efficient and productive way. Proficiency in ICT enables us to carry out tasks effectively and efficiently thus saving time for exploration of other developmental ideas. ICT advancement has had a significant impact on human achievements all over the world and any institution that seeks to compete with its contemporaries on a global level must adapt to and adopt ICT advantages. And parade personnel that are proficient in ICT skills.

The school is considered as an institution designed to provide learning and learning spaces for students, it is a place that builds up the character of its learners even as it directs them towards the understanding of particular disciplines. In school, students can have the opportunity to learn several valuable life lessons that would gear them towards self-development and make them responsible members of the society. Therefore, the principal, who is the person with the greatest responsibility of managing a school, through his abilities, will determine how well the students would develop these characteristics, thereby arriving at self and societal development. To achieve this, he must primarily, be an effective manager/leader. He must be organized; making himself available to teachers, parents, students, non-academic staff members, and the community; in order to execute his duties effectively, the principal become efficient at practices such as prioritizing, scheduling and organization (Meador, 2017).

Administration and Management applications of ICT are currently popular in schools due to its capabilities in facilitating administration activities from data storage to knowledge management and decision making (Ghavifekr, Afshari, Siraj, Seger, 2013). With the seemingly daunting task of educational leadership, the integration of educational technology, particularly ICT, in the administration of the school becomes necessary for success to be achieved. Educational technology is the study and ethical practice of facilitating learning and improving performance by creating, using, and managing appropriate technological processes and resources (Robinson, Molenda, Rezabek, 2016). Educational technology includes, but is not limited to ICT which refers to technologies that provide access to information through telecommunications with a primary focus on communication technologies. In order for the school principals in Nigeria to execute their duties and raise the current standard of education to a level closest to the ideal, ICT, which is a factor that can support and aid their achievement should not only be embraced by the school leaders but encouraged by all the educational stakeholders in Nigeria.

Basic ICT applications used by school administrators include word processing, data processing, internet as well as communication and messaging tools. Data processing is the collection and manipulation of items of data to produce meaningful information. The concept of data encompasses many kinds of information that help teachers and administrators to know their students, and staff, in depth (Morrison, 2009). The internet, a global computer network providing a variety of information and communication facilities, consisting of interconnected networks using standardized communication protocols is also necessary in school administration. In the last two decades, the internet and ICT application tools have been expended into the field of education all over the world. (Ghavifekr, Afshari, Siraj, Seger, 2013), and administrator's proficiency in the use of internet facilities would enable him gain access to information all over the world; communications and collaborations would be easier and his institution can run better as a unit with timely and accurate information circulation and distribution which would be made possible through the internet. Apart from information dissemination, the internet can be used by the administrator for cloud storage, emailing, online forums and research. He can and should also introduce a system where teachers set up tests and assignments online that can be automatically graded; this saves a lot of time doing correcting; they can afterwards generate result by using ICT. Also they can set up websites and online portals for students to access assignments (Kawade, 2012).

Messaging and communication through telephone and mobile devices is an aspect of ICT that must be utilized by every institution for its effective running. In Nigeria, statistics from Africa Infotech Consulting (AIC) showed that smartphone penetration has increased gaining about 30 per cent penetration with features phones having a 70 per cent penetration (Adepetun, 2016). The most important use of the cell phone is the ability of its user to stay in touch with anybody at any time including during emergencies. In addition to voice communication, mobile phones allow the transfer of data, which can be particularly useful for delivering educational content over long distances. Principals can collaborate with each other sharing their experiences and gleaning knowledge from each other's administrative strategies.

Governments have encouraged teachers and school administrators to acquire and develop ICT skills through Continuous Professional Development workshops. But to what extent has these workshops impacted on the school administrators ICT capabilities? Lifelong learning and Continuous Professional Development (CPD) is not a responsibility of the government alone. In order to keep abreast with global trends and best practices that can impact positively on his job performance and the nation as a whole, every administrator must embark on lifelong learning especially in ICT capabilities. The significance of ICT enabled communication capabilities such as the Internet is that it provides the professional with the opportunity to update his/her knowledge and skills in the chosen profession. If these facilities are embraced it can culminate to an educational professional man power with competencies that meet the emerging educational needs of the nation for a sustainable development.

What personal factors can influence administrators' embracing ICT as means of not only updating their ICT skills but as a necessity for effectiveness in their job as school administrators?

Area of Specialization: This refers to the subject specialization of the principal. If the subject of degree certification is ICT based or required the use of ICT for effective understanding, the principal would be more accustomed to ICT and its uses hence incorporating same while disseminating his duties. Howard, Chan, and Caputi (2015) revealed that teachers' readiness to integrate technology into instruction has significant associations with teacher's area of specialization. According to them subject areas involving a lot of research such as social studies would develop a principal's skills in use of internet to glean information; areas requiring use of software for statistics, projections and graphing such as Mathematics, would develop the data analysis skills of a principal while those of them who specialized in English and literary studies, which requires the use of computers for typing would have developed their skills in the area of communication. According to Zucker and Hug (2007), each subject constitutes a body of knowledge, concepts, and skills, and teachers use different teaching and learning strategies. In mathematics, students do drills and practice activities, while social studies' students conduct daily research, and English students use computers for writing regularly. However, Summak, Baglibel and Samancioglu, (2010) found no significant differences among teachers in their technology readiness across the subject areas.

The number of years a principal has spent in service can influence his ICT proficiency. Spending long years in service would enable some principals to adopt best practices for easier accomplishment of his duties, as he grows in service, he will more likely abandon non-productive or less efficient methods while adhering to skills that would increase his efficiency (Haward etal, 2015). According Lau and Sim, (2008) experienced teachers and principals implement technology more than beginner teachers. On the other hand, Baek *et al.* (2008) reported that principal with long teaching experience are less ready to integrate technology into their administration. Principals that have spent long years in service may find it difficult to let go of traditional modes of carrying out their functions. They are often older and less likely to adopt technology because of being accustomed to none technological methods. On one hand younger generation principals are more likely to use ICT simply because they are in an era where ICT is being emphasized. Papaioannou and Charalambous (2011) stressed that young and less experienced principals were more enthusiastic about ICT, felt less anxiety when using ICT and avoided using computer to a lesser degree than the older principals. However, Felton (2006) reported that level of experience does not play a significant role in determining educators' attitude towards computers.

## Statement of the Problem

With a fertility rate of 5.5 births per woman of child bearing age and a population of 174 million (National Bureau of Statistics, 2014) Nigeria will be experiencing a significant growth in enrolment in the nearest future and traditional and manual mode of school administration will not be sufficient to meet the educational needs of the society. Sustaining the development of the Nigerian economy requires that individuals and institutions engage in capacity building that can bring about long term survival of the nation. Hence, there is a need for principals to develop their ICT skills and apply it in their operations in order to meet the present and future educational need of the society. This study investigates some personal variables; areas of specialization and years of experience, to what extent do these variables influence principal's ICT proficiency?

### Research Questions

$Q_1$: To what extent does principals' ICT proficiency differ based on their area of specialisation?

$Q_2$: To what extent does principals' ICT proficiency differ based on their years of experience?

## Research Hypotheses

$Ho_1$: Principals' ICT proficiency in school administration does not significantly differ based on their area of specialisation

$Ho_2$: Principals' ICT proficiency in school administration does not significantly differ based on their years of experience.

## Methodology

The study was carried out in Calabar Municipality Local Government Area of Cross River State. Calabar is adjacent to the Calabar and Great Kwa rivers and creeks of the Cross River (from its inland delta). It is the capital of Cross River State and the most developed area in the state. Administratively, the city is divided into two Local Government Areas – Calabar Municipality and Calabar South LGAs.

The research design adopted for this study was the causal comparative research design. It sought to determine the cause and effect relationship between principals' personal variables and their ICT proficiency. The design was suitable because the information gathered was qualitative and the variables under investigation already exist; the study only sought to determine the influence the independent variable (principals' personal variables) affect the dependent variable (ICT proficiency).

The population of this study consisted of all the seventy three (73) principals in public (16) and private (57) secondary schools in Calabar Municipality Local Government Area. The sample size was 50 principals, consisting of thirty five (34) from private schools drawn by simple random sampling using balloting from the forty one (41) private secondary schools in the local government area and all the principals of the sixteen (16) public secondary schools in the area.

A researcher-developed instrument "Principals' Variables and ICT Proficiency Questionnaire" (PVIPQ) was used to elicit information from the principals. The instrument was divided into two (2) sections. Section A of the PVIPQ had items on personal/ professional data of the respondents regarding area of specialization, years of experience, and educational level. Section B of the PVIPQ consisted of forty-two (42) items eliciting information on attitude to technology (twelve items); ICT proficiency (thirty items) with declarative statements. The items in PVIPQ were structured in a 4-point rating scale of strongly agree -4points; agree -3points; disagree -2 points and strongly dis-agree -1 point.

Face and content validity were used to validate the items of the PVIPQ. They were reviewed by experts in Test and Measurements in the Faculty of Education, University of Uyo, Uyo. Their comments were incorporated into the final version of the instrument.

In order to determine the reliability of the PVIPQ, the instrument was tried out on twenty (20) principals of secondary schools who were not part of the research group. The instrument was subjected to Cronbach Alpha analysis; an overall reliability coefficient of 0.78 was obtained for the instrument. The instrument was administered to the secondary school principals in their respective schools with the researchers present to explain the objective of the research and how to respond to the items. The respondents were given ample time to reflect and respond accurately. 49 of the administered instruments were collected from the principals for analysis. Independent t-test was used to analyze the data obtained. The level of significance was placed at 0.05 and this served as the basis for accepting or rejecting the formulated hypotheses.

## Results

### Research Questions

$Q_1$: *To what extent does principals' ICT proficiency differ based on their area of specialisation?*

**Table 1: Mean, standard deviation of principals' ICT proficiency based on area of specialisation**

| Area of Specialization | N | Mean | Std. Deviation |
|---|---|---|---|
| Science | 22 | 99.36 | 8.375 |
| Humanities | 11 | 87.18 | 8.852 |
| Business | 5 | 95.55 | 7.488 |
| Language arts | 11 | 82.80 | 14.670 |
| Total | 49 | 94.08 | 10.681 |

In answer to research question one, Table 1 presents the mean ICT proficiency in school administration scores of school Principals according to their areas of academic specialization and it showed that their proficiencies differ based on areas of specialization. Thus, Principals who specialized in science related disciplines are more proficient in use of ICT in school administration (mean 99.36), followed by Principals that specialised in: Business disciplines (mean 95.55); Humanities (mean 87.18) and finally Language Arts (mean 82.80). Further examination of the standard deviations presented, showed less disparity in proficiency among Principals that specialized in Business and Sciences related disciplines as indicated by the lower standard deviation.

$Q_2$: *To what extent does principals' ICT proficiency differ based on their years of experience?*

**Table 2: Mean, standard deviation (SD) of principals' ICT proficiency based on their years of experience**

| Years of Principal Experience | N | Mean | Std. Deviation |
|---|---|---|---|
| 0-5yrs experience | 28 | 97.36 | 8.714 |
| Above 5 - 15yrs experience | 10 | 90.55 | 9.319 |
| Above 15 years | 11 | 88.80 | 13.881 |
| Total | 49 | 94.08 | 10.681 |

In answer to research question two, Table 2 presents the mean Principals' ICT proficiency scores in school administration based on their years of experience as Principals. It shows that Principals in the category of experience of 5yrs and below were more proficient (mean 97.36) in the use of ICT for school administration, followed by those with above 5yrs to 15yrs experience (mean 90.55) while those with over 15yrs experience as principals were less proficient in the use of ICT for administration (mean 88.80). Further examination of the standard deviations presented, confirm their superiority as indicated by less divergence in their proficiency scores represented by the lower standard deviations.

## Research Hypotheses

**HO$_1$:***Principals' ICT proficiency in school administration does not significantly differ based on their area of specialisation*

**Table 3: One way analysis of variance of principals' area of specialization and ICT proficiency in school administration**

| Specialisation Groups | Sum of Squares | df | Mean Square | F-cal | F-crit | P | Decision at 0.05 alpha level |
|---|---|---|---|---|---|---|---|
| Between Groups | 1797.419 | 3 | 599.140 | 7.330 | 2.82 | .000 | *Significant |
| Within Groups | 3678.255 | 45 | 81.739 | | | | |
| Total | 5475.673 | 48 | | | | | |

Table 3 is ANOVA table showing the result of the test for hypothesis one. It shows that the calculated F-value of 7.330 is greater than the critical F-value of 2.82 with P-value less than 0.05, F (3, 45) =7.330, P< 0.05. Therefore the null hypothesis is rejected. Hence Principals' proficiency in use of ICT in school administration significantly differs based on their areas of specialization. To determine the different areas of specialization where the mean significant differences occur, the mean differences were further subjected to Scheffe multiple comparison analysis as presented in Table 4.

**Table 4: Scheffe multiple comparison analysis of mean differences in use of ICT proficiency in school administration based on Principals' area of specialization.**

| (I) Area of specialization | (J) Area of specialization | Mean Difference (I-J) | Std. Error | Sig. | Decision at 0.05 alpha level |
|---|---|---|---|---|---|
| Science | Business | 3.818 | 3.339 | .728 | Not significant |
| | Humanities | 12.182* | 3.339 | .008 | Significant |
| | Language arts | 16.564* | 4.479 | .007 | Significant |
| Business | Science | -3.818 | 3.339 | .728 | Not significant |
| | Humanities | 8.364 | 3.855 | .210 | Not significant |
| | Language arts | 12.745 | 4.876 | .092 | Not significant |
| Humanities | Science | -12.182* | 3.339 | .008 | Significant |
| | Business | -8.364 | 3.855 | .210 | Not significant |
| | Language arts | 4.382 | 4.876 | .847 | Not significant |
| Language arts | Science | -16.564* | 4.479 | .007 | Significant |
| | Business | -12.745 | 4.876 | .092 | Not significant |
| | Humanities | -4.382 | 4.876 | .847 | Not significant |

The result of Scheffe multiple comparison analysis of mean differences presented in Table 4 showed that significant differences in use of ICT proficiency in school administration exist between Principals that specialized in Sciences and their counterparts in Humanities and Language Arts.

**HO$_2$:** *Principals' ICT proficiency in school administration does not significantly differ based on their years of experience*

**Table 5: One way analysis of variance of Principals' ICT proficiency in school administration and years of experience as Principal**

| Years of experience group | Sum of Squares | df | Mean Square | F | F-crit | P-value | Decision at 0.05 alpha level |
|---|---|---|---|---|---|---|---|
| Between Groups | 716.918 | 2 | 358.459 | 3.465 | 3.20 | .040 | Significant |
| Within Groups | 4758.756 | 46 | 103.451 | | | | |
| Total | 5475.673 | 48 | | | | | |

Table 5 is ANOVA table showing the result of the test for hypothesis two. It shows calculated F-value of 3.465 is greater than the critical F-value of 3.20 with P-value less than 0.05, F (2, 45) =3.465, P< 0.05. Therefore the null hypothesis is rejected. Hence Principals' proficiency in use of ICT in school administration significantly differs based on their years of experience. To determine the different years of experience groups where the mean significant differences occur, the differences were further subjected to Scheffe multiple analysis as presented in Table 6.

**Table 6: Scheffe multiple comparison analysis of mean differences in use of ICT proficiency in school administration based on Principals' years of experience.**

| (I) Years of experience | (J) Years of experience | Mean Difference (I-J) | Std. Error | Sig. | Decision at 0.05 alpha level |
|---|---|---|---|---|---|
| 0-5yrs Experience | Above 15 years | 8.557* | 3.747 | .045 | Significant |
| | Above 5 - 15yrs Experience | 6.812 | 3.619 | .182 | Not significant |
| Above 15 years | 0-5yrs Experience | -8.557* | 3.747 | .045 | Significant |
| | Above 5 - 15yrs Experience | -1.745 | 4.444 | .926 | Not significant |
| Above 5 - 15yrs Experience | 0-5yrs Experience | -6.812 | 3.619 | .182 | Not significant |
| | Above 15 years | 1.745 | 4.444 | .926 | Not significant |

The result of Scheffe multiple comparison analysis of mean differences presented in Table 6 shows that significant difference in use of ICT proficiency in school administration only exists between Principals in the experience category of 5years and below and their counterpart above 15 years of experience as Principals.

## Discussion of Findings

**Principals' Area of Specialization and their ICT Proficiency in School administration**

The research question one and hypothesis one sought to determine if the principal's area of specialization influenced their proficiency in the use of ICT tools in their school administration. The results reveal that Principals who specialized in science related disciplines are more proficient in use of ICT in school administration (mean 99.36), followed by Principals that specialized in: Business disciplines (mean 95.55); Humanities (mean 87.18) and finally Language Arts (mean 82.80). While there is a significant mean difference between the proficiency in school administration of principals who specialize in science disciplines and those who specialize in Humanities. Although the respondents have indicated reasonable proficiency in the use of ICT in school administration, these results imply that the discipline which a principal majored in can influence his ability to employ ICT tools effectively in his school administration. It is also revealed here that principals who majored in Science disciplines are significantly more proficient in the use of ICT in the running of their schools than their counter parts that majored in the Humanities. The findings collaborate with Howard, Chan, and Caputi (2015) who revealed that teachers' readiness to integrate technology into instruction has significant associations with teacher's area of specialization. But contradicts the Summak, Baglibel and Samancioglu, (2010) found no significant differences among teachers in their technology readiness across the subject areas. The findings of Summak et al (2010) is understandable if the respondents are living in a highly technology driven society unlike what prevails in Nigeria. In this study the principals who have a back ground in Humanities such as education are the ones that exhibit less proficiency. This accentuates the need for administrators especially those who have backgrounds in Language Arts and Humanities to continuously update their ICT knowledge and skills.

**Principals' years of experience and their ICT proficiency in School administration**

Research question and hypothesis two sought to find out if the principals' years of experience influenced their proficiency in the use of ICTs in school administration. The results revealed that principals in the category of experience of 5yrs and below were more proficient (mean 97.36) in the use of ICT for school administration, followed by those with above 5yrs to 15yrs experience (mean 90.55) while those with over 15yrs experience as principals were less proficient in the use of ICT for administration (mean 88.80).\ And that there is a significant difference in ICT proficiency in school administration only exists between Principals in the experience category of 5years and below and their counterpart above 15 years of experience as Principals. These results imply that the longer in the job the less proficient are the principals in the use of ICT tools for their job more experienced principals are not as good at using ICTs in the dissemination of their duties as principals as their less experienced counter parts. These findings are in accordance with the findings of Baek *et al.* (2008) that principals with long teaching experience are less ready to integrate technology into their administration. Principals that have spent long years in service may find it difficult to let go of traditional modes of carrying out their functions. They are often older and less likely to adopt technology because of being accustomed to none technological methods. On one hand younger generation principals are more likely to use ICT simply because they are in an era where ICT is being emphasized. However, Lau and Sim (2008) reported that experienced teachers and principals implement technology more than beginners. Again this can be the case in a technology driven society where the administrators have gained experience over the years on how to utilize technology in their job. In Nigeria the use of technology was not in existence previous decades thus these experienced principals will require to update their knowledge on emerging technologies for school administration in or der to be relevant and engender greater productivity for a sustainable national development.

## Conclusion

The study has that both the principals' area of specialization and their years of experience influences their proficiency in the use of ICT tools in their school administration. And that principals with specific subject backgrounds such as Language Arts and Humanities and principals who have been on the job for many years are not likely to be good at using ICT tools in executing their job as school administrators nor will the likely use ICT or Internet facilities to update their knowledge of ICTs. This should not be the case in the evolving technological era. A major tenant of sustainable development is building capacities of the manpower to be relevant to societal needs and global best practices. Thus, every worker should be continuously updating his knowledge and ICTs has made this possible. Thus there is a need for Lifelong learning in ICT usage among school administrators in order to be relevant in the technological era.

## Recommendations

Based on the findings of this study, the study recommends that:

- Knowledge and skills of basic ICT tools be made a prerequisite for promotion as and employment of school all school administrators.
- ICT skills centers should be set up by State governments, where government employees can go on courses to update their knowledge and skills periodically

- Government and private employers of labour should include ICT in compulsory Professional Development Programmes (CPD) for their employees

## References

Adepetun, A. (2016, July 8) Nigeria: Smartphone Penetration Hits 30%. *The Guardian.* Retrieved from http://allafrica.com/stories/201607080930.html

Beal, V. (2017) Word Processing (Word Processor Application). Retrieved from: http://www.webopedia.com/TERM/W/word_processing.html

Baek, Y. G., Jong, J. and Kim, B. (2008). What makes teachers use of technology in the classroom? Exploring the factors affecting facilitation of technology with a Korean sample. *Computers and Education*, 50(8), 224-234.

Central Intelligence Agency. (2015) *The World Factbook.* Retrieved fromhttps://www.cia.gov/library/publications/the-world-factbook/fields/2103.html#136

Felton, F. S. (2006). The use of computers by elementary school principals. (Doctoral Dissertation, Virginia Polytechnic Institute and State University, 181.

Ghavifekr, S., Afshari, M., Siraj, S., & Seger, K., (2013). ICT Application for Administration and Management: A Conceptual Review. *Procedia – Social and Behavioural Sciences.* 103, (13) P 112-118.

Ghavifekr, S., Afshari, M., Siraj, S. & Seger K. (2013). ICT application for administration and management: A conceptual review. *Procedia – Social and Behavioral Sciences 103*(2013) 1344-1351

Howard, S. K., Chan, A. and Caputi, P. (2015). More than beliefs: Subject areas and teachers' integration of lap- tops in secondary teaching. *British Journal of Educational Technology*, 46(2), 360-369.

Kawade, D. R. (2012). Use of ICT in Primary Schools. *Pioneer Journal.* Retrieved from: http://pioneerjournal.in/conferences/tech-knowledge/14th-national-conference/3798-use-of-ict-in-primary-school.html

Lau, B. T. and Sim, C. H. (2008). Exploring the extent of ICT adoption among secondary school teachers in Malaysia. *International Journal of Computing and ICT Research*, 2(2),19-36.

Meador, D (2017, March 24). The Role of The Principal in Schools. Retrieved from: https://www.thoughtco.com

Morrison, J. (2009) Why Teachers Must Be Data Experts. *ASCD -Educational Leadership.* 66 (4), 23-32.

National Bureau of Statistics. (2014, December). *Statistical report on Women and Men in Nigeria.*

Papaioannou, P. and Charalambous, K. (2011). Principals' attitudes towards ICT and their perceptions about the factors that facilitate or inhibit ICT integration in primary schools of Cyprus. *Journal of Information Technology Education*, 10. Retrieved September 7, 2014 from http://JITEV10p349- 369papaioannou958.pdt

Summak, M., Baglibel, M. and Samancioglu, M. (2010). Technology readiness of primary school teachers: A case study in Turkey. *Procedia Social and Behavioral Sciences*, 2, 2671–2675.

Zucker, A. A. and Hug, S. T. (2007). A study of the 1:1 laptop program at the Denver School of Science and Technology. Denver, CO: Denver School of Science & Technology. Retrieved February 25, 2017,fromhttp://www.scienceandtech.org/documents/ Technology/DSST_Laptop_Study_Report.pdf

# 4

# Leadership Style as Management Variable that Enhances Availability of Information Sources in Nigeria University Libraries in South-South

Ima M. P. Usoro Ph.D, Eboro Umoren Ph.D & Akwang Ph.D

## Abstract

*T his study was carried out to investigate Management Variable of Leadership Style and Information Sources Availability in Nigeria University Libraries in South-South University libraries. Seventy Three (73) practicing librarians were purposively used from the universities under study. The study adopted ex-post-facto design and questionnaire was used for data collection. The data collected were analyzed using simple percentages, mean score and chi square statistics. The result revealed that leadership style has significant influence on availability of information sources in the universities under study. The study recommended among others that management cadre of the library should ensure that leadership roles within the library should be discharged in a such a way that all key players (including the subordinates) are allowed to contribute their quota towards making available, information sources to library users.*

**Keywords:** *leadership style, information sources, availability, management*

## Introduction

The library plays a key role in delivering of learning resources to students and staff of the university. They are indispensable treasures for the acquisition of knowledge as they acquire and organize print, non-print and electronic information resources for utilisation by the users. The university library is known to be a service oriented organization with its primary objectives centered on the provision of information for the intellectual, academic and otherwise development of students, lecturers, scholars and professionals. It may be referred to as the heart of any institution and has the responsibility of providing necessary information resources to aid the attainment of academic and other purposes of the university.

Information sources constitute the essence of the library and as long as information sources continue to flow unhindered, the life and wellbeing of the library is assumed. Interfering with the supply of information resources to the library is like hindering the flow of blood within the human body which the consequences could be grave or tragic. A well-built library, stocked adequately with print, non-print and electronic information resources which are catalogued, classified and shelved together with qualified librarians becomes valueless if there is no good leadership. According to Usoro (2005), a functional library is one in which information sources are made available and accessible to users through a good leader who performs his/her duties diligently and responds to the needs of the clientele by making available and accessible the information resources needed by them at stipulated time with the help of his/her subordinates. This view is supported by Adeniran and Chidi (2015) who asserted that the issue of leadership cannot be downplayed in the effectiveness and efficiency of the library as hubs of information and knowledge to meeting the diverse information needs of the library users who depend on it.

The role of leadership as a vital tool in the achievement of any organizational goal cannot be underestimated, be it private or public. Leadership is a process by which a person influences others to accomplish an objective and directs the organization in a way that makes it more cohesive and coherent. In a definition given by Nwachukwu (2007), leadership is seen as a process whereby an individual influences a group of individuals to achieve a common goal. Similarly, Verber (2011) opines that leadership could be viewed as a community mobilization, initiation and motivation of employees to their involvement in the development of the organisation. Leadership is the ability to guide or move people in a particular direction and is a quality that must be possessed by a manager in order to induce, persuade and motivate others to identify with the goals of an institution. Leadership is a form of control during which a leader having assigned tasks to the subordinates follows up on the assigned duties to determine the level of adherence and the progress made towards the attainment of set objectives and goals; and initiating action where the need arises to correct deviations (Nkang and Usen, 2005). More so, leadership is important to all organizations to achieve goals as it is a key factor for improving the performance of the organization. The success or failure of an organization depends on the effectiveness of leadership at all levels as it is premised on the ability to influence attitudes, beliefs, and abilities of employees to achieve organizational goals.

Though there are several types of leadership styles ranging from autocratic leadership style (leadership style that is highly non-participative and requires little or no input or feedback from other members of the organisation), to democratic leadership style (leadership that allows for contributions and inputs from employees in the organisation thereby giving room for creativity and innovation in routine operations), transactional leadership style (leadership that is built on reward and punishment for tasks carried out. When assigned tasks are effectively executed reward follows and vice versa), transformational leadership style (leadership that clearly outlines goals and objectives to be achieved and positively drives subordinates to its achievement) and laissez-affaire leadership style (leadership that transfers decision making and power to subordinate staff) but the central underlying factor is that leadership is an essential predictor and has a central role in the working of any organization. Hence, Martindale (2011) suggested that there is no precise leadership style based on prior studies rather the professional manager should recognize the best style between other styles based on their operating environment in order to effectively engage the subordinate towards the achievement of organisation's goal. In other word, leadership is a management subordinate which is mostly directed towards persons and social communication (Wu, 2004).

The mention of social communication simply emphasizes that leadership requires communication as leadership cannot achieve the organisation's goal without effective flow of information between managers and subordinates. According to Nwachukwu (2005), all good leaders encourage effective communication by establishing channels of transmitting information to their subordinates whether formal or informal. Several studies have shown that effective organizational communication, such as high frequency, openness and accuracy, performance feedback, and adequacy of information about organizational policies and procedures are positively related to employees' feelings of happiness in the work place and job performance (Kacmar, Witt, Zivnuska and Gulley, 2003; Neves and Eisenberger, 2012). In line with the above, Proctor (2014) asserted that communication provides for avenues to recognize employee contribution and build organizational commitment. Thus, communication acts as a motivator in enhancing organizational commitment which is seen as the relative strength of an individual's identification with and involvement in a particular organization. Motivation on the other hand pertains to various drives, desires, needs, wishes and other forces that make an individual to behave in a certain way. Effective leaders need to understand what motivates the staff within the role they perform.

In the library, it is the place of the leaders to oversee and direct activities of the staff under them and give instructions on the set tasks relating to information sources and service provision without which information flow will be hindered thereby inhibiting the efficient delivery of information sources. Several studies have looked at the role of leadership styles on job satisfaction (Ahmed, Nawaz, Iqbal, Ali, Shaukat, and Usman, 2010; Azizi, Ghytasivand and Fakharmanesh, 2012; Bahadori, 2012; Bahrami, Ezzatabadi, Jamali, Dehghani, Tehrani and Ardakani, 2012; Khera and Gulati, 2012; Nasir, Fatimah, Mohammadi, Shahrazad and Khairudin, 2011; Olorunsola, 2012; Tiwari and Saxena, 2012; Yeop Yunus and Ishak, 2012); The role of leadership on employee performance (Shafie, Baghersalimi and Barghi, 2013) and leadership styles and job productivity of staff (Haenisch, 2012; Adeniran and Chidi, 2015). However, this paper intends to examine the influence of leadership style on the availability of information sources in university libraries.

## Assumption

This study assumes that the management variable of leadership is so indispensable that nothing tangible can be achieved without it. Especially in terms of making information sources available and accessible to users.

## Objective of the Study

The study seeks to determine the influence of leadership style on the availability of information sources in Nigerian university libraries in South-South Zone.

## Hypothesis

Leadership style has no significant influence on the availability of information sources in Nigerian university libraries in South-South Zone.

## Literature Review

The concept of managerial leadership permeates and structures the theory and practice of work organisations. In the management variables, leadership has been defined in terms of traits, behaviour, contingency, power and occupation of an administrative position. A general opinion that is supported by research results is that leadership style in an organisation is a major influence on the structure, strategy and the well-being of the organisation. Yuki (1998) believed that any definition of leadership is arbitrary and very subjective but defined leadership as the process wherein an individual member in a group or organisation enhances the interpretation of events, the choice of objectives and strategies, the organisation of activities, the maintenance of cooperative relationships, the development of skills and confidence by members, and the enlistment of support and cooperation from the people outside the group or organisation.

Usoro and Okon (2012) is the of opinion that leadership involves guiding and co-ordinating the work assigned to staff and all who are connected with tasks so much, such that instruction is effectively delivered and availability and accessibility of information sources is facilitated. Leadership style adopted by the head of any organisation including the library can lead to the success and this can also be an inhibition to the achievement of the organisational objectives. It is regarded as influences, the art or the process of influencing people so that they will strive willingly towards the achievement of goals (Evans, 2005).

Leadership is that phase of administration that focuses primarily upon the achievement of appropriate instructional expectations of an educational institution.

Through leadership, the goals of the library may be achieved as the leaders will work hand in hand with the other staff to implement the set task at the appropriate time. A leader that practices a good leadership style is an achiever because there is bound to be co-operation between him/her (leader) and the subordinates with free flow of information in the organisation which helps in decision making (Nkang and Usen, 2005). Leadership style used by academic librarians ensures cordiality and cooperation among staff and students in the library. Usoro and Okon (2012) state that when staffs are involved in decision making, they will also help to closely monitor the execution of such decisions. According to Covey (2004), the effectiveness of leadership is the ability to create an environment in which subordinates want to be a part of.

Empirical studies conducted by Lewin and Hite of the University of Lowa, cited in Nwachukwu (2007) identified three major leadership styles namely; autocratic, laissez-faire, and democratic/participative. The democratic/participative leader gets members involved in decision making, by guiding them to determine how the group functions. The autocratic leader provides the direction and determines policy, while the laissez-faire leader allows people in the group to determine their own direction and function without involvement. Chikere and Okafor (2011) summarised the activities of a leader as follows: providing new source of gains; designing organisational contexts to enable their followers to function effectively; motivating and inspiring the followers; driving goals to fruition; and acting as the moral compass of the organisation.

In the library context, Usoro and Okon (2012) asserted that the leader in acquisition section must lead the staff working under him/her to ensure that the newly acquired books are stamped, accession numbers are written, bar code are placed and the entire due process of the unit is carried out at stipulated time. The books are afterwards sent to the processing section; here the leader of the section must make sure that he/she leads the activities of processing of books by ensuring that all staff in the section works hand in hand. Catalogue cards must be prepared for proper filing in the catalogue cabinet if the library is not fully automated and the online catalogue must be updated. Once the books are sent to the circulation section the leaders ensures that the books are shelved accordingly on the appropriate shelves after it has been displayed on new arrival shelves for users to be aware. In addition, the leader of the circulation section manages the shelves by ensuring that books are shelved and the shelves are read to enhance availability and accessibility of the information resources in the library.

A good leader maintains a free flow of communication for greater productivity. He/she organises periodical meetings with his/her management staff and occasionally with all subordinates. Communication is the transfer of information ideas, understanding or feelings among people. Communication is pointed out as the hallmark of good management because it is through it that information flows in a clockwise, anticlockwise, lateral and vertically within the library (Usoro 2005). A good leader communicates effectively with his//her staff thus ensuring greater productivity.

Nwachukwu (2007) stated that all good leaders encourage effective communication by having established channels (formal and informal) of transmitting information to his/her subordinates. He maintained that when a leader sets the pace for open communication by encouraging subordinates to be frank, by soliciting information and sending out feedback, he/she sets a good organizational climate. In the library, communication is required to transmit the library's policies, programmes, schedules of duties, rules and regulation. Communication acts as a motivator. Motivation on the other hand pertains to various drives, desires, needs wishes and other forces that makes an individual to act in a way he/she does. A good leader motivates his/her staff members for greater productivity. A motivated staff functions effectively. It is the responsibility of the leader to discover the potentials in each staff and therefore apply the appropriate motivational technique because a motivated workforce will enhance availability of information sources in the library. Effective leader needs to understand what motivate the staff within the context of role they perform.

Without adequate leadership therefore, the objectives of the library cannot be achieved in terms of enhancing availability and accessibility of information sources which in turn will enhance quality teaching and learning in the universities in South-South Zone Nigeria.

## Research Method

The researcher used ex-post facto survey design. The study covered three federal universities out of five located in the South-South zone Nigeria namely; the University of Uyo, the University of Port Harcourt and the University of Calabar. The population was all academic librarians in the three universities under study. A purposive sampling technique was used to select 46 practicing librarians to form the sample for the study. The instrument for data collection was questionnaire tagged Management Variable of Leadership Style and Information Sources Availability (MVLSISA). The questionnaire used a four point rating scale with response from strongly agree to strongly disagree and asked respondents to tick the response that is applicable to the statements. The data obtained for the study were analysed using frequency distribution and percentages, while the hypothesis was tested using chi-square.

# Presentation of Result

The retrieved questionnaires were scored. The obtained data for influence of leadership style on the availability of information sources in Nigerian university libraries in South-South Zone libraries were collated and analysed. The summary of data analysis is presented in Table 1.

**Table 1: Respondents' Response to influence of leadership style on the availability of information sources in Nigerian university libraries in South-South Zone**

| S/N | Statements | N (%) | | Mean | Std. Dev. |
|---|---|---|---|---|---|
| | | Agree | Disagree | | |
| 1 | The leadership style used by my head encourages subordinates to work harder in order to make information sources available to the users | 69 (94.5) | 4 (5.5) | 3.55* | 0.76 |
| 2 | The leadership style used by my head encourages self-development for greater productivity which enhances availability of information sources | 69 (94.5) | 4 (5.5) | 3.33* | 0.75 |
| 3 | The leadership style used by my head is autocratically directed which hinders availability of information sources | 48 (65.8) | 25 (34.2) | 2.79* | 0.87 |
| 4 | The leadership style used by my head is democratic/participatory in nature and this enhances availability of information sources | 61 (83.6) | 12 (16.4) | 2.89* | 0.94 |
| 5 | The leadership style used by my head is laissez-faire which hinders availability of information sources | 51 (69.9) | 22 (30.1) | 2.89* | 0.91 |
| 6 | Exemplary leadership hinders mutilation and hoarding of information sources | 57 (78.1) | 16 (21.9) | 2.95* | 0.91 |
| 7 | Communication attributes of a leader exhibited by holding general/sectional meetings periodically enhances availability of information sources | 71 (97.3) | 2 (2.7) | 3.48* | 0.56 |

| 8 | Communication attributes of a leader exhibited by interacting with subordinates at leisure time enhances availability of information sources | 57 (78.1) | 16 (21.9) | 2.92* | 1.01 |
|---|---|---|---|---|---|
| 9 | Communication attributes of a leader exhibited by communicating effectively with other management staff enhances availability of information sources | 67 (91.8) | 6 (8.2) | 3.23* | 0.75 |
| 10 | Motivational attributes of a leader exhibited through positive response to subordinates' personal/official needs enhances availability of information sources | 69 (94.5) | 4 (5.5) | 3.16* | 0.69 |
| 11 | Motivational attributes of a leader exhibited by rewarding subordinates' performances enhances availability of information sources | 53 (72.6) | 20 (27.4) | 2.84* | 1.01 |
| 12 | Motivational attributes of a leader exhibited by disciplining of defaulting staff members enhances availability of information sources | 51 (69.9) | 22 (30.1) | 2.62* | 0.98 |

N = Frequency, % = Percentage; *Mean Scores above cut-off score of 2.5

The data on Table 1 shows the respondents responses to the questionnaire. The observed figures and the mean score reveal that the respondents know that leadership style is the prerequisite for the availability of information resources in the university libraries.

## Hypothesis Testing

The significance of the proposed hypothesis was tested using chi-square at .05 alpha as presented in Table 2.

**Table 2: Chi-square result for the influence of leadership style on the availability of information sources in Nigerian university libraries in South-South Zone**

| Variable | df | $X^2_{calc}$ | $X^2_{crit}$ | Contingency | Remark |
|---|---|---|---|---|---|
| influence of leadership style on the availability of information sources in Nigerian university libraries in South-South Zone | 11 | 206.99 | 19.66 | 0.82 | Reject $H_o$ |

As shown in Table 2, the calculated chi-square (206.99) is greater than the critical value (19.66 at df = 11); hence, the null hypothesis ($H_o$) of no significant influence of leadership style on the availability of information sources in Nigerian university libraries in South-South Zone is rejected. This means that leadership style as a management variable influences the availability of information sources in Nigerian university libraries in South-South Zone. The contingency coefficient of 0.82 shows that there is a very strong influence of leadership style as a management variable on the availability of information sources in university libraries. This implies that the choice of an appropriate leadership style will ensure the availability of information sources for library users.

## Discussion of Findings

The response distribution of respondents in Table 2 reveals that 94.5% of the respondents asserted that the leadership style as used by their heads encourages subordinates to work harder in order to make information sources available to the users. This is in line with the statement "the leadership style used by my head encourages subordinates to work harder in order to make information sources available to the users". This could be obtainable where the head ensures an accommodating and convenient environment for the discharge of duties within the library. This corroborates with the opinion of Covey (2004) that an effective leader should be able to create an environment in which people want to be a part of. That is, to encourage the subordinates to see to it that making information sources available is a thing they "want to" do rather than a thing they are "required to" do.

Also, the result in Table 2 reveals that the characteristic of leadership style adopted by head influences the subordinates so that they will strive willingly towards the achievement of goals which is to make information sources available in the university library. This was confirmed by 94.5% of the respondents who agreed that "The leadership style used by my head encourages self-development for greater productivity which enhances availability of information sources". This is in line with the opinion of Evans (2005). Effective leadership style adopted by the head will help to encourage the subordinates to develop appropriate skills towards their work in order to achieve library goals.

From the results, 65.8% of the respondents agreed to the statement that "the leadership style used by my head is autocratically directed which hinders availability of information sources". This implies that when a leader is autocratic; availability of information sources will be hindered possibly because the ideas are tailored to one direction being propounded by a single individual which is the autocratic leader. According to Nwachukwu (2007), an autocratic leader provides the direction and determines policy by himself.

In line with the statement "the leadership style used by my head is democratic/participatory in nature and this enhances availability of information sources", when a leader allows the participation of subordinates in decision making, they will help to closely monitor the execution of such decisions which will eventually enhance the availability of information sources this enhanced as supported by 83.6% of the respondents. This is supported by the findings of Usoro and Okon (2012) that the leadership style used by academic librarians ensures cordiality and cooperation among staff and students in the library.

On the other hand, 69.9% of the respondents confirmed that when a leader allows a care-free attitude to be exhibited by the subordinates as portrayed by the statement "the leadership style used by my head is laissez-faire which hinders availability of information sources", the availability of information sources will be hindered. According to Nwachukwu (2007), the laissez-faire leader allows people in the group to determine their own direction and function without involvement which may not be very suitable for the library which defines that all workers be dutiful and monitored for appropriate discharge of duties to enhance information sources availability.

Moreover, the results showed that 78.1% of the respondents agreed to the statement that "exemplary leadership hinders mutilation and hoarding of information sources". This implies that the leadership styles exhibited by the head in university libraries are such that is emulated by the subordinates prevent sensitive information from being mutilated or hoarded. This is in line with the assertions of Chikere and Okafor (2011) a leader is expected to act as the moral compass of the organisation. This implies that managerial staff in Nigerian university libraries are well versed with the technical know-how of library operations thereby are able to mentor and direct subordinates in cases of operational challenges. However, there are still lapses as indicated by the respondents who disagreed with the statement.

When the head exhibits good communication attributes by holding general/sectional meeting periodically to ensure a free flow of information for greater productivity which in turn will ensure availability of information sources in the library. This was asserted by 97.3% of the respondents in their responded to the statement "communication attributes of a leader by holding general/sectional meetings periodically enhances availability of information sources". This corroborates the findings of Usoro (2005) that communication is the hallmark of good management because it is through it that information flows in a clockwise, anticlockwise, lateral and vertically within the library.

Furthermore, for the statement "communication attributes of a leader exhibited by interacting with subordinates at leisure time enhances availability of information sources", 78.1% of the respondents confirmed that a leadership style which considers adequate communication with subordinates through established channels (formal and informal) and encourages subordinates to be frank, by soliciting information and sending out feedback, sets a good organizational climate for subordinates which will in turn enhance the availability of information sources. This is supported by the findings of Nwachukwu (2007) that all good leaders encourage effective communication with subordinates which is required to transmit the library's policies, programmes, schedules of duties, rules and regulation for effective functioning.

Also, when the leadership style adopted permits the head to communicate effectively with other top management staff, information sources could be made available to library users. Such communication is expected towards the achievement of library goals This was confirmed by the affirmative response of 91.8% of the respondents to the statement "communication attributes of a leader exhibited by communicating effectively with other management staff enhances availability of information sources". This is supported by the conclusions drawn by Nkang and Usen (2005) that a leader is an achiever when cooperation between him/her (leader) and the subordinates are encouraged with free flow of information in the organisation which helps in decision making and within the library setting; the primary aim is to make information sources available to intending users.

On the statement "motivational attributes of a leader exhibited through positive response to subordinates' personal/official needs enhances availability of information sources", 94.5% of the respondents affirm that a leader's interest in the welfare of subordinate staff will enhance availability of information sources in university libraries. This gives a sense concern and makes the subordinate to believe that his/her contributions are valued and to a great extent, it implies that the success of a leader depends on how much the cooperation of the subordinates can be commanded. The subordinates will tend to co-operate the more when they believe that their contributions are valued. According to Chikere and Okafor (2011), some of the activities of a leader is to function effectively, motivate and inspiring the followers.

Similarly, when hardworking staff are rewarded, it is imperative that they will be encouraged to be at their best in the discharge of their duties and seeming lazy ones would want to improve on their performances to receive such incentive and this would enhance availability of information sources in university libraries. This is confirmed by the positive responses of response of 72.6% of the respondents to the statement "motivational attributes of a leader exhibited by rewarding subordinates' performances enhances availability of information sources". It is imperative that a leader within the library motivates his/her staff members for greater productivity because a motivated staff functions effectively. Such rewards may come in the forms of accelerated promotion, award/honour, commendation letter, cash gift and material gifts. This helps in the leader to discover the potentials in each staff. According to Nwachukwu (2007), a motivated workforce will enhance availability of information sources in the library.

From the results, 69.9% of the respondents agreed that "motivational attributes of a leader exhibited by disciplining of defaulting staff members enhances availability of information sources". This implies that the characteristic of the head to be able to maintain standards and enforce orderliness within the university will enhance staff to be serious with their duties. Staff discipline for misconduct also helps to ensure that work ethics are strongly adhered to. This result is supported by Nkang and Usen (2005) who asserted that when a leader assigns tasks to the subordinates; must monitor and check to determine whether or not they are adhered to and whether the proper progress is made towards the attainment of set objectives and goals in order to serve as a pointer to act where the need arises to correct deviations.

## Conclusion and Recommendations

This study reveals that leadership style has a significant influence on the availability of information sources in Nigerian university libraries in South-South Zone. Where the appropriate leadership style is not adopted by the management cadre in the library, there is bound to be conflicting ideas which will not enhance the achievement of one of the cardinal goals in the library which is to make information sources available for the users. From the findings of the study, it is evident that management staff in Nigerian University libraries show a high sense of regard to their subordinates by allowing their participation in decision making process, ensuring effective communication and giving motivation to harness greater productivity. Having identified leadership style as a factor which could enhance or hinder the availability of information sources in the university library; the following recommendations are made:

i. Management cadre of the library should ensure that leadership roles within the library should be discharged in a such a way that all key players (including the subordinates) are allowed to contribute their quota towards making available, information sources to library users.

ii. The communication tool should be cautiously utilized to ensure that there are no breaks in information dissemination channels among all categories of library staff to ensure effective work flow which will enhance availability of information sources to users.

iii. Management staff in the library should endeavour to motivate subordinates using all classified motivation tools; be they material or non-material.

## References

Adeniran, S. & Chidi, D. (2015). Leadership styles and job productivity of university library staff: Interrogating the nexus. *Library Philosophy and Practice (e-journal).* Avaialable at http://digitalcommons.unl.edu/libphilprac/ 1269. Accessed 21st January 2017

Ahmed, I., Nawaz, M., Iqbal, N., Ali, I., Shaukat, Z. & Usman, A. (2010). Effects of motivational factors on employees job satisfaction a case study of University of the Punjab, Pakistan. *International Journal of Business and Management, 5*(3): 70-80.

Anchor, S. (2010). *The Happiness Advantage.* New York, NY: Crown Business

Azizi, S., Ghytasivand, F. & Fakharmanesh, S. (2012). Impact of brand orientation, internal marketing and job satisfaction on the internal brand equity: The case of Iranian's Food and Pharmaceutical. *International Review of Management and Marketing, 2*(2), 122-129.

Bahadori, M. (2012). The effect of emotional intelligence on entrepreneurial behavior: A case study in a Medical Science University. *Asian Journal of Business Management, 4*(1), 81-85.

Bahrami, M. A., Ezzatabadi, M. R., Jamali, E., Dehghani Tafti, A., Tehrani, A. G. & Ardakani Entezarian, S. (2012). Job motivation factors: a case study of an Iranian Medical University. J*ournal of Management and Business Studies,* 1(10), 345-352.

Bennett, N. & Anderson, L. (2003). *Rethinking educational leadership.* London: Sage Publication.

Chikere, A. A & Okafor, J. C. (2011). Management of Organisational Behaviour II. Enugu: Hipuks Additional Press.

Covey, S. R. (2004). *The 8th Habit: From Effectiveness to Greatness,* New York: Free Express.

Duckett, H. & Macfarlane, E. (2003). Emotional Intelligence and Transformational Leadership in retailing. *Leadership & Organization Development Journal,* 24, 309-317.

Eisenberger, R. & Stinglhamber, F. (2011). *Perceived organizational support: Fostering enthusiastic and productive employees.* Washington, DC: APA

Evans, G. E. (2005). Management Techniques for Librarians. London: Academic Press Inc.

Gannon, M. (1997). *Organisational Behaviour: A Managerial and organisational Perspective,* Boston: Little Brown and Company.

Khera, S. N. & Gulati, K. (2012). Job satisfaction: A ray of sunshine even in burnout times: Perceptual analysis of IT organizations. *International Journal of Management & Information Technology,* 1(3), 111-117.

Lewin & Hite cited in Nwachukwu (2007). *Management Theory and Practice.* Onitsha: Africana Press

Lewin & Hite, cited in Nwachukwu (2007). *Management Theory and Practice,* Onitsha: Africana.

Martindale, N. (2011). Leadership styles: How to handle the different personas. *Journal of Strategic Communication Management,* 15(8), 32-35.

Mehrad, A. & Fallahi, B. (2014). The role of leadership styles on staff´s job satisfaction in public organizations. ACTA Universitaria: Multidisciplinary Scientific Journal, 24(5): 27-32

Nasir, R., Fatimah, O., Mohammadi, M. S., Shahrazad, W. S. W. & Khairudin, R. (2011). Demographic variables as moderators in the relationship between job satisfaction and task performance. *Journal of Social Science and Humanities,* 19, 33-40.

Neves, P. & Eisenberger, R. (2012). Management communication and employee performance: the contribution of perceived organizational support. *Human Performance.* 25:5, 452-464. Available at www.psychology.uh.edu/faculty/Eisenberger/files/Neves-Eisenberger-communication.pdf. doi: 10.1080/08959285/2012/721834

Nkang, I. E. & Usen, H. (2005). Supervision of Primary School Teacher for Effective Instruction: Implication for Implementing School Curriculum in Nigeria. Nigerian Journal of Curriculum Studies. pp. 12.

Nwachukwu, C. C. (2007). *Management Theory and Practice.* Onitsha: Africana Press

Olorunsola, E. O. (2012). Job satisfaction and personal characteristics of administrative staff in South West Nigeria Universities. *Journal of Emerging Trends in Educational Research and Policy Studies, 3*(1), 46-50.

Proctor, C. (2014). Effective organizational communication affects attitude, happiness, and job satisfaction. M. A. Thesis, Southern Utah University, United States of America.

Rhoades, L., & Eisenberger, R. (2002). Perceived organizational support: A review of the literature. *Journal of Applied Psychology*, 87, 698–714.

Tiwari, P. & Saxena, K. (2012). Human resource management practices. *Journal of Pakistan Business Review, 13*(4), 669-705.

Usoro, I. M. P. (2005). Management Variables and Information Sources Availability in Nigerian University Libraries in the South-South Zone. Ph. D. Dissertation.

Usoro, I. P., & Okon, H. I. (2012). Supervision as a management Variable that Enhances Availability of Information Sources in Nigerian University Libraries. The Information Technologist. Pp. 67-69.

Wu, M. (2004). A review of relationship between principal's leadership style and teacher's job satisfaction. *Journal of Meiho Institute of Technology*, 23(2), 235-250.

Yeop Yunus, K. N. & Ishak, S. (2012). The Relationship between Internal Satisfaction and External Satisfaction amongst Hotel Customers in Malaysia. *International Journal of Economics Business and Management Studies,* 1(1), 21-29.

Yuki, G. A. (1998). Leadership in Organisation. Upper Saddle River: Hill.

# QUALITY ASSURANCE ISSUES

# 5

# Program Accreditation and Licensure Examination Performance of Philippine Higher Education Institutions with Engineering Program in CALABARZON Region and Manila

Jake M. Laguador PhD

## Abstract

*Program accreditation is a function of quality assurance that measures the performance against the vision and mission of the Philippine Higher Education Institutions as well as to the defined criteria and standard. This study aims to explore the influence of program accreditation to licensure examination performance between private and public higher education institutions with engineering programs in CALABARZON Region and Manila, Philippines. Results of licensure examinations for Mechanical Engineers, Electrical Engineers, Civil Engineers and Electronic Engineers were taken from the website of Professional Regulation Commission (PRC). Results showed that there is a moderate level of accreditation of Engineering Programs in CALABARZON and Manila. CALABARZON schools obtained higher performance than Manila in the overall result of licensure exam with repeaters. Public schools performed higher than the private both for the first timers and the result with repeaters. Program accreditation is a factor that can determine the performance of schools in the licensure exam for engineers. Senior High School students may be advised to enroll in engineering programs within the CALABARZON area for they can still achieve the quality education that schools in Manila can offer.*

**Keywords:** *Program Accreditation, Engineering, Quality Assurance, CALABARZON, Manila*

## Introduction

There are various measures of performance to determine certain level of quality. It is always part of the mission of Philippine institutions of higher learning to promote the culture of academic excellence that strengthens the foundation of school reputation and image to the local and global communities. Laguador and Dotong (2015) stated that the seal of quality is what people want to ensure to get from the goods and services they acquire from the providers and this assurance can only be certified by external bodies and agencies who already established greater reputation in assessing and evaluating the performance of the industries.

Program accreditation is one of the strategies of HEIs in submitting themselves to external evaluators and to scrutinize their educational inputs, processes and outputs as quality assurance mechanism (Laguador, Villas & Delgado, 2014) based on the standards of the selected accrediting body.

The accreditation system in the Philippines started in 1957 through the Philippine Accrediting Association of Schools, Colleges and Universities (PAASCU) which is the oldest and largest accrediting agency in the country when they developed evaluation instruments, trained the accreditors and performed public information about the importance of voluntary accreditation (Arcelo, 2003; Pijano, 2010). There are several accrediting agencies in the Philippines which are all under the umbrella of Federation of Accrediting Agency of the Philippines (FAAP) such as: Philippine Association of Accrediting Agencies of Schools, Colleges and Universities (PAASCU), the Accrediting Association of Chartered Colleges and Universities of the Philippines (AACCUP), the Philippine Association of Colleges and Universities-Commission on Accreditation (PACU-COA), the Association of Christian Schools and Colleges (ACSC), PACUCOA has 150 member institutions and 1,067 accredited programs in various levels as of April 2013 while AACCUP is a non-profit, non-stock corporation now composed of 111 State Universities and Colleges (AACCUP Institutional Members, 2015).

In the Philippines, the Commission on Higher Commission (CHED) supports the initiatives of HEIs to undergo voluntary accreditation of self-regulation and peer evaluation through giving incentives and greater autonomy therefore, accreditation is now viewed as a means of promoting educational excellence ("CHED Accreditation in the Philippines"). CHED policy clearly benefits accrediting agencies, the amount of control it exerts is also a threat to the private voluntary nature of the accreditation system, which is one of its strengths (Pijano, 2010). Compliance to certain international standards and practices of most developed countries makes one organization from a third world country like the Philippines more trusted and regarded as forerunner in the field.

Accreditation stimulates the interest and motivation of the management to pursue higher level of assessment to sustain and certify the quality of education they provide for the youth. Conchada and Tiongco (2015) mentioned that "accreditation is one way that HEIs keep themselves in check with the standards. With the growing number of HEIs in the country and the demand for skilled workers in the global market, there is an urgent need to further enhance quality of education". Quality assurance is applied in HEIs to achieve "quality education" (Al Tobi& Duque, 2015).

Meanwhile, one of the evidences in the criteria of Instruction and student achievements of the degree program with board exam is the result of licensure exams. Laguador and Dizon (2013) mentioned that the Licensure Examination for Engineers is a tool that measures and ensures the quality of engineers who would join the workforce of various manufacturing industries in the Philippines and abroad. The Professional Regulations Commission (PRC) as the duly constituted body created for this function has been consistent in its task of screening who among the graduates from all board courses will be granted the professional licenses based on the board exam results.

This study investigated the board performance of private and government engineering schools for the last 3 years. Based on the initial data, there is only one-third of the government schools offering engineering programs with board exam in CALABARZON and half in Manila area. The study would like to explore the probability of variation between private and public engineering schools in two areas of investigation. CALABARZON as one of the regions in the Philippines with the fastest growing economic activities due to large number of industrial and science parks that were established in Batangas, Laguna and Cavite. With the increasing number of Techno Parks in the region, there is also demand for engineering graduates. HEIs and Industries are working together to produce competitive graduates who will become part of both local and global labor market. Therefore, providing quality education to the students is always in the forefront.

This study also dealt with the likelihood of obtaining consistent higher board exam performance if there is a higher level of program accreditation. It provides basic analysis if program accreditation has a direct impact to Engineering Licensure Examination Performance through various quality measures implemented by the Philippine HEIs in meeting the standards of these accreditations. It is also the concern of the present study to look into the possibility if there are some variations in the board exam performance of engineering programs with and without accreditation.

In the marketing aspect of the study, some people believed that universities and colleges in Manila area are better training grounds than provincial schools. But this can be considered just a notion or misconception that people cannot derive any generalization, provided they have a scientific basis. That is why, this study is concerned on determining if there is underlying difference in the Engineering Licensure Exam performance between schools in CALABARZON and Manila. It investigated the Manila schools achievement in board examination; that can also be achieved by provincial schools in the CALABARZON. But this study is limited in the result of Licensure Examination as basis of school performance while other aspects of quality will not be taken into account.

The result of the study will serve as baseline information to HEIs in providing better delivery of instruction and effective educational leadership and management to strengthen the performance of Engineering Licensure Examination with the help of program accreditation.

## Objectives of the Study

This study aims to conduct a comparative analysis of Program Accreditation and Licensure Examination Performance of Private and Government Engineering Schools in CALABARZON and Manila. It specifically aims to determine the level of program accreditation of Higher Education Institutions in CALABARZON and Manila with Engineering degree programs; determine the number of Public and Private Schools with and without Accreditation Across Four Engineering Programs; determine the passing percentage in Licensure Examination for Engineers for the last three years in terms of Location, Type of School; Degree program; and Program Accreditation; test the correlation between the level of program accreditation and Engineering Licensure Examination Performance; test the difference in engineering licensure examination performance in terms of Location, Type of School, Degree Program, level of Accreditation and province; and provide the implication of the findings to the practices of HEIs in terms of quality assurance.

## Methods

### Research Design

Descriptive method of research will be employed in the study. In quantitative descriptive research, the researcher's purpose is to answer questions about a variable status by creating numerical descriptions of the frequency with which one of the variables occurs (Zulueta & Costales, 2003).

## Subjects

**Table 1: Frequency Distribution of Schools in CALABARZON and Manila**

|         | Private | Public | Total |
|---------|---------|--------|-------|
| Cavite  | 11      | 4      | 15    |
| Laguna  | 7       | 6      | 13    |
| Batangas| 6       | 2      | 8     |
| Rizal   | 5       | 2      | 7     |
| Quezon  | 1       | 3      | 4     |
| Manila  | 10      | 5      | 15    |
| **Total** | **40** | **22** | **62** |

Table 1 shows the frequency distribution of schools in CALABARAZON and Manila. There are 42 private schools and 22 public engineering schools with a total of 64 will serve as subjects under study. Only schools with at least 3 licensure examination results will be included in the study

Table 2: Frequency Distribution of Engineering Programs

| Engineering Degree Programs | | f |
|-----|------------------------------------|-----|
| 1.  | Electronics Engineering            | 52  |
| 2.  | Electrical Engineering             | 37  |
| 3.  | Civil Engineering                  | 33  |
| 4.  | Mechanical Engineering             | 33  |
| 5.  | Chemical Engineering               | 10  |
| 6.  | Marine Engineering                 | 4   |
| 7.  | Geodetic Engineering               | 2   |
| 8.  | Manufacturing Engineering          | 2   |
| 9.  | Agricultural Engineering           | 2   |
| 10. | Environment & Sanitary Engineering | 2   |
| 11. | Mining Engineering                 | 1   |
| 12. | Petroleum Engineering              | 1   |
| 13. | Food Engineering                   | 1   |
| 14. | Instrumentation & Control Engineering | 1 |
| 15. | Construction Engineering           | 1   |

Table 2 presents the frequency distribution of engineering programs in CALABARZON and Manila. Only those engineering programs that almost half of the colleges and universities within the areas under study will be included in the study. Electronics Engineering (52), Electrical Engineering (37), Civil Engineering (33) and Mechanical Engineering (33) will serve as the degree programs under investigation.

## Instrument and Procedure

Documentary analysis of the result of performance of engineering schools in the licensure examination was obtained from the website of Professional Regulation Commission in the last three (3) years. Present level of program accreditation was taken from PACUCOA, PAASCU and AACUP. Data were gathered from March to May 2016. Only those data published and made available during that period were included in the study.

## Data Analysis

Frequency count and percentage were used to quantify the result of data gathered from the program accreditation while arithmetic mean was used to interpret the result of the board examination performance. Eta-square was used to test the correlation between the level of program accreditation and performance in licensure examination and chi-square was used to test if there is difference between public and private schools in terms of program accreditation while independent sample t-test was used to determine if there is significant difference in the performance between Private and Government Schools, between CALABARZON and Manila; as well as between with and without program accreditation. Analysis of Variance (ANOVA) was used to test the difference in the licensure examination performance among provinces in CALABARZON, level of accreditation and across four engineering programs.

The given scale was used to interpret the result of percentage of degree programs with and without accreditation: 0.00 – 20.00: Very Low (VL); 20.01 – 40.00: Low (L); 40.01 – 60.00: Moderate (M); 60.01 – 80.00: High (H); 80.01 – 100.00: Very High (VH)

## Results and Discussion

Table 3 presents the level of program accreditation of Higher Education Institutions with Engineering Degree Programs in CALABARZON and Manila. Out of 150 engineering programs across CALABARZON and Manila, there are 68 or 45.3 percent have program accreditations in various levels while 82 or 54.7 percent have no accreditation at all including those programs with preliminary status.

**Table 3: Level of program accreditation of Higher Education Institutions with Engineering Degree Programs in CALABARZON and Manila**

| | Level | | | | | % of Programs w/ Accreditation | VI | No. of Programs | No of Schools |
|---|---|---|---|---|---|---|---|---|---|
| | 0 | 1 | 2 | 3 | 4 | | | | |
| Cavite | 16 | 3 | 1 | 1 | 0 | 23.8 | L | 21 | 15 |
| Laguna | 21 | 5 | 3 | 0 | 4 | 36.4 | L | 33 | 13 |
| Batangas | 13 | 1 | 1 | 4 | 0 | 31.6 | L | 19 | 8 |

| | | | | | | | | | |
|---|---|---|---|---|---|---|---|---|---|
| Rizal | 3 | 4 | 0 | 0 | 0 | 57.1 | M | 7 | 7 |
| Quezon | 3 | 3 | 5 | 0 | 0 | 72.7 | H | 11 | 4 |
| Manila | 26 | 2 | 15 | 7 | 9 | 55.9 | M | 59 | 15 |
| **Total** | **82** | **18** | **25** | **12** | **13** | **54.7** | **M** | **150** | **62** |

*Scale: 0.00 – 20.00: Very Low (VL); 20.01 – 40.00: Low (L); 40.01 – 60.00: Moderate (M); 60.01 – 80.00: High (H); 80.01 – 100.00: Very High (VH)*

Engineering Programs with International Accreditation were considered have Level 4 status as its equivalent in local accreditation. Engineering program with Level 2 Accredited Status has the highest number followed by Level 1 Status while Level 4 and Level 3 have the least. In the CALABARZON region considering the four identified engineering programs, Laguna has the most number of engineering degree programs followed by Cavite and Batangas while Quezon and Rizal have the least number of engineering programs due to less number of schools offering the engineering program.

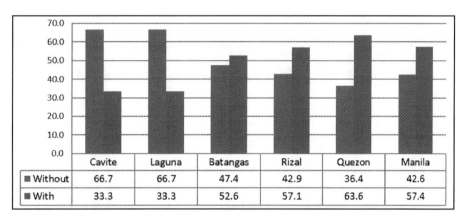

**Figure 1: Comparison of Percentage of Schools in Engineering between With and Without Accreditation across CALABARZON and Manila**

Figure 1 reveals that there are more schools with engineering programs in Laguna and Cavite which are not yet accredited by any accrediting body while Quezon and Rizal have the highest percentage.

However, Rizal and Quezon have the least number of schools with engineering program as shown in Table 3. Meanwhile, Batangas and Manila have more than 50 percent of schools with engineering programs are accredited by PACUCOA and PAASCU. The program accreditation in CALABARZON and Manila is considerate moderate in which more than half of their program offerings in engineering with board exam are accredited. This signifies that Universities and Colleges in both regions are still trying to exceed the minimum requirements of the Commission on Higher Education.

**Table 4: Frequency and Percentage Distribution of Public and Private HEIs in terms of Accreditation across Four Engineering Programs**

|  | Without | | | | | With | | | | | |
|---|---|---|---|---|---|---|---|---|---|---|---|
|  | Public | | Private | | Total % | VI | Public | | Private | | Total % | VI |
|  | f | % | f | % | | | f | % | f | % | | |
| ME | 1 | 14.3 | 10 | 47.6 | 39.3 | L | 6 | 85.7 | 11 | 52.4 | 60.7 | H |
| EcE | 5 | 38.5 | 27 | 73.0 | 64.0 | H | 8 | 61.5 | 10 | 27.0 | 36 | L |
| EE | 7 | 53.8 | 13 | 50.0 | 51.2 | M | 6 | 46.2 | 13 | 50.0 | 48.7 | M |
| CE | 3 | 30.0 | 12 | 48.0 | 42.9 | M | 7 | 70.0 | 13 | 52.0 | 57.1 | M |
| **Total** | **16** | 37.2 | **62** | 56.9 | 51.3 | **M** | **27** | 62.8 | **47** | 43.1 | 48.7 | M |

*Scale: 0.00 – 20.00: Very Low (VL); 20.01 – 40.00: Low (L); 40.01 – 60.00: Moderate (M); 60.01 – 80.00: High (H); 80.01 – 100.00: Very High (VH)*

Table 4 presents the frequency and percentage distribution of public and private HEIs in terms of accreditation across four engineering programs. When considered the type of school in terms of accreditation, overall, in every 10 engineering programs, there are 6 from Private schools having no accreditation and 4 with accreditation. Mechanical engineering program has the highest percentage of programs with accreditation both public and private schools followed by Civil Engineering while Electrical Engineering has the same percentage for private school with and without accreditation. This signifies that there is a high level of program accreditation in Mechanical Engineering in CALABARZON and Manila and moderate level in Civil and Electrical Engineering programs.

However, Electronics Engineering has the highest percentage of private schools without accreditation and lowest percentage of degree programs with accreditation from private schools. This signifies that Electronics Engineering has low level of program accreditation in the CALABARZON and Manila.

It is also good to note that there are less non-accredited programs in Mechanical Engineering and Civil Engineering from the Public Schools while the Private schools have almost similar number of engineering programs both with and with accreditation except for Electronics Engineering with higher percentage of non-accreditation.

**Table 5: Mean Passing Percentage in Licensure Examination for Engineers**

|  | First Timer | | Total | |
|---|---|---|---|---|
|  | Mean % | Std. Deviation | Mean | Std. Deviation |
| CALABARZON (N=96) | 49.95 | 28.06 | 47.94 | 25.19 |
| Manila (N=56) | 50.66 | 26.95 | 45.11 | 25.00 |
| Public (N=43) | 57.25 | 24.56 | 53.61 | 22.62 |
| Private (N=109) | 47.43 | 28.29 | 44.24 | 25.60 |

| | | | | |
|---|---|---|---|---|
| ME (N=28) | 69.49 | 23.62 | 63.92 | 24.11 |
| EcE (N=50) | 30.58 | 18.93 | 32.85 | 17.93 |
| EE (N=39) | 61.89 | 24.32 | 55.02 | 24.99 |
| CE (N=35) | 49.81 | 26.93 | 44.29 | 23.63 |
| No Accreditation (N=82) | 38.1796 | 26.07274 | 36.5537 | 23.78416 |
| Level I Status (N=18) | 60.8489 | 21.72457 | 55.3083 | 19.65700 |
| Level II Status (N=25) | 54.8720 | 23.40521 | 51.1224 | 21.00110 |
| Level III Status (N=12) | 72.6125 | 16.44736 | 64.0417 | 18.02881 |
| Level IV Status (N=13) | 77.4877 | 17.70419 | 73.3931 | 18.64811 |
| **Total** | **50.21** | **27.57** | **46.89** | **25.08** |

Table 5 shows the mean passing percentage in licensure examination for engineers. Colleges and Universities in Manila obtained 50.66 percent for First Timers of passing percentage in licensure examination for engineers which is higher than the performance of schools in CALABARZON with 49.95 percent with lower degree of dispersion in favor of Manila schools. However, CALABARZON has a total of 47.94 percent of passing percentage with repeaters which is higher than Manila with 45.11 percent with almost comparable standard deviation.

Public schools obtained higher score of 53.61 percent in the licensure exam compared to private schools with 44.24 percent. When computed for the chi-square between public and private schools in terms of program accreditation as shown in Appendix B, the result shows that there is a significant difference between private and public schools wherein there are more private schools without accreditation than public schools. Therefore, program accreditation can be a factor in the licensure examination performance of public schools.

When compared the performance between engineering programs, Mechanical Engineering (ME) obtained the highest score of 69.49 percent and 63.92 percent both for first timers and with repeaters respectively, followed by Electrical Engineering (EE) with total percentage of 55.02 percent and Civil Engineering with 44.29 percent while Electronics Engineering (EcE) obtained the least score of 32.85 percent.

Out of 150 engineering programs across CALABARZON and Manila, there are 68 or 45.3 percent have program accreditations in various levels while 82 or 54.7 percent have no accreditation at all including those programs with preliminary visit status. Results showed that engineering programs with Level IV status have the highest passing percentage for both first timers and with repeaters followed by programs with Level III Status and Level I Status while Level II Status obtained the least percentage among programs with Accreditation while evidently that these engineering programs without accreditation obtained the least passing percentage of 38.18 percent and 36.55 percent for first timers and with repeaters, respectively.

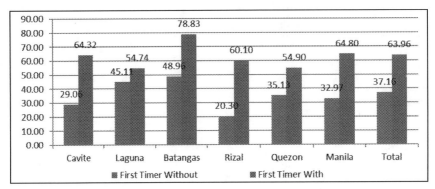

**Figure 2: Comparison of Performance of Schools in Engineering Between With and Without Accreditation**

It is highlighted in Figure 2 the comparison of performance of school in engineering for first timers between with and without accreditation. Results show that schools with program accreditation performed better in Licensure Examination for Engineers compared to those without program accreditation. Batangas obtained the highest percentage of passers for first timers followed by Manila, Cavite and Rizal while Quezon and Laguna obtained the least ratings. Likewise, schools without accreditation in Batangas still obtained the highest passing percentage followed by Laguna, Quezon and Manila while Cavite and Rizal obtained the least passing percentage.

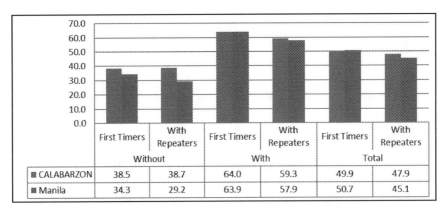

**Figure 3: Comparison of passing percentage Between CALABARZON and Manila in terms of Accreditation**

Figure 3 illustrates the comparison of passing percentage Between CALABARZON and Manila in terms of accreditation. The passing percentage of schools with and without accreditation in CALABARZON is higher than Manila both for first timers and with repeaters. However in total, schools in Manila obtained higher passing percentage with 0.08 difference for first timers but schools in CALABARZON still obtained higher passing percentage in overall with repeaters. The performance in the Licensure Examination for four engineering programs of provincial schools compared to HEIs in Manila is not substantially different with very minimal variation. It is good to note that the quality of education of HEIs in CALABARZON can be considered comparable with the schools in Manila. CALABARZON Schools in engineering have the capacity to produce similar percentage of passers.

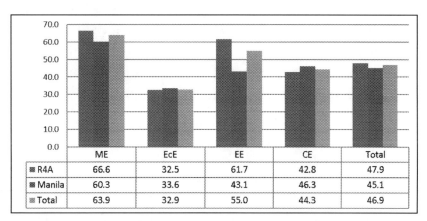

| | ME | EcE | EE | CE | Total |
|---|---|---|---|---|---|
| R4A | 66.6 | 32.5 | 61.7 | 42.8 | 47.9 |
| Manila | 60.3 | 33.6 | 43.1 | 46.3 | 45.1 |
| Total | 63.9 | 32.9 | 55.0 | 44.3 | 46.9 |

**Figure 4: Total Passing Percentage between CALABARZON and Manila Across Programs**

Figure 4 reveals that the passing percentages in terms of ME and EE are higher in CALABARZON than in Manila while the result in terms of EcE and CE is higher in Manila than CALABARZON. Meanwhile, in overall passing percentage, the results show that CALABARZON (47.9%) obtained higher performance than Manila (45.1%). Furthermore, in terms of degree program, licensure examination for Mechanical Engineers has the highest rating of 63.9 percent followed by EE (55%) and CE (44.3%) while EcE obtained the least passing percentage of 32.9 percent.

**Table 6: Relationship between the Level of Accreditation and Performance of Schools in Licensure Examination**

| | r-value | p-value | Remarks |
|---|---|---|---|
| Level of Accreditation and Performance Rating | .475(**) | .000 | Significant |

** Correlation is significant at the 0.01 level (2-tailed).

Table 6 reveals the relationship between the level of accreditation and performance of HEIs in Licensure Examination. There is a significant relationship between the level of accreditation and the performance of schools in Licensure examination for four engineering programs as denoted by the p-value of 0.000 which is less than the 0.01 level of significance.

This implies that the program accreditation is a factor that can determine the performance of schools in the licensure exam for engineers. It is one of the major objectives of the program accreditation to improve the delivery of all educational services to the students that could either directly or indirectly affect the knowledge, skills and attitude of the future engineers. With the finding of this study, it is good to note that accreditation has really an impact to the program being accredited as the result of licensure examination is concerned. The efforts of the colleges and universities in taking time to prepare for the accreditation really contributed to the reputation of the organization and to the personal and professional career of their graduates. Conchada and Tiongco (2015) emphasized that those who undergo accreditation experience an improvement in their programs because of the process of internal and external quality assurance and it keeps the institution motivated to adhere to its prescribed vision, mission and goals.

Table 7 reveals the test of difference on passing percentage across variables. There is no significant difference in the passing percentage of Licensure Examination for Engineers between schools in Manila and CALABARZON as denoted by the computed p-value of 0.503 which is higher than the 0.05 level of significance. This signifies that the performance of provincial schools in national board examination is somewhat comparable in the performance rating of schools in Manila.HEIs in the CALABARZON are evolving to provide the same level of quality which schools in Manila can offer. The growing number of Industrial Parks in CALABARZON makes it a good training ground for the future engineers to practice their profession as trainees.

**Table 7: Test of Difference on Passing Percentage**

| Variables | | Passing Percentage | t-value | p-value | Remarks |
|---|---|---|---|---|---|
| Location | Manila | 45.11 | .672 | .503 | Not Significant |
| | CALABARZON | 47.94 | | | |
| Type of School | Private | 44.24 | 2.214 | .029 | Significant |
| | Public | 53.61 | | | |
| Accreditation | Without | 35.68 | -6.39 | .000 | Significant |
| | With | 58.71 | | | |
| | | | f-value | p-value | |
| Program | ME | 63.92 | 13.828 | .000 | Significant |
| | ECE | 32.85 | | | |
| | EE | 55.02 | | | |
| | CE | 44.29 | | | |

| | | | | | |
|---|---|---|---|---|---|
| **Province** | Cavite | 40.05 | 2.012 | .080 | Not Significant |
| | Laguna | 47.44 | | | |
| | Batangas | 62.19 | | | |
| | Rizal | 39.96 | | | |
| | Quezon | 41.85 | | | |

Meanwhile, there is a significant difference in the performance rating between private and public schools as indicated by the computed p-value of 0.029 which is less than the 0.05 level of significance. Public colleges and universities in the CALABARZON and Manila perform higher in the licensure examination for engineers than Private institutions.

The result of ECE licensure exam is significantly lower than ME, EE and CE while ME is significantly higher than EcE and CE. It signifies that there are more mechanical engineering examinees passed the licensure exam than EcE and CE while EcE has the lowest passing percentage.

The performance rating of schools with no accreditation is significantly lower than those schools with accreditation. It is always part of the criteria of accreditation especially for the board programs is the result of licensure examination. Before an engineering program gets accredited, it needs to meet the requirements of accreditation. Although when tested the difference per level using ANOVA, level 2 status of accreditation is not significantly higher than the result of licensure exam of no accredited program, it is still closed to the average performance of Level 1 status. Other factors may be considered in the next study to identify the reasons for a little drop on the performance rating of those engineering programs with Level 2 status. But in overall, definitely, program accreditation in engineering is really something that needs to consider by the school administrators of putting quality assurance on their programs. It is one way of improving the educational practices and processes of delivering instruction and other related curricular activities for a holistic development of the students.

Furthermore, there is no significant difference on the performance ratings among schools in the CALABARZON when grouped according to province. Although Batangas obtained the highest performance mean rating for the last three years, the computed mean variance is not enough to consider its difference. This signifies that schools anywhere in CALABARZON especially those with program accreditations could be able to produce engineers without any significant variation in performance rating in the result of board examination.

## Implications to Quality Assurance

The increasing trend of program accreditation in most higher education institutions in the Philippines is one way of expressing the interest of school administrators to adapt quality assurance mechanism to distinguish and uplift their status from the rest of the institutions who are only complying with the minimum requirements of the Commission on Higher Education (CHED). Since the concept of quality and quality assurance differs from one person to another; and from one institution to another, defining what quality is for the institution will help in setting the HEIs' quality goals and objectives, as well as directions (Al Tobi & Duque, 2015). Being accredited is putting something different and added value to the curricular offerings. People might not see it as an advantage because of their lack of awareness on the rationale of accreditation but it should something to be aspired and aimed by the HEIs especially during the K to 12 transition and ASEAN integration.

On the result of this study, the impact of program accreditation to the delivery of educational services to the students is evident on the result of licensure examination for engineers. The program accreditation itself has no direct influence on the performance rating of any institution in the licensure examination but the process of complying with the requirements, following the standard procedures and considering various aspects of quality on the student development are some of the best practices derived from the program accreditation. It is gearing towards the accomplishment of targets from the strategic plans and making realized the vision and mission of the organization.

Being an HEI in the CALABARZON region wherein going to Manila is just in couple of hours, being complacent for what the institution has achieved today would not be relevant tomorrow due to high competition in the region. CALABARZON is the second region with the highest number of private and public HEIs next to National Capital Region. It is indeed appropriate to keep the program offerings notable, updated and in-demand with the current trends in science and technology especially that the CALABARZON is highly industrialized region where most of the techno parks are situated. In order to keep abreast with the latest information and updates, faculty members should always be sent to seminars, training and conferences so that they could grasp fresh ideas from other HEIs and partner industries. Investing in human capital is always important part of the institutions' thrust through empowering people and strengthening their knowledge and skills with innovation and creativity. Providing quality education to future engineers and professionals is like preparing the nation to the next level of competitiveness.

## Conclusion

There is a moderate level of accreditation of Engineering Programs in CALABARZON and Manila wherein only Mechanical Engineering program obtained a high level of program accreditation and Electronics Engineering obtained the least. There are 68 or 45.3 percent have program accreditations in various levels mostly in Level 2 while 82 or 54.7 percent of the programs have no accreditation at all.

Majority of the engineering programs in the public HEIs are accredited while almost half of the engineering programs in private schools are accredited except for EcE but in general, there are more than half of the engineering programs in private schools are without accreditation.

Engineering schools in Manila performed a little higher than CALABARZON in the result of licensure exam for the first timers but CALABARZON schools obtained higher performance than Manila in the overall result with repeaters. Meanwhile Public schools performed higher than the private schools both for the first timers and the result with repeaters. Licensure Exam for Mechanical Engineers has the highest passing percentage while Electronics Engineers obtained the least rating. Engineering programs with accreditation performed better in the Licensure exams than those without accreditation.

Program accreditation is a factor that can determine the performance of schools in the licensure exam for engineers. The result of licensure exam of Manila and CALABARZON Region has no significant difference as well as the result per province. Public HEIs performed better in the licensure examination than private and engineering programs with accreditation significantly performed higher than those without accreditation. Meanwhile, the result of licensure examination for Mechanical Engineers is significantly higher than the other programs under study while the result of Electronics Engineers is significantly the least.

The result of this study is a confirmation and justification of having the degree programs accredited could have significant impact on the delivery of educational services to the students which in this case is the result of Licensure Examination.

## Recommendation

School administrators especially the private schools may include in their strategic plans the future program accreditation not only engineering but also other board programs. Senior High School students may be advised to enroll in engineering programs within the CALABARZON area for they can still achieve the quality education that schools in Manila can offer. HEIs with Electronics Engineering program are advised to keep on monitoring the progress of students enrolled in the program in order to increase their chances of passing the national board exam. The EcE program of a certain institution may not be qualified for accreditation due to low passing percentage in the licensure exam, therefore, the management is still encouraged to make the EcE program feasible for accreditation.

It is very beneficial for any academic institution to have a Quality Assurance Office that will cater to the needs of program accreditations and other certifications either national or international level.

This study is limited only for four engineering programs in the CALABARZON and Manila areas therefore, future studies may be investigated other degree programs with licensure exams for other provinces or regions. Other factors that possibly affect the result of schools' performance in licensure examination can be considered to further assess the educational services of HEIs aside from program accreditation.

## References

Al Tobi, A. S., & Duque, S. (2015). Approaches to quality assurance and accreditation in higher education: A comparison between the Sultanate of Oman and the Philippines. Internationalisation in Higher Education: Management of Higher Education and Research, 3(1), 7-14.

Arcelo, A. A. (2003). In pursuit of continuing quality in higher education through accreditation. International Institute for Educational Planning, Paris.

CHED Accreditation in the Philippines, url: http://goo.gl/vD9JfS, date retrieved: April 27, 2015.

Conchada, M. I. P., & Tiongco, M. M. (2015). *A Review of the Accreditation System for Philippine Higher Education Institutions* (No. DP 2015-30).

Dotong, C. I. & Laguador, J. M. (2015). Philippine Quality Assurance Mechanisms in Higher Education towards Internationalization, *Studies in Social Sciences and Humanities*, 3 (3),156-167

Laguador, J. M., Dizon, N. C. (2013). Academic Achievement in the Learning Domains and Performance in Licensure Examination for Engineers among LPU's Mechanical And Electronics Engineering Graduates, *International Journal of Management, IT and Engineering*, 3(8): 347-378

Laguador, J. M., Villas, C. D., Delgado, R. M. (2014). The Journey of Lyceum of the Philippines University-Batangas Towards Quality Assurance And Internationalization of Education, *Asian Journal of Educational Research*, 2(2)

Pijano, C. V. (2010). Quality Assurance and Accreditation: The Philippine Experience, Japan-ASEAN Information Package Seminar, retrieved from: http://goo.gl/xGDsFT, date accessed: September 29, 2015.

Zulueta, F. M. & Costales Jr., N. E. B. (2003) Methods of Research: Thesis-Writing and Applied Statistics, Navotas, Metro Manila, Philippines: Navotas Press, 75-76.

# 6

# Are Character Education Programmes Achieving their Stated Goals? A Case Study of Character Education Programmes in Private International Schools in Egypt

Rania M. R. A. Khalil

## Abstract

*Research related to character education programmes in Egypt and North Africa is limited. Consequently, there is little research on the effects of character education on students from K-12 in private schools in Egypt. Character education is defined as a conscious effort to optimise students' moral conduct. Character education is said to have been initiated in the 1600s (Vardin, 2003). By the end of the 1800s, character education had adopted two approaches: the traditional and the relativist. Most of the character education programmes run in private schools in Egypt follow the relativist approach and are taught through a developmental curriculum with clear learning objectives that are both academic and moral. Developing the teaching strategies of instructors in the area of moral development could not be more urgent. However, what is paramount and which is the main focus of this paper is the strong need and urgency in designing effective direct evaluation tools of character education programmes. This paper highlights the benefits of character education, the drawbacks of current evaluation methods and makes recommendations for future research in the area of character education.*

**Keywords:** Character education, Egypt, Evaluation of character education programmes

## Introduction

Research related to character education programmes in Egypt and North Africa is limited. Consequently, there is little research on the effects of character education on students from K-12 in private schools in Egypt. Howard et al. (2004) state that, in general, research on the effect of character education on students, is vague and scarce when one considers the numerous character education programmes in place. A close look at the outcome measures used to arrive at the conclusion of general effectiveness of the character education programmes indicates that current character education programme outcomes in Egyptian private schools, are measured indirectly.

Today, a large number of teachers involved in character education, tend to come to the same conclusions regarding what the intended outcomes of a character education programme should be: which are honesty, loyalty, dedication, citizenship, integrity, courage, perseverance, and self-motivation. Consequently, it becomes exceptionally challenging to measure changes in integrity that might result from character educational programmes. Berkowitz and Bier (2004), state that it is difficult to discuss the effectiveness of character education without considering the goals of any character education programme.

## Character Education Defined

Character education is defined as a conscious effort to optimise students' moral conduct (Berkowitz & Hoppe, 2009; Katilmis, Eksi, & Öztürk, 2011) and is often prized as the "engine of social change" (Cooley, 2008 p.203). From a psychological and philosophical perspective, character education is a way of reforming the behaviour of students in order to become good citizens of the future. Hoge (2002) promotes the idea that through pedagogy, virtues can be taught and learned.

Character education is said to have been initiated in the 1600s (Vardin, 2003). By the end of the 1800s, character education had adopted two approaches: the traditional and the relativist. The first approach aims at teaching students traditional values with the teacher providing constant modeling of moral behaviour (Howard, Berkowitz & Schaeffer, 2004; Altekar, 1944; Keay, 1959). The second approach focuses more on developing students' abilities to think critically and arrive at sound decisions when faced with ethical dilemmas. Most of the character education programmes run in private schools in Egypt are a consequent of this relativist approach and are taught through a developmental curriculum. Researchers suggest that by connecting experiences and values, stories serve as role models (Sanchez & Stewart, 2006) and hence, the easiest way to promote character education is through literature.

## Training Teachers to Teach Character Education

How to teach character education should be an integral part of the training of pre-service and in-service teachers. That is, it should be part of the curriculum of teacher education. Revell and Arthur (2007) argue that teachers' awareness of the importance of character education plays a critical role in the successful process of implementing character education programmes in schools. The justification behind this, is that those teachers will be involved in elementary and middle school in which values and character development are easier to introduce to students. Adequate knowledge and training of how to instill character education in young learners and adolescents, would make teachers more credible in the eyes of their learners as they engage in character and moral development. Developing the teaching strategies of instructors in the area of moral development could not be more urgent. Few schools in Egypt intentionally prepare teacher for this task through in-service training in moral character education (Lapsley and Woodbury, 2016; Lickona, 2013; Naraez and Lapsley, 2008; Schwartz, 2008; Willemese, Lunenberg & Korthagen, 2008).

## The Benefits of Implementing Character Education Programmes

Character education, is a pedagogy that benefits the community as whole. Research has identified a number of positive outcomes as a result of applying character education programmes in schools. Katilmis et al., (2011) name some of these positive outcomes which include higher academic achievement, a sense of community, and less aggressive behaviour. Accordingly, many international schools in Egypt have adopted character development as a aim, and have started promoting core values, such as honesty, responsibility, kindness, fairness, respecting differences, developmental discipline, and cooperative learning. Studies show that students who take part in character education programmes tend to be more respectful, empathetic and thoughtful to one another (Gage & Berliner, 1998). Williams et al. (2003) found, that the beneficial learning experience which participants obtained was not only in developing intellectual, experiential and ethical, foundation of character, but that those experiences also continued to extend throughout their lives. This can easily be linked to Gardner's views on multiple intelligences. Gardner argues that an emphasis on intellect or academic achievement alone abandons other significant characteristics of the individual such as his/her interpersonal capacity for sympathy and empathy which are crucial to students' personal and social development (Carr, 2000).

## Evaluating the Effectiveness of Character Education Programmes

Evaluating change in the overall school environment and culture can be best measured with qualitative methods, but behavioral transformation in students is best evaluated with objective methods. It is worth noting that it is flqawed to assume that evaluating beliefs about the effect of a character education programme is identical to measuring the behavioral transformations resulting from the programme. It has been noted in evaluations of character education programmes that teachers are inclined to develop greater expectations for student behaviour and, as a result, after the implementation of a character education programme, the measures used to assess student conduct are based on higher standards (Dunn & Wilson, 1997). Should this point of view be correct, then this means that:

> "the problems of validity with using only indirect measures of behavior (self-report and others-report) and not including quantitative measures of behaviour when evaluating character education programs. However, there is evidence of behavioral change directly measured from behavior records. This is the type of data necessary to make a solid argument that character education programs have a significant impact on the type of behaviors that are targeted as objectives of these programs. However, if, educators, administrators, wish to effectively promote the use of character education in schools, it is necessary to continue to collect...qualitative data and [undergo] analyses based on sound techniques [which] are certainly an important part of the process" (Dunn and Wilson 1997).

Researchers encourage schools collecting data to evaluate change as a result of implementing a character education programme to stay true to rigorous qualitative and quantitative methods in their pursuit of the evaluation process and endeavor to answer the questions: Does character education really transform students' behaviour? What outcomes are reasonable to expect? Are some methods more effective than others? Two evaluation approaches are currently common for measuring the effectiveness of character education programmes: surveys based on the perception of administrators and teachers of the character education programme, and interviews with parents and students related to how far the character education programme helps in fostering a sense of community and wholeness (Leming, 1993). Perry (2002) adopts the view that a strong sense of community ensures that there is an abundance in positive behaviour. However, we must not jump to the conclusion that a strong sense of community immediately indicates positive interpersonal behaviour in all individuals. Accordingly, the steady practice of using direct quantitative measures to evaluate behavioral outcomes of a character education programme through pre-tests and post-tests allows administrators in schools and teachers to measure actual changes. The data collected is integral to the evaluation process. The use of pre-tests and post-tests ensures that progress in moral development through the implementation of the character education programme is made. Stoppleworth (2001) who also studied the perception of students and teachers in character education programmes, supports the above and believes that one of the main underlying research questions that any academic institution must ask itself is how has the character education programme impacted the environment and culture of the school, as well as the students' behaviour?

## Case Study: Hayah International Academy, New Cairo, Egypt

Hayah International Academy (HIA) was established in 2002 in Cairo, Egypt. It is committed to deliver to the Egyptian society and the world distinguished adults who honour their cultural identity, maintain personal growth and strive for academic excellence. All of these are qualities which enable its high school graduates to live a future life with purpose and make a difference in a challenging global environment.

The Character Education Programme (CE) at HIA was designed in-house and has been put to practice since in elementary, middle school and high school. The CE programme is designed to cover intended behavioural and academic outcomes related to positive character development, pro-social behaviour, and academic performance. At HIA, character education is viewed as an asset for all learners as it strives through a tailored programme to achieve equity, efficiency, and excellence lateral to the cultural necessities of the Egyptian community. According to Thomas Lickona (1993), schools must help children understand core values, adopt or commit to them, and then act upon them in their own lives.

Over the past fifteen years, HIA has set its self apart from the many public and private schools in Egypt, which have long focused on knowledge and skills targeting only the mind and body, failing to produce self-motivated individuals who can live with the challenges and ambiguities of today's world. It is from here, this gap in educational transformation, that the need for a character education programme which would deepen the students' commitment to life-affirming values and an interest to take action on those values arose.

The HIA website outlines the following:

"The role of the Hayah's Character Education program is to provide an emotionally and socially safe environment in which students can internally and externally explore themselves. As the pioneer Character Education school in Egypt, the program is supported by a dedicated team of teachers for kindergarten, elementary, middle and high school, who take up multiple roles as teachers, coaches, mentors and activity coordinators. They passionately interact and network with students in and out of class through one-on-one and group discussions, reflections, activities, trips, camps, weekend events and activities. In addition to building a strong relationship with the students, the Character Education team closely allies with teachers and parents to achieve the program's individual and collective goals. School wide, the program is reinforced holistically through interdisciplinary integration of the core values" (CE Program – HIA).

## CE Activities

"The Character Education program is supported with a number of activities that include weekend trips, camps and sleepovers. One of our main tools is the quarterly TGIT (Thank God It's Thursday) outings or sleepovers that aim at bonding with the students, getting to know them in their context, challenging them, and finally providing a safe environment for them to explore themselves and each other. Activities are held on and off campus, and vary in their goals throughout the year. The second important tool provided by the program are Egypt excursions and/or camps that aim at challenging them, getting them out of their comfort zone, and finally getting them to know themselves better. Most camps happen in Egypt, in different governorates across the country. International camps are also held yearly to support the above aims as well as to interacting with new cultures and people and learning from their collective and personal experience" (CE Program – HIA).

## Designing and Evaluating the Hayah International Academey Character Education Programme

Khalil and Mattar, (2011) in their research *Character Education Seeking the Best of Both Worlds: A Study of Cultural Identity and Leadership in Egypt* state that "[t]he Character Education (CE) sessions designed at Hayah are based on the concept of service learning to ensure the applicability of the program to real life situations and give the students hands-on experience as opposed to the traditional classroom lecture. Activities in the classroom promote cycles of empowerment and excellence, through a values-based atmosphere, which allow students to move to increasingly higher levels of moral development. Discussions around the core values of Hayah and case studies allow space for critical thinking and problem solving skills to develop" (p.26).

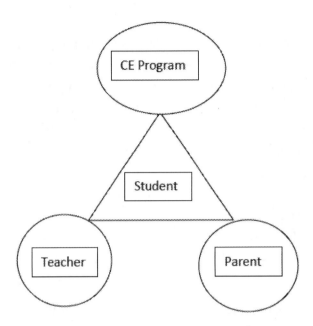

**Figure 1: The Three Pillars of the HIA Character Education Programme**

The HIA CE team during the early stages of the programme's implementation was content with the effort made and the quality of the material used, only to realize later that they had no way of really knowing if the students implemented what was taught in class at home with family, neighbours and friends out of school (Khalil and Mattar, 2011).

In order to be able to assess the programme, the HIA CE team's "weekly department meetings became discussions of teacher observations and impressions of how students in the classroom and around the school were applying the values taught in the Character Education sessions. It is important to note that data collection and observation has been on-going since 2003" (Khalil and Mattar, 2011 p. 34).

Khalil and Mattar (2011) found that the challenge which faced the HIA CE team was collecting data from the younger students and in particular the K and Pre-K. The HIA CE team's data collection methods included: surveys prepared by them, as well as a survey for parents to accompany a CE newsletter in addition to an invitation for a monthly interactive parent CE training workshop. Both formal and informal methods of data collection were used at HIA ranging from "teacher -parent meetings at the end of every quarter, peer observations, class teacher observations, teacher observation during recess, one to one discussions with students during teacher office hours, after school Character Education activities and the ... Parent Teacher Association" (p.35).

## Controversies with Implementing Character Education

We live in a free world, and accordingly, some families choose to raise their children in ways they feel to be more fitting for them and their life styles. Those who do not advocate for character education, believe that children should be entirely independent in making up their mind without moral signposts or external influences. The mindset of these people is that "character education is an infringement of children's rights" (Pike, 2010, p.311).

## Reliable and Valid Evaluation

According to character education consultants, David Brooks and Mark E. Kann (1993), implementing a valid and reliable character education programme must include a pre-assessment of goals and a post-assessment of outcomes. We must admit though that measuring behavioural and societal constructs that have real-life implications on students is challenging. Romanowski (2005), as well as other researchers, highlight the complications associated with assessing behavioural outcomes such as attitudes and values of students based on the perceptions of others who might have different motives, and experiences such as administrators, teachers and parents. Character education programme outcomes are often measured based on the perceived behaviours which are obvious and which we can measure objectively such as student attendance and academic achievement.

## Conclusion

Factors such as family, social, and cultural constructs have a strong impact on school students accordingly, we cannot consider character education as a modern day solution for students' negative behaviour. The student's character is shaped by the social context in which he/she thrives and which is beyond the scope of the school's academic setting (Romanowski, 2005). Character development is "the dynamic interplay between internal determinants and external influences in order for positive growth to occur" (Gallien & Jackson, 2006, p. 133). Schools need to create the right environment where students are challenged to reflect on moral values and be given the opportunity to apply its principles. Lickona (1989) sums up formal character education into three parts: knowing the right, valuing the right, and making the right choices. Taking advantage of the students' immediate community, role modeling and teachable moments are all informal ways to encourage the development of character and values, these can be done in the form of activities during school hours or as extra- curricular activities on or off the school campus.

Despite the challenges in objectively evaluating the outcomes of character education programmes, character education can still be considered as one of the best ways to prepare young individuals and students for the challenges of a rapidly changing and complex world. In order for character education to yield the desired results, it must be regarded as a mission that is embedded in everyday school life and beyond its walls. Students need to practice good values and go beyond their school existence in order to see for themselves the effectiveness of their moral behaviour and the impact of their moral decisions (Milliren & Messer, 2009). Most importantly, the promotion of character education should have an action plan for practice and effective evaluation tools (Cooley, 2008). Administrators, students, parents and teachers, must all join forces in order to manifest the good values of character education in their everyday lives. At the same time, assessment experts in education, must find objective and direct evaluation tools to accurately assess the outcomes of current and future character education programmes not just in Egypt but in different parts of the world. Objective evaluation is where character education falls short.

## Recommendations

It is important to incorporate qualitative data collection in order to assess the intended outcomes of any character education programme. A mix between participant observation and classroom discourse analysis of character education sessions help assess students' character development. Romanowski (2005) provides some beneficial suggestions for the implementation of character education: (1) teachers when involved in the planning of material and identifying intended learning and behavioural outcomes, are committed, this in turn improves the effectiveness of the character education programme; (2) the character education curriculum, should be meaningful and challenge for students academically, emotionally, and socially; (3) administration must ensure a supportive learning environment where teachers have enough space and autonomy in using flexible character education pedagogy for developing specific behavioural traits; (4) allow teachers to facilitate class discussions in order to allow students to both reflect on and engage in the character education programme effectively; finally, (5) the overall school environment should reinforce moral behaviour where students can practice and exhibit positive conduct as a reflection of the character education programme.

In terms of the evaluation of the outcomes of character education programmes, future research needs to put more emphasis on including different perspectives as a means of measuring the intended behavioural outcomes of character education programmes. This emphasis could facilitate a better understanding of the impact of character education on young individuals (Gallien & Jackson, 2006).

## References

Altekar, A. S. (1944). Education in ancient India. Benares: Nand Kishore & Bros.

Berkowitz, M. W., & Bier, M. C. (2004). Research-based character education. *The Annals of the American Academy*, 59 (1), 72–85.

Berkowitz, M. W., & Hoppe, M. (2009). Character education and gifted children. *High Ability Studies,* 20 (2), 131-142. doi:10.1080/13598130903358493

Brooks, D. & Kann, M. (1993). What Makes Character Education Programs Work? *Character Education* 51 (3) 19-21 http://www.ascd.org/publications/educational-leadership/nov93/vol51/num03/What-Makes-Character-Education-Programs-Work%C2%A2.aspx

Carr, D. (2000). Emotional intelligence, PSE and self-esteem: A Cautionary note. *Pastoral Care in Education* 18, 27-33.

Cooley, A. (2008). Legislating character: moral education in North Carolina's public schools. *Educational Studies,* 43(3), 188-205. doi:10.1080/00131940802117563

Dunn, L. T., & Wilson, D. (1997). A research report—moral classrooms: The development of character and integrity in the elementary school. Kansas City, MO: The Teel Institute.

Gage, N. L. & Berliner, D. C. (1998). Educational psychology. New York: Houghton Mifflin Company.

Gallien, L. B., & Jackson, L. (2006). Character development from African-American perspectives: to-ward a counter narrative approach. *Journal of Education & Christian Belief, 10 (2), 129-142.*

Hoge, J. (2002). Character education, citizenship education, and the social studies. *Social Studies,* 93 (3), 103-109.

Howard, R. W., Berkowitz, M. W., & Schaeffer, E. F. (2004). Politics of character education. *Educational Policy,* 18 (1), 188–215.

Katilmis, A., Eksi, H., & Öztürk, C. (2011). Efficiency of social studies integrated character education program. Educational Sciences: *Theory & Practice,* 11 (2), 854-859.

Keay, F. E. (1959). A history of education in India and Pakistan. Calcutta: Oxford University Press.

Lapsley, D. & Woodbury, R. (2016). Moral Character Development for Teacher Education. *Action in Teacher Education* 38 (3), p.194-206. http://dx.doi.org/10.1080/01626620.2016.1194785

Leming, J. S. (1993). Character education: Lessons from the past, models for the future. Camden, ME: The Institute for Global Ethics.

Lickona, T. (1989). Educating the moral child. *Education Digest, 55* (1), 45–48.

Lickona, T. (1993). The return of character education. *Educational Leadership*, 51(3), 6–11.

Lickona, T. (2013). Educating for character in the sexual domain. Peabody Journal of Education, 88, 198-211. DOI: 10.1080/0161956X.2013.775873

Mattar, Nevien & Khalil, Rania. (2011). Character Education Seeking the Best of Both Worlds. *The International Journal of Interdisciplinary Social Sciences*: *Annual Review,* 5, 23-52. 10.18848/1833-1882/CGP/v05i11/51941.

Milliren, A., & Messer, M. H. (2009). Invitations to character. *Journal of Invitational Theory & Practice,* 15, 19-31.

Narvaez, D., & Lapsley, D. K. (2008). Teaching moral character: Two alternatives for teacher education. *Teacher Educator*, 43 (2), 156–172. doi:10.1080/08878730701838983

Perry, C. M. (2002). Snapshot of a community of caring elementary school. *School Community Journal*, 12 (2), 79–102.

Pike, M. A. (2010). Christianity and character education: faith in core values? *Journal of Beliefs & Values: Studies in Religion & Education,* 31(3), 311-312.

Revell, L., & Arthur, J. (2007). Character education in schools and the education of teachers. *Journal of Moral Education*, 36, 79–92. doi:10.1080/03057240701194738

Romanowski, M. H. (2005). Through the eyes of teachers: High school teachers' experiences with character education. *American Secondary Education,* 34 (1), 6-23.

Sanchez, T. R., & Stewart, V. (2006). The remarkable Abigail: story-telling for character education. *High School Journal,* 89 (4), 14-21.

Schwartz, M. (2008). Teacher education for moral and character education. In L. Nucci & D. Narvaez (Eds.), Handbook of moral and character education (pp. 583–600). New York, NY: Routledge.

Stoppleworth, L. (2001). An ethnographic study of participants' perceptions of character education including students, parents, teachers, club sponsors, administers, and community support people. *Dissertation Abstracts International*, UMI No. 3025154.

Vardin, P. (2003). Character education in America. *Montessori Life*, 15 (2), 32–34.

Willemse, M., Lunenberg, M., & Korthagen, F. (2008). The moral aspects of teacher educators' practice. *Journal of Moral Education*, 37, 445–466. doi:10.1080/03057240802399269

Williams, D. D., Yanchar, S. C., Jensen, L. C., & Lewis, C. (2003). Character education in a public high school: A multi-year inquiry into Unified Studies. *Journal of Moral Education,* 32 (1), 3-33.

# 7

# Developing and Assessing Physics Prospective Teachers Conceptual Understanding of the Problem Solving Aspect of Some Selected Physics Concepts

Sa'adatu M. Abubakar

## Abstract

*The study developed and assessed physics prospective teachers' conceptual understanding of the problem solving aspect of some selected physics concepts. The design was quasi experimental research design. The study was carried out in two of the federal universities of technology in North Eastern Nigeria. The two instruments used for data collection developed by the researcher were test for conception of physics knowledge (TCPK) and test for conceptual understanding of problem solving in physics (TCUPSP). The result was analysed using mean, standard deviation and t-test. The findings revealed that physics prospective teachers' success in conceptual understanding aspect of problem solving in physics is based on two factors: Knowledge base and skills base. These also contribute in their high achievement in conceptual problem solving task of physics. It was generally recommended that physics teacher educators should endeavor to attend workshops and conferences on the integration of knowledge base and skills base for proper conceptual understanding.*

**Keywords:** Conceptual understanding, Problem-Solving Strategy, Problem Posing Strategy, Knowledge base, skills base, Prospective Teachers.

## Introduction

Physics plays an important role in scientific and technological advancement, in this regard, prospective teachers are expected to have developed a deep understanding of physics concepts for higher level of performance in scientific thinking, reasoning and problem solving (Benbow, & Stanley, 2012). Physics Teacher Subject Matter Competencies (PTSMC, 2011) also emphasizes the necessity of understanding physics concepts. Teachers with insufficient content knowledge are bound to make mistakes when delivering the content knowledge, thereby causing problems in students learning (Ball & McDiarmid, 1989; Çekbaş & Kara, 2009; Kahyaoğlu & Yavuzer, 2004). Teachers having proper understanding of content knowledge, on the other hand, know how to teach the subjects and implement their lesson for meaningful learning (Kahyaoğlu & Yavuzer, 2004).

Meaningful learning is not about learning facts by rote, but by understanding which helps the learner to remember certain fact. Rote learned knowledge is not usable in forms or in contexts, different from that in which it was obtained. In such a case, failure to use the information would imply that their understanding was poor. Oversby (2002) presented contrasting knowledge learned with understanding by characterizing it as knowledge that can be transformed, applied in other contexts and used in various ways, such as in making predictions, attempting explanations or solving problems. Teachers' level of understanding the concepts they teach is one of the obvious factor affecting their effectiveness in the class and this effectiveness in the classroom is very crucial in the formation of concepts by the students. Hence our starting point for any remediation should be the teacher, because the conceptual understanding of the teachers must first be improved upon before any meaningful improvement can be expected in students learning and understanding of physics concepts.

Several science education researchers have revealed that many conventional teaching methods do little to improve students' conceptual understanding (Cummings, Marx, Tornton, & Kuhl, 1999; Hoellwarth, Moelter, & Knight, 2005; Kohl, Kuo, & Ruskell, 2008). Thus, there seems to be only a marginal gain in students' achievement. They further stated that for most science teaching, students and teachers are preoccupied with the acquisition of numerous facts and problem-solving algorithms usually by rote learning. Kim & Park, (2002) found that students in a physics course are given a great deal of practice in problem solving skills via problem sheets and tutorial exercises. Inevitably, students concentrate on developing these skills rather than developing conceptual understanding since problem solving skills are the likely one to be tested in the final examination.

Moreover, Hill, Rowan and Ball (2005) stated that teachers' knowledge should give them chance to understand their students, explain the content knowledge and evaluate their students understanding through problem solving. Teachers who can make connections between ideas and process across topics seem to have students who learn more science and better science (Novak and Gowin 1983, Hipkinsb et al 2002). They further state that this form of interconnectedness is something that teachers start in their initial teacher education and can continue to develop whilst teaching. Problem posing strategy takes increasing attention in recent year. Main reason that lie behind this attention are establishing connection between concepts, processes and daily life (Abu-Elwan, 2002; Dickerson, 1999; Knott, 2010), transitions between representations (English, 1998; Işık, Işık & Kar, 2011) and it contributes to acquisition of problem solving skills. The problem posing hierarchical steps was adapted from the polya, 1957 problem solving model as follows;

**a) Understanding the problem:** Ask yourself questions such as: "What is the problem all about?" "What am I given and not given?" "What do I need to find?"

**b) Devising a plan:** What strategy of which you know (look for pattern, making table or work backward) you will use.

**c) Carrying out the plan:** Perform the necessary computations and describe the steps that you take.

**d) Looking Back:** Check if there might be other solutions or other strategies which will yield the same solution. Student teachers must indicate all questions, attempts, frustrations or any restrictions they may have placed on a problem. Within the context of solving a given set of problems, probing questions are posed such as: Are all the given data relevant to the solution? Do any assumptions have to be made? Are there different ways interpreting the given information or conditions? As the questions are posed, students reach a good understanding of each problem. The most important step is to encourage students to "generate an extension of the given problem" or "posing a related problem" as is suggested by Gonzales (1994). She suggested a fifth step which is:

**e) Posing a related problem:** Using the given problem and modify it to obtain a variation of the given problem. A student poses a related problem by changing the values of the given data and by changing the context of the original problem, that does not mean he has to modify or change the solving strategy used in the original problem.

Problems-posing education solves the student-teacher contradiction by recognizing that knowledge is not deposited from one (the teacher) to another (the student) but is instead formulated through dialogue between the two (Bybee, 2000; Hofstein & Lunetta, 2004). It is against this background that the present study aims at developing and accessing the conceptual understanding of the problem solving aspect of physics prospective teachers in some selected physics concepts.

## Statement of the Problem

Physics teaching in both high schools and colleges give more emphasis on problem solving (Bogno & Eylon, 1997; Tuminaro & Redish, 2007; Walsh, Howard & Bowe, 2007). Though student teachers demonstrate reasonable competence in traditional assessments of problem solving skills, there is evidence that understanding of fairly fundamental concepts is weak or lacking following completion of introductory courses (Kim & Park, 2002; Maloney, O'kuma, Hieggelke & Van Heuvelen, 2001). When exposed to introductory physics courses, they solve problems largely using a process termed means-ends analysis, search for equations containing the quantities in a problem and try to reduce the "distance" between the goal state and their current state in the solution process (Walsh, Howard & Bowe, 2007; Docktor, Mestre & Ross, 2012). They are also not taught to solve problems simply by manipulating equations since instructors typically mention the concepts and principles that they are applying, but they rightly perceive the equations as being central to obtaining quantitative answers and tend to ignore conceptual information. This approach can be effective at getting answers, but falls short in understanding the conceptual underpinnings of the solution process. It is, therefore, not surprising that student teachers learn or retain little conceptual knowledge following introductory physics courses. Hence, the need for developing and assessing the conceptual understanding of the problem solving aspect of physics prospective teachers in some selected physics concepts.

## Purpose of the Study

The following objectives were formulated for the study

  i.  Develop prospective teachers' conceptual understanding in physics
  ii. Examine prospective teachers' conceptual understanding in physics.

## Research Questions

For the purpose of the study the following questions were asked:

  i.  How are prospective teachers' conceptual understanding in physics developed?
  ii. What is the prospective teachers' conceptual understanding in physics?

## Research Hypothesis

The following research hypothesis was tested at 0.05 level of significance.

**Ho$_1$** There is no significant difference between the achievement score of prospective physics teachers' taught using problem posing and those in the control group.

## Research Methodology

The design for the study is quasi experimental research design. The study was carried out in two of the federal universities of technology in North Eastern Nigeria (Abubakar Tafawa Balewa University, Bauchi and Federal University of Technology Minna, Niger State). Being an intact class, student teachers involved were nine and eleven nine 300L physics education students respectively. The prospective teachers' studying physics education in ATBU that formed the experimental group, were exposed to treatment on the topics "work and energy" using problem posing strategy for one month to improve their level of conceptual understanding of problem solving aspect of the selected physics concept. The physics prospective teachers in Federal University of Technology Minna, Niger State serve as the control group.

The two instruments used for data collection, that is nine items test for conception of physics knowledge (TCPK) and five items test for conceptual understanding of problem solving of physics (TCUPSP) were developed by the researcher and validated by experts in physics and physics education in Modibo Adama University of Technology, Yola, and their corrections and suggestions were made before pilot testing. The pilot test result was used to ascertain the appropriateness of test items before data collection. The groups were pre-tested to know their background level of conception of physics knowledge, using TCPK on the topics force and motion. They were later assessed using TCUPSP instrument. The result from the assessment of the group was analyzed using mean, standard deviation and t-test.

## Result of the Study

### Research Question 1:

How are physics prospective teachers conceptual understanding developed?

The physics prospective teachers conceptual understanding was developed using problem posing strategy based on experts problem solvers characteristics. The general characteristics are the acquisition and application of knowledge base and skills base. Success in problem solving is based on two factors: Knowledge base and skills base (Gick, 1986; Taconis, Ferguson-Hessler & Broekkamp, 2001). Knowledge base consists of knowledge within a particular subject, such as laws of motion, as well as general or "common" knowledge. Skills base consists of specific cognitive activities or abilities, such as the ability to rearrange equations to isolate a variable.

**Research Question 2:**

What is the conceptual understanding of physics prospective teachers on some selected topic?

**Table 1: Mean Gain Result of the Experimental and Control Groups**

| Groups | n | Pre-test Mean | Post-test Mean | SD | Mean Gains |
|--------|---|---------------|----------------|-----|------------|
| Experimental | 9 | 7.5 | 15.3 | 14.3 | |
| | | | | | 6.2 |
| Control | 11 | 7.8 | 9.5 | 3.4 | |

Table 1 shows the pre-test and post-test mean score of the experimental and the control groups as experimental group has pre-test 7.5 and post-test 15.3, while that of control group has pre-test 7.8 and post-test 9.5 respectively. The post-test mean gain as compared was 6.2. This indicates a relatively high gain compare to the pre-tests mean and the control group post-test mean.

**Hypotheses 1:**

$Ho_1$ There is no significant difference between the achievement score of prospective physics teachers' taught using problem posing and those in the control group.

**Table 2: t-test Result Comparing the Mean between Experimental and Control Groups**

| Groups | n | Mean | SD | df | t-cal | p | Decision |
|--------|---|------|-----|-----|-------|-----|----------|
| Experimental | 9 | 15.3 | 14.3 | | | | |
| | | | | 18 | -3.43 | 0.01 | Rejected |
| Control | 11 | 9.5 | 3.4 | | | | |

Table 2 shows the post-test means of the group as 15.3 and 9.5 respectively, df as 18, t-cal was -3.43 and the probability was 0.01. Being that the probability value is less than 0.05, the hypothesis is rejected. Therefore, there is significant difference in the mean conceptual score of the experimental and the control groups, whereas the experimental group performed better than the control group.

## Discussion of Findings

The result revealed that physics prospective teachers' exposed to treatment using problem posing strategy obtained higher post-test mean score; which shows that the achievement is based on the treatment given. The result of the analysis of the overall post-test score using t-test indicates that the hypothesis is rejected, this means that there is significant difference in the mean achievement score of physics prospective teachers in the experimental group and physics prospective teachers in the control group. This is in agreement with Ingels, & Dalton, (2008) who found that prospective teachers' own conceptual understanding were closely related to how they respond to numerical solutions to problems. It also agrees with Al Swidi (2010) who argued that prospective teachers should have knowledge of instruction which promotes retention, and further, that they should be able to provide alternative representations and to recognize and analyze alternative methods before they can teach with understanding.

The findings of this study is also in contracts with the findings of Parikh, (2011) who asked pre-service teachers to solve five problems, and found them to have adequate knowledge of answering problems but the time between recalling principles differs. This is because some showed "bursts" of quick access while some have delayed time which was consisted with the pattern for accessing the information randomly.

## Conclusion

The conclusion for the study is that physics prospective teachers' success in conceptual understanding aspect of problem solving in physics is based on two factors: Knowledge base and skills base. These also contribute in their high achievement in conceptual problem solving task of physics.

## Recommendations

Based on the findings of the study, the following recommendations are made

1. Teacher educators should be encouraged to give more emphasis on conceptual understanding of problem solving when teaching physics at tertiary level.
2. Prospective teachers should be trained on integration of the knowledge base and skills base in physics.
3. Curriculum planners of physics education should also adopt the integration of knowledge base and skills base in restructuring physics curriculum at tertiary institution.
4. Teacher educators should endeavor to attend workshops and conferences on the integration of knowledge base and skills base for proper conceptual understanding.

# References

Abu-Elwan, R. (2002). Effectiveness of problem posing strategies on prospective mathematics teachers' problem solving performance. *Journal of Science and Mathematics Education,* 25(1), 56-69.

Al-Swidi, B. (2010). Grade nine mastering level of science process skills. *Damasus University Journal,* 26(1), 209 –234.

Bagno, E., & Eylon, B. S., (1997). From problem solving to a knowledge structure: An example from the domain of electromagnetism, *Am. J. Phys. 65, 726.*

Ball, D. L., & McDiarmid, G. W. (1989). The subject-matter preparation of teachers. *Advances in Research on Teaching* (Vol. 2), 437–449.

Benbow, C, P., & Stanley, J. C. (2012). Sex differences in mathematics ability: Facts or artifact? *Science, 210 (12), 1262-1264.*

Çekbaş, Y., & Kara, İ. (2009). Evaluation of basic physics subject matter knowledge of prospective elementary science teachers. *Eurasian Journal of Physics and Chemistry Education,* 1(1), 1–7.

Cummings, K., Marx, J., Tornton, R., & Kuhl, D. (1999). Evaluating innovation in studio physics. *American Journal of Physics Supplement,* 67(S1), S38– S44.

Dickerson, V. M. (1999). *The impact of problem posing instruction on the mathematical problem solving achievement of seventh graders.* (Unpublished doctoral dissertation). University of Emory, Atlanta.

Docktor, I., Mestre, J. P., & Ross, B. H. (2012). Impact of a short intervention on novices' categorization criteria, Phys. Rev. ST Phys. Educ. Res. 8, 020102.

English, L. D. (1998). Children's problem posing within formal and informal contexts. *Journal for Research in Mathematics Education,* 29(1), 83-106.

Gick, M. L. (1986). Problem-solving strategies. *Educational Psychologist, 21,* 99-120.

Gonzales, N. A. (1994). Problem formulation: Insights from student generated questions. *School Science and Mathematics, 96* (3), 152-157.

Hoellwarth, C., Moelter, M., & Knight, R. (2005). A direct comparison of conceptual learning and problem solving ability in traditional and studio style classrooms. *American Journal of Physics*, *73*(5), 459– 62.

Ingels, S. J., & Dalton, B. W. (2008). Trends among high school seniors, 1972–2004 (NCES 2008-320). Washington, DC: *National Center for Education Statistics*, Institute for Education Sciences, U.S. Department of Education.

Işık, C., Işık, A., & Kar, T. (2011). Öğretmen adaylarının sözel ve görsel temsillere yönelik kurdukları problemlerin analizi. *Pamukkale Üniversitesi Eğitim Fakültesi Dergisi*, 30, 39-49.

Kahyaoğlu, H., & Yavuzer, Y. (2004). Öğretmen adaylarının ilköğretim 5. sınıf fen bilgisi dersindeki ünitelere ilişkin bilgi düzeyleri. *İlköğretim-Online*, *3*(2), 26–34.

Kim, E., & Park, S. J., (2002). Students do not overcome conceptual difficulties after solving 1000 traditional problems, *Am. J. Phys. 70, 759.*

Kohl, P., Kuo, V., & Ruskell, T. (2008). Documenting the conversion from traditional to studio physics formats at the Colorado School of Mines: Process and early results. *PER Conference Series*, *1064*, 135– 38.

Maloney, D., O'Kuma, T., Hieggelke, C. J., & Van Heuvelen, A. (2001). Surveying students' conceptual knowledge of electricity and magnetism, *Am. J. Phys. 69, S12.*

Novak, J. D. & Gowin, D.B. (1983). *Learning how to learn.* Cambridge, UK: Cambridge University Press.

Parikh, S. E. (2011). *Characterizing expert and novice differences in problem-solving in heat transfer.* Ph. D. Dissertation, Stanford University.

Physics Teacher Subject Matter Competencies (PTSMC) (2011). Retrieved, January 11, 2011, from http://otmg.meb.gov.tr/ttkfiz.pdf.

Oversby, J., (2002). Assessing conceptual understanding in Amos, S & Boohan, R. (Ed). Aspects of Teaching Secondary Science: Perspectives on practice, The open University.

Taconis, R., Ferguson-Hessler, M. G. M., & Broekkamp, H., (2001). Teaching science problem solving: An overview of experimental work. *Journal of Research in Science Teaching, 38,* 442-468.

Tuminaro J., & Redish, E. F., (2007). Elements of a cognitive model of physics problem solving: Epistemic games, Phys. Rev. ST Phys. Educ. Res. 3, 020101.

Walsh, L. N., Howard, R. G., and Bowe, B. (2007) Phenomenographic study of students' problem solving approaches in physics, Phys. Rev. ST Phys. Educ. Res. 3, 020108.

# MANAGEMENT ISSUES

# 8

# Student Personnel Administration in Higher Education: Implication for Repositioning Tertiary Education in Nigeria

Ekaette E. Iroegbu

## Abstract

*Student personnel administration in Nigerian higher education has been a source of concern of late and the students form an integral part of this activity. Effective administration of student personnel plays a vital role in repositioning Tertiary education in Nigeria. Based on that fact, this paper focuses on student personnel administration in higher education. This activity or service is an integral part of student's life and it is provided by the educational institutions through specialized systems designed to develop and align student's personality positively. Academic, social and emotional support given to students through these services boosts their awareness and enhances the quality of higher education. The paper was supported by the Chikering Theory of Seven Vectors which stipulates that college students experience seven vectors of development throughout their college experience and that these vectors of development must reach resolution for the students to achieve identity. The services to be administered to the students as outlined in the paper include: orientation exercise, students' registration, guidance and counseling services, co-curricular activities, student records, school discipline, school medical services, hostel accommodation, academic library, student union government, security and safety services, communication services, transportation services, multi-faith services, Automated Teller Machines/banking services, lecture halls and laboratory services, electricity and water services, Information and Communication Technology, and student feeding services. The paper ended with recommendations among others that the federal and state governments should ensure that adequate funds are allocated to the education sector as this will enable the tertiary institutions to provide most, if not all the essential services to students.*

**Keywords:** Student, personnel, administration, higher education, repositioning, tertiary, institutions

## Introduction

Education in all spheres of life the world over, is regarded as a vehicle identified and used for cultural, social and cognitive transmission from one generation to the next. Education is seen as a process of acculturation through which individuals are assisted to attain the development of their potentials in order to ensure moral, social, economic, political and technological development of any society (Okpaga, 2013). Education is all encompassing in the sense that it is concerned with the all-round development of a person to meet diverse goals of the individual, educational institution and the society at large. Hence, one of the national education goals is the acquisition of appropriate skills and the development of mental, physical, and social abilities and competencies as equipment for the individual to live in and contribute to the development of the society (Federal Republic of Nigeria [FRN], 2004).

Higher education is the educational level following the completion of secondary education and the term can be used interchangeably with tertiary education/institution. Nigeria has a very robust tertiary education and according to the National Policy on Education FRN (2004), tertiary education includes universities, colleges of education, polytechnics and monotechnics. Others are colleges of agriculture and colleges of health technology. They are commonly called higher institutions in Nigeria since they are the next stage of education after the successful completion of the post-primary education. They are owned by private proprietors, state or federal government. According to Teboho (2013), the role of higher education in development encompasses all aspects of development, and in rethinking this role, there is the need to keep in mind all aspect of development and not be skewed towards economic development alone. Venkotaih and Sandhya's study as cited in Nwaka (2012) submitted that value education is a critical component of the roles of higher education since value education has the capacity to transform a diseased mind into a very young, fresh, innocent, healthy, natural and attentive mind capable of higher sensitivity and heightened level of perception.

A major concern of any educational institution should be the commitment to implement specified student personnel administration. It is the realization of the symbolic role of the curricular and co-curricular services in the realization of educational objectives in tertiary institutions that the Federal Republic of Nigeria (FRN, 2003) in the National Minimum Standard (NMS) prescribed mandatory student personnel services that the school administration should make available to students that will go along with curricular activities.

The word 'administer' is derived from the Latin word 'ad' and 'adminstrar' which means to serve, care for, look after people or to manage affairs. Administration may be defined as an activity which involves the cooperation and coordination of people and resources for the purpose of achieving desired goals and objectives. The idea of goal achievement is central to the concept of administration. Administration of student personnel in tertiary institution is an integral part concerned with promoting the achievement of the institution's objectives by carefully using available resources (both material and non-material) to accomplish predetermined goals. The term administration does not refer to any single process or act. It is like a broad umbrella encompassing a number of processes such as; planning, organizing, directing, coordinating, controlling and evaluating. Liverpool and Jacinta (2013) stated that in an institutional setting, administration has been extended as a service activity or tool through which the fundamental objectives of the institutional process may be more optimized efficiently when allocating human and material resources as well as to make the best use of existing resources.

Repositioning the higher education system and by extension, achieving quality tertiary education in Nigeria, requires fashioning ways of addressing the poor state of infrastructure, insufficient funding, abysmal administration of student personnel, lack of planning, and implementation problems. These challenges has led to the weakening of university administration; poor teaching and learning outcomes; questionable services to the students and community. Mostly affected are the recreational facilities, student welfare and orientation, infrastructure and knowledge facilities. The essence of this paper is to outline how tertiary institutions can be repositioned through highly effective administration of student personnel.

## Theoretical Framework

Chikering's Theory of Seven Vectors (1969) is an identity development theory and arguably one of the most widely known and widely applied theories of student development. Chickering first outlined this theory in a landmark book titled Education and Identity (1969). While employed at Goddard College, Chickering was responsible for evaluating the impact of innovative curricular practices on student development. The theory delves into the idea that college students experience seven vectors of development throughout their college experience. These vectors of development must reach resolution for the student to achieve identity. Though Chikering, and later as revised by Reisser (1995), did not necessarily state that a student's movement through these seven vectors were sequential, the theory indicates that students must resolve through a specific group of vectors as a springboard of foundation towards progressing through later vectors (Foubert, Nixon & Sission, 2005).

As to the revision of the vectors as instigated by the definition of development meant students were proceeding along the seven vectors of developing competence, managing emotions, moving through autonomy towards inter-dependence, developing mature interpersonal relationship, establishing identity, developing purpose, and developing integrity (Foubert, *et al,* 2005) during their college experience. Chickering and Reisser (1993) went on to postulate that students can experience several vectors at once rather than having to resolve one before moving on to the other. The vectors build upon each other leading to greater complexity, stability and interaction (Evans, Forney, Guido, Patton, & Renn, 2010). Chickering and Reisser also acknowledged that the educational environment plays an enormous role in a student's ability to progress and resolve each vector. They suggested seven educational environmental influences that impact a student's development as follows: institutional objectives, institutional size, student-faculty relationship, curriculum teaching, friendships, student communities, and student development programs (Evans et al, 2010). These influences do not only affect a student's ability to progress through all seven vectors, but also, affects the rate at which they do so.

The application of Chickering's theory and seven vectors in higher education is most apparent in the inherent differences between incoming fresh student and a graduating senior. It is clear in most cases that a graduating senior will have resolved many of Chickering's vector by the time they are ready to enter the 'real world'. Fresh incoming students on the other hand are in a transition period where they are starting to build a foundation of basic college student developmental needs before attempting to address such vectors as 'developing purpose' or 'establishing identity' which most seniors may have already experienced. Student affair administrators or academic counselors have different expectations when a fresh incoming student enters their office versus when a senior enters. In such a scenario, an administrator can use Chickering's vectors to assess where the student is on their developmental journey simply by knowing what class they are in. Again, it would be prudent to utilize Chickering's theory and vectors as a guideline to addressing students' need rather than trying to assess sequentially where the student is and where the student should be going as their next stage of development.

## Concept of Student Personnel Administration

Student personnel administration refers to programmes or services that are 'student centered' and are provided by educational institutions through specialized systems designed to develop and align student's personality positively. These services are also targeted at ensuring that students are assisted to be well informed about the learning processes they have to undergo in school. Student personnel administration as defined by Ejionueme (2010) refers to those school services that supplement and support the instructional programme of a school. Effective administration of these services in higher education institution is not only important, but necessary for the achievement of the desired educational goals of inculcating the right type of values, attitude, skills and the development of mental and physical abilities as equipment for producing good quality citizens of Nigeria (FRN, 2004). Student personnel administration are viewed as welfare services provided in educational institutions in order to prevent unnecessary increase in the rate of anti-social activities among the students and to encourage positive thinking and actions that would promote the attainment of their academic pursuit and choices of future career (Akinnubi & Kayode, 2012). Efficient student personnel administration that is focused on its necessities should be created in these institutions in order to provide the needed support for academic activities, social skills, personal and cognitive development as well as cultural values. These services enhances and supports student's welfare, academic and social development right from their first contact with the institution to when they become alumni of such institutions.

The overall objective of the student personnel administration is to ensure that the students are socially conscious of their environment, maximize their full potential and boost the institutions academic programme. Precisely student personnel administration focuses on the ways that learning and development occur beyond the classroom in all dimensions of life in a post-secondary institution. Vanshival (2009) stated that the specific objective of student personnel administration is to select the right type of student for admission with regards to qualifications and conducts; to ensure proper orientation and classification of students; and to ensure that facilities are available for effective teaching and learning. However, Oboegbulem (2004, p.165) specifically identified nine objectives of student personnel administration to be;

1. To make the students think effectively
2. To help them communicate their thoughts clearly
3. To help them develop the skills of making relevant judgment
4. To help them play their parts as useful members of their homes and families
5. -To make the pupils understand the basic facts about health and sanitation
6. To help the students understand and appreciate their roles as citizens of Nigeria
7. To help the students develop good moral principles
8. To help the pupils understand and appreciate their cultural heritage; and
9. To make them recognize the dignity of labour.

## Student Personnel Administration Activities/Services

School administrators and educators are the major role players in student personnel administration. Student personnel administration has to do with all activities or services that are put together by an educational institution that supplements or supports the usual instructional programme. It also involves meeting the needs of all students especially the new entrants in ensuring that their transition into higher education life becomes seemly while also ensuring that returning students' needs are adequately met. Oboegbulem (2004) defined student personnel administration as all the activities and services, apart from the normal classroom instruction rendered to students by the school and even the community that are geared towards making an individual in the school an all-round educated, law abiding citizen of his community. In order to reposition higher education in Nigeria, it is quite crucial to ensure that student personnel are adequately administered in these institutions of learning so that students can benefit maximally from the laudable objectives of each of the higher institutions in Nigeria. These activities or services are identified as;

**1. Admission Exercise of Students:** Admission of new entrants should be well planned in accordance with the capacity of available physical facilities and material resources. It is expected that the new students are registered first and made to resume earlier than the old students to enable the school carry out the preliminary services to get the students acquainted with the new environment. Some tertiary institutions do carry out internal qualifying examination away from the general Joint Admission and Matriculation Board (JAMB) examination and the successful students are admitted.

**2. Orientation Exercise of Students:** The first week of resumption should be set aside as orientation week to introduce the freshmen to a whole new college life that is an upgrade of the previous institution. This is to put the student at ease and to help in adjusting to new college life. Unfortunately, most students miss out on this important programme due to varying reasons. The newly admitted students are formally introduced into the various programs of the school, they get them acquainted with campus life, school traditions, hostel living, institution standard, health services, methods of study, infrastructural facilities, equipment, rules and regulations as well as library usage. It aims to let the new students know what to expect from the institution and what the institution expects from them. According to the University of Cape Coast (2012), orientations are organized to purposively introduce new students to the variety of student services available on and off campus so that they are able to navigate the university and its environment on their own.

**3. Registration of Students:** Students who have met the minimum requirement for the programme and has been admitted are expected to pay a pre-registration fee also known as acceptance fee. They are also expected to commence the process of the online registration and then present themselves for physical screening at the university with copies of acceptance fee receipt, admission letter, JAMB offer of admission and result slip, secondary school testimonial, certificate of local government of origin (If non-Nigerian, permit), birth certificate/declaration of age, passport photographs and medical certificate of fitness from a registered hospital duly signed by medical officers. Akpanumoh (2011) stated that compliance with registration formalities confers status to the students as bona-fide members of the school community.

**4. Guidance and Counseling Services to Students**: This is one of the pivotal aspects of student personnel services whose main purpose is to provide the students with the necessary information needed to solve personal problems and aid the students in the development of a more wholesome personality. It encourages constructive utilization of the student's abilities, time, and energy in pursuing academic goals. The National Universities Commission (NUC, 2011) directed every tertiary institution in Nigeria to establish the Counseling and Human Development Centre (CHDC). This unit is responsible for developing and deploying career management initiatives that will enable students develop critical life skills, assist them make informed decisions on their future and also plan and implement social responsibility and advocacy programs. Students come from diverse backgrounds with myriads of personalities, problems, belief system and other issues. Similarly, students from varying backgrounds and socio-economic status all come together to cohabit and this brings to bare the importance of counseling especially to those exhibiting inferiority complex. This service helps to boost the students' self-confidence and also prevents them from succumbing to negative peer influence. All the students will not adjust to college life easily and at the same time, and this therefore makes it expedient for them to avail themselves the counseling services offered by the institution. Oboegbulem (2014, p.347) stated that guidance is of two types as outlined below;

a.   **Vocational Guidance:** These includes;

    i.   Letting the students know the various occupations relating to rewards, conditions of employment, opportunities for advancement and requirements to succeed in an occupation.

    ii.   Giving the students the opportunities to know their special capacities, aptitudes, interest, traits of personality and character with regards to vocational life.

    iii.   Letting the students know the right studying habits which will enable them succeed in making appropriate vocational decisions.

b.   **Educational Guidance:** These involves;

    i.   Giving the students the opportunity to discover their interest, abilities and capacities in their career choice.

ii. Giving them a wide range of courses that would help contribute to the realization of his/her vocational and educational plans.

iii. Providing courses of study as well as guiding them in the choice of courses to study.

iv. Acquainting the students with the curricular and co-curricular opportunities of the school that will help them in future life.

v. Acquainting them with the opportunities and methods of using the school library most effectively.

One of the high points of repositioning tertiary education in Nigeria in the recent past is the introduction of the CHDC in every tertiary institution in the country to take care of students counseling needs. This has extended the frontiers of counseling which have hitherto been limited to career counseling for career choice.

**5. Co-Curricular/Extra-Curricular Activities:** Co-curricular activities refer to those activities that complement learning experiences and programs that are connected to, or that mirrors the academic programme organized to help students have a better understanding of his/her course. Examples of co-curricular activities are quiz, seminars, conferences, workshops, exhibition, debate, discussion, etc. Extra-curricular activities on the other hand, which is sometimes referred to as Extra Academic Activity (EAA) refer to those activities which are totally outside the realm of normal curriculum, but are essential for the all-round development of students. These activities particularly help in diversifying the curricular to cater for the differences in talents and provide opportunities and roles which are open to students. Examples are swimming, gymnastics, athletics, weaving, tailoring, singing, acting, etc. Being only brilliant in academics will not help the students in our society of today due to the high level of competition and low rate of employment. This is a good reason to ensure that the students are equally talented in other fields or at least show some interest of which when developed or harnessed, could also serve as an additional source of income and promotion of self-reliance.

These activities enrich the student's learning, livens the school environment, and helps them discover what they have passion for. The Office for Standard in Education (OFSTED, 2009) pointed out that students acquire many subtle learning like human values, beliefs, manners and thinking patterns through hidden curriculum which is also manifested in extra-curricular activities and improved learning outcome. Recreational activities foster students' creative abilities; build self-esteem and self-confidence; and enhances social and psychosomatic development. Time for extra-curricular activities is a time of relaxed nerves for the students as the atmosphere is usually less formal compared to lecture time. This gives them more room to be expressive, develop interpersonal skills and improve their social and emotional health. Borhade (2012) stated that students suffering from high anxiety got relieved of it through regular participation in extra-curricular activities.

**6. Students Record:** Students record is an aspect of student personnel services that should be taken seriously. These records help in storing and retrieving students' information speedily and efficiently for inferences. Accuracy of the records and regular update as at when due should also be a priority because wrong information or a mix up of these records will lead to chaos and project inefficiency. Appropriate record is essential for the provision of school facilities, classification, health services, allocation of funds, resources and other purposes. A students' file should contain personal data such as passport photograph, personal data form, copies of credentials like birth certificate, certificate of local government of origin, First School Leaving Certificate (FSLC), JAMB and WAEC/NECO (West African Examination Council/National Examination Council) results, health information and so on. It should also contain academic data such as course registration form and up-to-date results of the student. Database Management System (DBMS) for students' records should be introduced in Nigerian tertiary institutions to avoid loss of relevant student information due to burglary, riot, flood or fire incident which may destroy all traces of records with no hope of recovery. Nosiri and Nwagbo as cited in Ejinueme (2010) observed that student's cumulative records in our institutions of higher learning are not properly kept, and where they are kept, do not contain all the details such as personal and home records, test scores, summary of academic records and student activities.

**7. School Discipline:** School discipline is a required set of action, punishment, rules and regulations by the institution to the students whenever their behaviour disrupts the ongoing institutional activity or they break pre-established rules created by the school system. Discipline helps to keep students in check and it requires knowledge, skills, sensitivity and self-confidence. The term discipline is often times confused with classroom management; discipline is one dimension of classroom management and classroom management is a general term. Adesina as cited in Oboegbulem (2014, p. 357) sees discipline as a situation which results when students are taught to respect the school authorities, to observe the school laws and regulations, and to maintain an established standard of behaviour. Oboegbulem (2011) identified eight attitudes that promotes discipline to be; respect for authority; frankness; adherence to rules and regulations; use of commendation; good sense of humour; taking responsibility for one's action; justices, firmness and fairness; use of punishment that will lead to reform. Students are expected to comply with the school rules and codes of conduct especially in the area of time keeping, dressing, social behaviour and work ethics.

**8. School Medical Services:** School medical services can be explained as those services that caters for the health needs of the school community especially the students. The essence of this is to provide services that promote and maintain the health of students through limited ambulatory nurse practitioner services, health promotion and public health services. Achalu as cited in Oboegbulem (2014, p. 349) identified the objectives of school health services to include:

i.   To understand each child's health needs and develop high level health for each student.
ii.  To prevent defects, disorder, and continuously appraise a student's health.
iii. To develop in each student a positive health awareness and reduction in the incidents of diseases.
iv.  To develop personal and helpful hygienic life.
v.   To provide emergency measures, health school environment and maintenance of good sanitary practices and surrounding.

The services to be provided amongst others are; health history from all new entering students; first aid treatment with referral to physician; women's health services; immunizations; HIV testing; isolation of sick students; notification of parents concerning outbreak of communicable diseases; and reporting any diseases or infection to appropriate quarters.

**9. Hostel Accommodation for Students:** The concept of accommodation for tertiary institutions can be both classroom and hostel which are very crucial to the meaningful and well-being of students on campus. Okebukola, Ibrahim, Bola, and Ayo (2003) opined that Nigerian universities were established with the intention of providing comfortable and on-campus hostel accommodation for all students. Living in the school premises allows the students ample opportunity to meet many people and create lifelong friendships, participate in a wide variety of academic, educational and social events. It also affords the students the opportunity to live in a culturally diverse environment while developing an independent lifestyle away from parents and guardians. The tertiary institutions residence halls are more than just a place to live in. In addition to safe and comfortable surroundings, living in an adult environment with limited supervision provides students with a glimpse of what living in the society is all about; interacting with people from various backgrounds; learning how a political governing system works; taking responsibility for personal behaviour; learning how to have fun; and get along with friends and neighbours.

**10. Academic Library:** These are libraries attached to tertiary institutions such as universities, polytechnics, colleges of education, colleges of agriculture, and colleges of technology and research institutes (Akporhonor, 2005). School library is an important aspect in the academic development of students, and it serves as the foundation stone and centre of the school learning programme of any tertiary institution. Library can be defined as an institution with a collection of printed, digital and audio-visual materials which serves as a knowledge and reading centre as well as a repository of information well catalogued for both the learner and the teacher. Singh and Kaur (2009) stressed that preservation and access to knowledge and information is the main mandate of academic libraries alongside supporting the mission of their parent institutions which is teaching and research. Oboegbulem (2011) defined library as a room or building in a school where books, magazines, journals, periodicals, cassettes, films, filmstrips and projectors are stored for students' use. In other words, it is a central laboratory of the whole school which stakes books in all subject areas including non-book materials. Academic libraries have shifted from the contemporary practice of high dependency on remote learning resources like textbook due to the growing access to the internet and the World Wide Web (www). Today's library focuses more on the virtual and digital libraries without borders accompanied by sophistication in the changing pattern of information needs of users. Singh and Kaur (2009) also observed that there is a paradigm shift from stand-alone libraries to library and information networks; from printed publications to digital documents; and from ownership to access. Since the library is an indispensable element in the life of the student and the school, it should be properly planned and effectively managed in order to achieve the institution's objectives.

**11. Student Union Government:** This refers to the rights accorded to students by the school administration to govern and represent the student community. The student government is vested with the responsibility of coordinating, planning, controlling and carrying out strategic plans and actions that are geared towards meeting the needs of the students in the institution. This is a highly recognized body in the institutions and the officials are usually elected into the various positions by the students. The programs carried out by the student government provides opportunities for students to interact, relate and collaborate with themselves, the school board, the community, neighbouring institutions, national student bodies, local and state government and other academic partners. Foubert and Grainger (2006) stated that many have their first substantive leadership experience through Registered Students' Organizations (RSO) and that these organizations are the most potent mechanisms for the school to reinforce academic experiences with strong leadership trainings that are reflective of the kinds of citizens the country needs. These organizations should be adequately monitored by the student affairs division for proper accountability and this view is also shared by Arikewuyo and Adegbesan (2009) who state that the monitoring of students' union activities becomes absolutely essential to prevent the menace of secret cults in schools.

**12. Security and Safety Services:** The word security emanated from the Greek word 'Se-cura', meaning to be in a state of no fear. Security is the degree of resistance to, or protection of life and property of a person from harm. It is a form of protection where a separation is created from between the assets and the threat. According to Fasasi (2008), security service is primarily to maintain peace and order that will promote a peaceful atmosphere. This will aid the academic performance of the student which is their primary objective. This service is provided for adequate and total protection of life and properties of the students in the academic institutions. Institutions designed to be centers for learning should be safe, secured and peaceful, but in a situation where the school premises seem unsafe for learning, students will always be reluctant to go to school. Special attention should be given to perimeter security and access control issues. The institutions should have clearly defined perimeters for schools through the use of fences, gates, environmental designs, signage, and other professional security means. This is very essential due to the high rate of bombings, terrorists attack, kidnapping, robbery, riots, herdsmen attack, rape and so many issues that have bedeviled our institutions of higher learning.

Students should be oriented to report any suspicious activities observed around the premises which may include suspicious vehicles on and around the campus, suspicious persons in and around school buildings, including those taking photographs or video recording. Students should be educated to avoid staying in lonely places alone; to always move away from any car that pulls up beside them and is driven by a stranger, even if that person looks lost or confused; should not be found loitering around areas that has been prohibited by the school authorities within the school premises. The school security can also be improved upon by controlling visitor access to the school, have one or two designated entrances with adequate security; use designated parking areas especially for visitors; use of car tally for identification; verify the identity of service personnel and vendors visiting the school; and provide adequate safety measures for both teaching and non-teaching staff on how to respond to bomb scare, use of fire extinguisher, crime scene management, lockdown and evacuation procedures, etc.

**13. Socio-cultural Services:** Tertiary institutions are considered to be one of the best venues for cultural exchange and integration. Multicultural services and experiences should be provided to students as it has a great potential to help students understand the value of diversity and how it helps them to become well rounded individuals and professionals in their various fields of endeavour. When students are exposed to diverse cultures, they have multiple opportunities to compare and construct a more diverse world view. Severiens and Wolff (2008) found out that student who feel at home, who are well connected to fellow students and lecturers, and who take part in extracurricular activities are more likely to successfully graduate from school. As posited by Wilcox, Winn and Fyvie-Gauld (2005) that support from family and society has a positive influence on the study-success of students.

**14. Communication Services:** Communication services works side by side with the security services. As part of effective student personnel administration, a functioning network communication is very essential. There should be a free and favourable flow of information from the management to the students. The communication department should ensure that students are well informed about programs, events, and services that enrich the students' experience. Effective communication supports the values of student learning and development by providing communication vehicles that help students connect to the institution. Many problems in and out of schools can be directly traced to whether information was communicated, how it was communicated and who communicated it.

**15. Multi-Faith Programs and Services:** These programs and services afford students the opportunity to learn more about their own faith as well as learning about other faith backgrounds. It also allows the students to celebrate, worship and to join in fellowship with others. The school provides variety of religiously acceptable activities that are contributory to student's development and supportive of the school's educational objectives. The institutions are categorized as diverse communities and are thereby encouraged to exercise their rights with the belief that religious formations are an integral part in the development of life-long characters which can shape the values, ethics and attitudes of students towards a fulfilling work and life.

**16. Transportation Services:** This service is very essential as it is a means of moving students from one location to another in the course of their academic activities. A good means of transport is an indispensable part of the school system (Arikewuyo & Adegbesan, 2009). Most tertiary institutions operate two or more campuses or large campuses where the hostel area is a considerable distance from the academic and other service buildings. Where the university does not have buses or taxis to cater for students' transportation need at subsidized rate, private transport companies should be deployed to provide these services in liaison with the university transport unit.

**17. Automated Teller Machine (ATM)/Banking Service:** ATMs and other banking services should be provided for within the campus as this will help to reduce time wastage of trying to get out of the campus to get banking services. The high rate of robbery and ATM fraudsters operations will also be hugely avoided. This will give the students seamless access to funds anytime of the day and this will also stop them from keeping more cash than needed in their hostels or bags. Community banks or branches of the conventional banks are allowed to plant branches on the campus giving the students opportunities to operate savings account or bank transfer activities.

**18. Lecture Halls and Laboratories services:** Spacious, well equipped, well ventilated and conducive lecture halls and laboratories should be provided and easily accessed by students for academic activities. A conducive academic environment has far-reaching effects on the students' learning process. The school management should ensure that the lecture halls and laboratories are not overcrowded and over-stretched to avoid rapid decay of the facilities. Laboratory equipment provided for should be put into proper and efficient use to avoid them becoming obsolete as a result of the rapid trend in technological development.

**19. Electricity and Water Supply Services:** Provision and availability of these two services should be a constant in the tertiary institutions. The schools with electronic libraries cannot serve the academic community effectively when electricity generation is not constant. This is also applicable to the malfunctioning of the school's resource centers, laboratories, lecture halls, and even the availability of water will also be affected as electricity is needed to pump water in most cases. Constant electricity supply will reduce or eliminate the proliferation of generating sets which brings about noise and fumes pollution on campus and this is in contrast to the expected serene, calm and pollution free environment needed for qualitative academic activities.

**20. Information and Communication Technology (ICT) Services:** Access to ICT is one of the services that the tertiary institution is expected to provide to students. Adomi and Kpangban (2010) defined ICT as a diverse set of electronic technologies and technological tools and resources used to communicate, create, disseminate, store and manage information. ICT has the ability to widen access to educational resources, improve the quality of learning and improve management efficiencies of the education system (Ibe-Bassey, 2013). ICT centers helps to deliver education to the door steps of those who yearn for it, especially the students. Other necessary student support services for students include printing press and well stocked bookshops where students can secure materials and print their manuscripts without stress.

**21. Students' Feeding Service:** Provision of quality and adequate food service at subsidized rate by the institution's approved vendor is also considered paramount and a service that cannot be overlooked. The university management through the student affairs should control the feeding service and ensure that the quality meets a set standard. The catering services and environment should also be decent. Absence or inadequacy of this service adds to the psychological, emotional and physiological stress of the students' thereby constituting distraction and low concentration in academic activities.

## Conclusion

The quality of higher education depends directly on the student personnel administration services provided in various modes of higher education. Student personnel administration should ensure that the services as earlier stated are made sufficiently available as this will develop the students intellectually, socially, psychologically, physically and educationally. Most of these services are available in Nigerian higher education institutions but they are in dire need of revamping. The present state of student personnel administrative services is not a hopeless one as it could be controlled and improved upon if some measures are adopted.

## Recommendations

- The tertiary institution administrators should take cognizance of the available student personnel services when admitting new students for the various programs and ensure the services available can cater for the number of students enrolled, as well as the returning students.
- The federal and state government should ensure that adequate funding is allocated to the education sector as this will enable the higher education institutions to provide most, if not all the essential services to students.
- The school management should inculcate a high-level maintenance culture into the staff and students. Sanctions should be placed on anyone who misuses or damages school facilities.
- Non-governmental bodies like the alumni associations, corporate organizations, philanthropists, and international organizations should be appealed to by the tertiary institutions to assist in the provision of these services.

## References

Adomi, E. E., & Kpangban, E. (2010). Application of Information Communication Technologies in Nigerian secondary schools. *Library and Philosophy and Practice (e-journal),* March, 1-8. Available at: http://digitalcommons.unl.edu/libphilprac/345. Accessed: August 21, 2017.

Akinnubi, O. P., & Kayode, D. J. (2012). Student personnel services and students' behaviours in University of Ilorin, Ilorin. *Global Journal of Applied Sciences, Management and Social Sciences,* 1: 1-14.

Akpanumoh, U. D. (2011). Students' personnel management in higher education. In S. U. Bassey & U. U. Bassey (eds.). *Management of Higher Education in Africa.* Uyo: Abaam.

Akporhonor, B. A. (2005). Library funding in Nigeria: Past, present and future; The bottom line. *Managing Library Finances,* 18(2): 63-70.

Arikewuyo, O. M., & Adegbesan, S. O. (2009). Practicum on administration of personnel in education. In J. B. Babalola & A. O. Ayeni (eds.). *Educational management: Theories and tasks* (pp. 323-337). Lagos: Macmillan.

Borhade, S. (2012). Open distance education and sustainable development. *International Journal of Research in Commerce, Economics and Management,* 2 (12): 72-77

Chickering, A. W. (1969). *Education and identity.* San Francisco: Jossey-Bass.

Chickering, A. W., & Reisser, L. (1993). *Education and identity* (2nd ed.). San Francisco: Jossey-Bass.

Ejionueme, L. K. (2010). Management of student personnel services in federal and state universities. Unpublished Ph.D. Thesis, Department of Educational Foundations, University of Nigeria, Nsukka.

Evans, N. J., Forney, D. S., Guido, F. M., Patton, L. D., & Renn, K. A. (2010). *Student development in college: Theory, research and practice* (2nd ed.). San Francisco, CA: Jossey-Bass.

Fasasi, I. V. (2008). *Educational planning and administration in Nigeria.* Ibadan: Daily Graphics Ltd.

Foubert, J., Nixon, M. L., & Sisson, V.S. (2005). A longitudinal study of Chickering and Reisser's Vectors: Exploring gender differences and implications for refining the theory. *Journal of College Student Development,* 46: 461-471. doi: 10.1353/csd.2005.0047

Foubert, J. P., & Grainger, L. U. (2006). Effects of involvement in clubs and organizations on the psychosocial development of the first year and senior college students. *NASPA Journal,* 43(1): 166-182.

Federal Republic of Nigeria (2003). *Education reports on student welfare services in Nigeria.* Abuja: FGN Press.

Federal Republic of Nigeria (2004). *National policy of education.* Lagos: NERDC Press.

Ibe-Bassey, G. S. (2013). Human capacity building for Information and Communication Technology (ICT) integration in teacher education in Nigeria. A paper presented at 2nd AFTRA teaching and learning in Africa conference at Pride Inn Sailrock Beach Hotel, Mombasa City, Kenya, from June 24-28, 2013.

Liverpool, E. O. & Jacinta, A. O. (2013). Information and Communication Technologies (ICT): A panacea to achieving effective goals in institutional administration. *Middle-East Journal of Scientific Research,* 15(2): 200-207.

National Universities Commission (NUC) (2011). Guidelines for the establishment of counseling centres in Nigerian Universities. Stakeholders Seminar, July 12, Abuja.

Nwaka, N. G. (2012). The state of tertiary education in meeting the needs of the modern Nigerian society. In O. Ibeneme., B. Alumode & H. Usoro. *The state of education in Nigeria.* Onitsha: West and Solomon Publishing Coy. Ltd.

Oboegbulem, A. I. (2004). Pupil personnel administration. In T. O. Mgbodile, (ed.). *fundamentals of educational administration and planning.* Enugu, Nigeria: Magnet Business Enterprises.

Oboegbulem, A. I. (2011). *Classroom organization and management- issues and concerns.* Nsukka: Great A.P. Express Publishers Ltd.

Oboegbulem, A. I. (2014). Student personnel administration in secondary school. In G.O. Unachukwu & P. N. Okorji, (eds.). *Educational management: A skill building approach.* Anambra, Nigeria: Rex Charles & Patrick Ltd.

Office for Standard in Education (OFSTED, 2009). Education for sustainable development. Available at: www.ofsted.gov.uk/ofsted-home/publications. Accessed: July 15, 2017.

Okebukola, P., Ibrahim, A., Bola, B., & Ayo, B. (2003). *Private sector participation in university hostel development and management.* National Universities Commission, Abuja 2003, Abuja.

Okpaga, A. (2013). Repositioning education in Nigeria to tackle the challenges of poverty, self-reliance and national development. *Journal of Teacher Perspective,* 7(4):719-730.

Reisser, L. (1995). Revisiting the seven vectors. *Journal of College Student Development,* 36: 505-512.

Severiens, S. & Wolff, R. (2008). A comparison of ethnic minority and majority students: Social and academic integration, and quality of learning. *Studies in Higher Education,* 33(3): 253-266.

Singh, J & Kaur, T. (2009). Future of academic libraries in India: Challenges and opportunities. A paper presented at the International Conference on Academic Libraries (ICAL) held at the University of Delhi, India, p.52.

Tehobo, M. (2013). Re-envisioning higher education in Africa: *African Journal of Higher Education Studies and Development (AJESD),* 1(2): 133-158.

University of Cape Coast (2012). *Orientation programmes for fresh students 2012/2013 academic year.* Cape Coast: UCC Press, Ghana.

Vanshival, I. (2009). Human resource management index. Available at File://E:/ PersonnelAdministration.html. Accessed: July 24, 2017.

Wilcox, P., Winn, S. & Fyvie-Gauld, M. (2005). It was nothing to do with the university, it was just the People: The role social support in the first year experience of higher education. *Studies in Higher Education,* 30(6): 707-722.

# 9

# Innovation, Issues and Challenges of Higher Education: Implications for University Education in Nigeria

Maria E. Maxwell & Inimbom I. Edet

## Abstract

*The problem of adapting to the changing global trends in tertiary institutions, especially in Nigeria, has been on the limelight in recent times. This paper therefore examined innovation, issues and challenges in higher education: an implication for university education in Nigeria. The paper further looked at the importance and the challenges of innovation in these tertiary institutions. Issues from both the internal and external communities were identified as attacking the university system and consequently, has affected the standard in all ramifications. The paper concluded, among others that multi-dimensional approaches, methods and tools should be put in place to revitalize the system to breed learners' autonomy. Recommendations included that government should immediately and urgently increase financial allocation to university education.*

**Keywords:** Innovation, Issues, Challenges, Higher Education, University Education

## Introduction

In this contemporary era of globalization, the relevance of higher education is recognized for improving economic performance, increasing social integration as well as promoting civil laws. Education is the core factor for the development of human capital, the most influential form of the capital which is also a central factor in the development of the society. Institutions of higher learning not only reflect, but also create and augment the stock of knowledge through research and innovation. Innovation means successfully exploring exploiting and utilizing new ideas that would enhance the attainment of educational goals.

This means some new ways of doing things or a change that result in improvement of administration or scholarly performance in institutions of learning in Nigeria.

Higher education in this country is faced with great challenges related to financing and equitable accessibility of education, staff development, skills-based training, quality education in teaching and research, relevance of programs to the growth and development of the country, out dated curricula, non-implementation of learner-centered learning approach and other modern methods of learning. The growing trend of globalization, fueled by information and communication and the internet as it affects higher education, become issues of great concern in relation to the economic development of the nation. It has been generally observed that the educational sector in Nigeria has suffered setback in a number of areas. With all the federal, state and private universities, polytechnics and other higher institutions of learning across the country, millions of Nigerian youths are still very desirous of higher education, principally university education but find it difficult to access it.

As Nigerians prefer university education, every year, universities exceed "get admission quota". Some universities are constantly being inundated with admission request they cannot meet (Okoroafor, 2013). The number of candidates who apply annually exceeds by far the vacancies available. There is also the issue of rise in proliferation of illegal degree awarding institutions with illegal degree meals, thereby preying on the desperation of Nigerians for university education. Most of them claim affiliation to already established universities in United States, United Kingdom and Canada. Other issues are proliferation of expensive private universities, unemployable graduates with inadequate skills and competency in their areas of specialization, absence of National Economic Empowerment and Development (NEEDS) driven curriculum to address national needs, difficulty in development and retention of qualified university teachers among others.

These trending issues have rendered the pursuit of educational goals for higher education unattainable. The society is never static. It continues to change. Education is the hub of that change. Therefore the educational system must change to take care of the societal changes which are deemed vital for the continuity of that society. As new scraps of information, ideas and practices and so on are evolved, and drowned across boarders by globalization, human organizations and institutions are forced to introduce changes. This paper therefore examines innovation, issues and challenges of higher education: implications for university education in Nigeria.

## The Concept of Innovation

The concept of innovation in higher education is backed up by the theory of Diffusion of Innovation (DOI) by Everett Rogers 1962 (Sahin, 2006). Diffusion of innovation is a theory that seeks to explain how, why and at what rate new ideas and technology spreads. Rogers views diffusion as the process in which an innovation is communicated through certain channels overtime among members of a social system (Rogers in Sahin, 2006). The theory proposes four main elements influencing the spread of a new idea to include: the innovation itself, communication channels, time and a social system. This process relies heavily on human capital. It is the human capital that should adopt the new idea. Adoption is a decision of full use of an innovation as the best course of action available.

Adoption of a new idea follows three steps which are: knowledge, persuasion and decision. Innovation is linked to technology according to the theory. Communication channels allow the transfer of information from one unit to the other. Time is the passage of time necessary for innovations to be adopted. The social system is the combination of external influences (mass media, organizational or governmental mandates) and internal influences (strong and weak social relationship).

## Innovation in Higher Education in Nigeria

The innovation process involves five steps namely: knowledge, persuasion, decision, implementation and confirmation. Innovation in education is expedient because education plays a crucial role in creating a sustainable future. Innovation is a change that creates a dimension of performance that would lead to the achievement of desired goal. From institutional perspectives, it means successful exploitation of new ideas (White and Glickman, 2007). This applies to higher education, where innovation can refer to some new way of doing things, or a change that improves administrative or scholarly performance, or a transformational experience based on a new way of thinking.

Although certain people use the word innovation to represent improvements, Clayton in White and Glickman (2007) has explained innovation in two perspectives: sustaining and disruptive innovation. Sustaining innovation according to the author is a process, system or modification that improves an existing product or system. It may make it better, bigger, more efficient and/or more beneficial to the end user. Disruptive innovation on the other hand is innovation that creates significant change. This represents an innovation that brings to market a product or service that is not as good as the best traditional offerings, but is more affordable and easier to use (particularly in the beginning) of the product life. Put differently, disruptive innovation replaces the original, complicated, expensive product with so much more affordable and simple product that a new population of customers now has enough money and skills to buy and readily use the product. Examples of disruptive innovation include the introduction of the home computer and Apple's development of iTunes

Innovations in higher education is multifaceted covering various perspectives such as ownership of universities and other higher educational institutions, funding strategies, quality assurance practices. These include innovative planning (strategic planning), innovative programme contents, human and material resources development, admission procedures, carrying-capacity regulations, use of ICT in teaching and learning, innovative programme appraisal procedures and standards among others. One of the impact of globalization on higher education is bringing to bear innovation in funding of universities as funding forms the foundation on which all other challenges build on. Higher education in Nigeria is expected to borrow a leaf from American institutions by not being unduly dependent on government for funding (Juma in Etuk, 2015). As posited by Soludo in Etuk (2015) Universities in Nigeria are advised to source for funds from other sources such as foundations, the private sector, endowments and from the alumni. They are also expected to generate their own revenue by engaging in businesses, entrepreneurial activities and in marketing.

The use of the model of funding called "marketing mix conceptual framework" as recommended by Lamptey in Etuk (2015) has four Ps (product, price, place and promotions. This includes marketing through diversification of admissions and outsourcing (product mix), innovative funding through charging discriminatory price (price mix), funding by utilizing innovative education distribution channels (place mix) and innovative funding through the use of marketing communication strategies (promotion).

It is widely held that qualitative education should help students acquire innovative skills, variously called "employability" daily-living skills, generic skills, life-coping skills, fluency in information and communication technology (ICT) and the capacity to embrace learning as a new way of life. Quality assurance activities therefore include innovative educational curriculum enriched with general studies courses, standardization of admission procedures and quality assurance in planning, innovation of the learning contents, innovations in human and materials resources development and quality control through accreditation of programmes.

Global trends have led to the widespread adoption of new teaching technologies which is reinforcing the move towards student-centered learning and assessment. This has enhanced the development of the new approaches to distance education. We are living in a continually evolving digital world and technology is making dynamic changes in the society. Innovations in higher education include the use of ICT for active learning, collaborative learning, creative learning and integrative as well as evaluative learning.

Application of technology in education include e-learning (synchronous and asynchronous), blended learning, e-library, use of smart board to replace the traditional overhead projectors, use of smart phones, computers, education chat groups, repository, cloud computing etc. use of internet and www has led to the development of borderless education such as Corporate Universities created by the merger of Company training and Research Departments. These are all in response to the challenges of the new knowledge economy and for profit universities. Global alliances can also be established as a result of partnership between global multimedia and communications corporations to replace more conventional types of academic exchange among universities worldwide. This alliance as asserted by Iroegbu and Maxwell (2017) enhances internationalization of higher education across the borders.

## Importance of Innovation in Higher Education

Transformation in the objectives of higher education has necessitated a fundamental review of polices of tertiary education. Innovations in educational policies should result in producing graduates that can produce, discovers and export ideas, goods, drugs, equipment etc. and not depend on other nations to solve their developmental challenges. It enhances a shift towards a problem-based mode of knowledge creation, away from the classic discipline led approach and the blurring of the distraction between basic and applied research.

- Consequently, innovation brings about a shift from the traditional departmental approach to interdisciplinary approach that recognizes research and training as a major tool for solution to complex socio-economic problems of our immediate community.
- Enables educators in higher education adopt technology that has value in their instruction. This would also help in providing helpful experiences for themselves and their students.
- Innovations helps to balance the fiscal pressures of running a large organization influenced by external forces (such as rankings and increased competition for students and faculty), as well as internal stresses produced by boards and assessment bodies or accrediting agencies.
- It would make room for more transparency, accountability, and tangible evidence of success, in curricula programmes, delivery mechanisms, support services and operations.

Higher education in Nigeria, not only needs new ideas and inventions that shatter the performance expectations of today's status quo to make a meaningful impact, but should also provide new solutions that should be adequate to serve millions of students and teachers as well as the underserved populations. Lack of innovation can have profound economic and social repercussions. Higher education in Nigeria requires innovations that are either or evolutionary. As explained by Osolind in Serdyukov (2017), evolutionary innovations lead to incremental improvement but require continuity: revolutionary innovations bring about a complete change, totally overhauling and/or replacing the old with the new, often in a short time period.

## Barriers to Innovation

Though innovation is a welcomed idea in the educational system, there are certain factors that can impede this process in the Nigerian higher education system. These include:

- Interrelatedness sand interdependency of all the educational levels. These are the primary, the post primary, colleges, polytechnics and the universities. These sub systems are closely webbed in such a way that one sub system constitutes the intake of the other. If innovation does not cut across all these levels of education, it might not give the expected and desired result.
- Another structural change which might impede innovation is a methodological or curricular change in one subject area which might necessitate a ripple effect on other subjects.
- Lack of support from the society for innovations, thus, education will stagnate and produce mediocre outcome.
- Human beings are historically slow in adapting to change, more so, when it involves a large army of people who are intellectuals and who cannot be completely controlled. While it is easy to remove an obsolete machinery for the purpose of modernization, it is not exactly so with human beings. Higher education industry is filled with highly educated people who hold advanced degrees; many of whom are seen as national and international experts in their fields of study. These individual have conducted researches that resulted in creative ideas and improvements in certain aspects of education and may be generally wary of changes that challenges old assumptions and require new skills to succeed.
- Tradition and culture – tradition and culture can be extremely powerful forces both from within and outside the institution, when planning change of any kind. Many institutions of higher learning have been protected by the prestige of their brands and lack of any real competition. This attitude of continuing to rest on the reputation of their institution does not encourage innovation in spite of any external pressure for change.
- Promotion of teachers – it is becoming conventional for educational institutions to gauge promotion of teachers on the number of years put in, rather than on how hard working the teacher is. A committed and enthusiastic teacher, whose primary concern is how to effectively and efficiently impart on the student, is placed on the same salary with a colleague who is busy, always out-of-school with activities like paper presentations, publications, money-earning efforts etc. This system does not

encourage the hard worker to work harder, rather it discourages them from working to maximum capacity.

- There is also the issue of publication and mobility in tertiary institutions. Teaching and research are the two key roles of higher institutions of learning. The primary role is teaching, but this role is now taking the secondary position as efforts of academia are directed towards publications in reputable professional journals. This is predicated on the fact that upward mobility in academic hinges on the number of such publications made, rather than on the quality of their teaching and inventions. The quest for innovation is hereby strangulated by the desire for publication.

- Another impediment to innovation is the leadership style; internal systems structures and decision making processes. It has been observed that the concept of shared governance is engrained in the culture of higher education. Shared governance connotes a system that attempts to balance maximum participation in decision making with clearly defined accountability. Although this system encourages members of the institution to make input into decisions, it can as well cloud the decision making process and slow down innovation.

- Inadequate or lack of infrastructure needed for innovation may hinder it, such infrastructures include: buildings dorms, classrooms, athletic facilities, technology etc. if these infrastructures may have created significant overhead in the business model, or if the changes or innovations would change the business model, it possess a challenge.

- Funding – financial support for higher education is in its most conflicting position recently, especially with the current trend of economic recession in the country thereby impeding innovation.

- Another barrier to innovation in higher education is the formulation of educational policies by non-educationist, borne out of politics and achievement of selfish interest. These policies suffer setbacks during the implementation process as they end up being "square pegs in round holes" as far as the business of education is concerned. The result is stagnation and maintenance of status quo, without any form of creativity, improvement or innovation.

- Accreditation – nearly all accreditation processes and standards are designed to maintain the status quo. This is because, these regulatory and assessment bodies gear their standards and polices towards maintaining and increasing excellence in higher education. Notions of excellences remain mostly focused on measures that reinforce the existing state of affairs rather than invention of new ideas.

- Staffing and recruitment processes – the search processes for most new academic positions tend to place greater weight on preserving the status quo. Diversification of the faculty is one of the most essential tools that can enhance innovation.

- Faculty governance – the traditional faculty socialization and tenure processes is also a strong barrier to change. Tenure track plays an important role due to their oversight and control of teaching and learning experiences. Any effort directed towards change is seen as a threat to academic excellence or integrity. The process of earning tenure is one that rewards and reinforces status quo in the educational system.

• Organizational silos – many educational administrators tend to work in silos, cutting off from the broader inputs and influences that could shape their future. Thus, the institution becomes too internally focused and rigidly structured, missing the signs of change

## Issues and Challenges in Higher Education

Higher education is the level of tertiary education attained after the successful completion of post-primary level of education. Federal Republic of Nigeria (2013) in the National Policy on Education defines higher education as the education given after secondary education that is in universities, colleges of education, polytechnics, monotechnics among others. According to Ayo-sobwale and Akinyemi in Ekankumo and Kemebaradikumo (2014) higher education in all nations, is specially designed to provide the needed manpower for the overall turnaround of a nation. Education and specifically higher education, is seen and assumed to be the most important instrument of change, as any fundamental change in the intellectual and social outlook of any society should be perceived by an educational revolution. It is only through functional education, backed-up by innovations that this role can be fulfilled. The goals of higher education are very laudable but have been faced with many challenges affecting the achievement of tertiary educational goals.

The National policy on University Education as stipulated by Federal Republic of Nigeria (2013) stated that university education shall make optimum contribution to national development by:

(a) Intensifying and diversifying its programmes for the development of high level manpower within the context of the needs of the nation.
(b) Making professional course contents to reflect our national requirements.
(c) Making all students part of a general programme of all-round improvement in university education, to offer general study courses such as history of ideas, philosophy of knowledge, nationalism, and information technology (IT); and
(d) Making entrepreneurial skills acquisition a requirement for all Nigerian universities.

Some researchers have observed that, what is on ground is contrary to the exposited roles of university education as the system is not yet prepared to contribute to national development as stated by Federal Republic of Nigeria. The system is grossly dysfunctional as it has failed to equip its beneficiaries with the needed skills necessary for economic, scientific and technological development.

Higher education is under attack. What was sometime considered a climate of good will and respect for institution of higher education, founded in the belief that the administrators, faculty and staff who worked within the prestigious auditorium of learning institutions, were doing good to the society at large, is now replaced with a general sense of skepticm. These observations are borne out of increasing cost of operating universities, as well as a general lack of understanding of the breadth of work conducted in higher education today. There is no doubt that today's climate of higher education is placing more pressure on leaders of universities, polytechnics, colleges etc, to think differently about how they manage their institutions. Institutions of higher learning are expected to be more accountable especially in terms of performance. That is, defining the outcomes of that institution as it relates to students' learning, how the institutions meet those outcomes viz-a-vizs students' needs in line with global standard.

National accrediting and assessment bodies, which were thought of as the "quality enforcers" of higher education, appear to be directed by the federal government to be more demanding of institutions. There seems to be a progressing climate of mistrust of these accrediting bodies themselves, seeing them as "good-old-boy networks" rather than as quality control organizations. It is axiomatic that the economic, scientific and technological development of any nation depends on the quantity and quality of skills acquired and offered by the school system to the society at large. In this age of technological advancement, ignited by the fire of Information and Communication Technology (ICT), www and the internet, the education that we need is one that is capable of producing Nigerians who can manufacture raw materials, machines, tools, equipments as well as possess the skills needed for the industries in an industrialized society.

Higher educational institutions should produce individuals who can produce enough food for local and international markets, invent new designs, make new equipments, discover new drugs that are capable of curing these incurable diseases and thereby move this country to a level of being a producer or manufacturer of goods and services. For this type of education to be achieved, Williams and Anekwe (2010) posited that certain parameters should be adhered to. These are:

- The qualities of lecturers in terms of their trainings and qualifications.
- Availability and adequacy of lecturers
- Quality and availability of teaching materials
- Quality and content of the instruction and curriculum
- Quality and quantity of the instructional facilities which include classrooms, libraries, laboratories, workshops and other physical facilities.
- Availability of modern teaching materials and techniques such as the use of computer, slides, film projectors, television, video, radio, the internet, teleconferencing etc.

- Availability of specialized lecturers
- Consideration of the recommended class size and lecturers workload
- The use of modern management/administrative techniques and quality of monitoring and evaluation system for both students and lecturers.

It is believed that, if all these parameters are given full consideration, and the National universities Commission (NUC) and other assessment bodies, use them as parameters in accrediting a department, then the goals of higher education in the country would be achieved. From the foregoing, it can be deduced that higher education is Nigeria is confronted with a lot of issues that is traced to the type of education that was imposed on Nigeria by the colonial masters, which the country is now experiencing the long terms effects. It has been observed that educational system is far below standard which is not in tandem with best practices globally. The indicators used for measuring, from teaching, research, research impact, innovation and international outlook were used to rank the universities. As at 2017, only two African Universities appear is the top 200 of worldwide rankings: the University of Cape Town was 1st in Africa and at 148th position in the world, while University of Ibadan, Nigeria was 18th position in Africa and at the 801 in the world. Followed by University of Lagos 29th position in Africa, Obafemi Awolowo University 35th, University of Benin 71, University of Abuja 81st, University of Port Harcourt 82nd (Obiajura, 2017,).In the same vein, Bothwell and Grove (2018) reported that University of Cape Town was 1st in Africa and now at 171 position, while University of Ibadan is at 801 position in the world.

Considering University education, Nigeria has the largest university system in Sub-Saharan Africa. The university system offers numerous graduates and post-graduates programs that serve as magnets for students even from neighbouring countries. Nigerian Universities are grouped into first, second and third generation universities engineered by the ever increasing population of the citizens thirsty for university education, which led to the imperative establishment of private universities. The 2017 ranking of universities by the National Universities Commission (NUC), revealed that University of Ibadan was the 1st, followed by University of Lagos, Obafemi Awolowo University Ife, Amadu Bellow University, Zaria. The University of Uyo is the 26th on the lists (Olawale, 2017). There seems to be students migration based on this ranking of universities by National Universities Commission. All these accrediting bodies expect universities and colleges to address issues related to poor performance of students and to improve student retention and graduation rates across board. This becomes a concern for education leaders in all types higher institutions of learning.

As observed by Ebersole in White and Glickman (2007), one of the top issues facing higher education is the increasing cost, which is being attributed to reduce tax support for public institutions and has forced an offset through increase in tuition fees. The current economic recession has had a devastating impact on Nigerian economy and subsequently on the administration of university education. This implies that the system of higher education in Nigeria has failed to meet the needs and aspirations of the society. The university and other higher educational system ends up producing graduates for white collar jobs and individuals who are very "bookish' with every impressive, well certificated, and lengthy curriculum vitae, who cannot relate or implement the content of what they learnt in the university at their workplaces. Commenting on the relevance of university education, Aguba in Williams and Anekwe (2010) observed that the system breeds half-baked graduates who are found lacking in terms of intellectual capacity, moral disposition and skills development.

Many people are faced with the fact that the university education system in Nigeria has been in a state of permanent crisis which to name a few include financial inadequacy, irrelevance, unequal expansion, un-planned expansion etc. corroborating this view, Anowor in Williams and Anekwe (2010) remarked that the history of the Nigerian Education system generally has been a history ridden with crisis beyond the imagination of the proponents, initiators and propagators. This is also affirmed by certain scholars including Erinsho in Ajayi and Awe (2007) who asserted that the issues and challenges facing higher education in Nigeria are linked to the role of their proprietors and administrators, as well as those that are self-inflicted by the universities, that is, internal and external problems. The internal challenges include; weak internal governance and internal politics, while the external ones are related to inconsistent policies, polities and under-funding. Others include; poor academic preparation, enrolment explosion, shortage of qualified personnel, examination malpractice sexual harassment, decline in staff training programme, unconducive learning environment, effects of unionism, lack of modern standard instructional facilities (example e-library, internet facilities, ICT technologies devices etc) among others.

The overall effects of all these inadequacies usually result in many universities producing low quality graduates, general decline in the standard of higher reeducation as well as withdrawal of accreditation of some programmes from some of these institutions in the country. These recurrent challenges have also led to a good number of lecturers and researchers leaving the shores of Nigerian in search of greener pastures elsewhere. As observed by many researchers including Olugbile in Williams and Anekwe (2010) a gale of brain drain is now blowing away whatever remains of scientists and researchers in nation's research institutes, and this ill wind portends danger for national development because research institutes are the pivot upon which any meaningful growth can be achieved in any nation.

There is also the issue of quality of higher education provided for the citizens of Nigeria as a nation. As observed by Ajayi in Williams and Anekwe (2010), due to the impact of considerable fall in the standard of university education, a university degree is no longer a guarantee of good communication skills and professional competence. The resultant effect is our higher educational institutions producing "unemployable and half-baked graduates. The internal mechanism for quality university education are stipulated in the powers given to the Senate in the universities to control admissions, instructional supervision at departmental and faculty levels, conduct examinations, certifications and well as discipline of students and staff. To strengthen the internal control measures for quality education in the university, the university has the power to appoint external examiners in order to ensure an objective assessment by providing an impartial advice on performance in relation to specific programmes. This regulatory framework is sometimes being politicized to the extent that the primary objective of obtaining that impartial assessment becomes defeated.

Higher institutions in Nigeria are losing the expected value at a fast rate and it is high time something is done to correct the situation. Discussions about all these issues and trends in higher education make news on a regular basis. Increase in enrolment, accreditation of courses, philosophical questions on the purpose of education, competency of Nigerian graduates, deregulation and privatization of education at all levels and many more calls for creativity and innovations in the administration of higher education in Nigeria.

## Conclusion

Higher education in Nigeria is faced with issues and challenges that is taking them on a journey of losing their value or becoming dysfunctional. The issue of dysfunctioning emanates from challenges which include poor funding, population explosion and low admission capacity, declining academic standard, crumbling infrastructure, inadequate/lack of modern instructional facilities and equipment, examination malpractice, half-baked and dropouts' students, policy issues, capacity issues, socio-cultural issues etc. Nigeria education desperately needs effective innovation on a scale that can help produce high quality learning outcomes across the system and for all students.

As the price of education, especially higher education continues to rise; cost and time, efficiency of learning, effective instructional approaches, methods and tools capable of fulfilling the primary goals of education, should become critical areas of research and inventive solutions. Therefore, a multidimensional approach to revitalizing the educational system, such that, it breeds learners' autonomy, self-efficacy, critical thinking, creativity, and a common culture that support innovative education should be encouraged. Innovative education should be a collective matter for all society, generating public responsibility; otherwise all efforts to build an effective higher education system will be a mirage.

## Recommendations

- Federal Government of Nigeria should increase financial allocations to education sector. This will enable the universities and other higher institutions of learning expand educational facilities to cope with the increase demand for higher education as well as innovative practices.
- Staff development programmes should be given priority attention by educational administrators and should be directed towards activities that encourage innovative practices that would enhance effective teaching and learning.
- Education policies should be formulated by educationist who have "worn the shoes and knows where it pinches"
- The envisaged innovation must offer apparent and globally acceptable advantage over current practices and procedures. Where such an alternative exists, it is more likely to win support and acceptability than the one which does not.
- Adequate coherent and systemic support services such as advisory teams, resource centres and professional organizations should be available to back up innovations; else educational system will eventually collapse.
- Researches focusing on bringing innovations, raising productivity, efficiency and improving the quality of learning should increase in all critical areas of education.
- Students learning, their mind, attitudes, behaviors, character, cognition and work ethics should form an important part of the innovation process. This implies that educational administrators should create a conducive learning environment that enhances effective communication, critical thinking skills, independent and self-directed entrepreneurship for learners at all levels of education.

## References

Ajayi, I. & Awe, B. (2007). Challenges of autonomy and quality assurance in Nigerian Universities. Available at: (www.academia.edu/.../challenegs_of _...) Retrieved on 18th December 2017.

Bothwell, E. & Grove, J. (2018). World university ranking 2018 Time Higher Education (THE). Available at: (https://www.timeshighereducation.com>...) Retrieved on 12th January, 2018.

Ekankumo, B. & Kemebaradikumo (2014). Quality financing of higher education in Nigeria: A Nostrum for the provision of quality education, *Journal of Education and Practice*. 5, 19. Available at: (http://www.IIste.org). Retrieved on 17th December, 2017.

Etuk, G. (2015). Innovations in Nigerian Universities: Perspective of an insider from A "Forth Generation" University. *International Journal of Higher Education*. Vol. 4 No.3

pp. 218-232. Available at: (http://dx.dol.org/10.5430/Ijhe.V4n3p218). Retrieved on 11th December, 2017

Federal Republic of Nigeria (2013). National Policy on Education 6th Ed. Lagos: Nigeria NERDC Publishers.

Iroegbu, E. & Maxwell, M. (2017). Internationalization of higher education in Nigeria: A cross-border education perspective. In *Revolutionizing Education in Nigeria.* Pp. 66-84. Onitsha: West and Solomon Publishing Coy Ltd.,

Obiajura, N. (2017). University of Ibadan ranked among top 25 Universities in Africa. Available at: (https://www.naija.ng>) Retrieved on 18th December 2017.

Okoroafor, J. (2013). Nigeria: the challenges of higher education –addressing the brain drain/infrastructure rot. Educational Issues, National Issues. Available at: (www. opinionNigeria.com>Nigeria-at the) Retrieved on 20th December, 2017.

Olawale, J. (2017). Top 100 best universities in Nigeria 2017. Available at: (https://www. naija.ng>.) Retrieved on 3rd January, 2018.

Sahin, I. (2006). Detailed review of Rogers' diffusion of innovations theory and educational technology related studies based on Rogers' theory. *The Turkish Online Journal of Educational technology – TOJET,* April 2006, vol. 5, Issue 2. article 3 Available at: (eric.ed.gov/fulltext/ED501453 pdf.) Retrieved on 10th July 2017.

Serdyukov, P. (2017). Innovation in education: what works, what doesn't and what to do about it. *Journal Research in Innovative Teaching and Learning.* Vol. 10. 1pp4-33. Available at: (https://dai.org/10.1108/JRIT-10-2016-0067). Retrieved on 11th July, 2017

Swanger, D. (2016). Innovation in higher education: can colleges really change. Available at: (https://www.fmcc.edu/about/files/2016/innovationin-higher-Education.pdf.) Retrieved on 17th July, 2017

White, S. & Glickman, T. (2007). Innovation in higher education: Implications for the future. Wiley Interscience. Available at: (https://pdfs.semaniticssscholar.org/ d43f/20527ae602f0d6934bOc/faaf91788.pdf). Retrieved on 18th July 2017.

Williams, C. & Anekwe, J. (2010). Nigeria University education and functionality in the 21st century. In E. C. Iloputaife, B. U. Maduewesi, and R. O. Igno (eds.), *Issues and challenges in Nigerian education in the 21st century.* Onitsha: West and Solomon Corporate Ideals Ltd.

# 10

# Transforming Primary Education in Nigeria

Binta Sani Ph.D

## Abstract

*E* *ffective implementation is very vital if primary schools are to be transformed to achieve its goals. The government has to lay a sound and effective foundation by providing a sound curriculum, funds, classroom infrastructures, facilities, qualified teachers and mother tongue amongst others. Primary education is the level that develops the individual the capacity to read, write and calculate. It is the core of development and progress in modern society. Primary education is the only level of education that is available everywhere in the developed and the developing countries as well as urban and rural areas. This explains why primary education is the largest sub-sector of any educational system that offers the unique opportunity to contribute to the transformation of the societies through the education of the young ones.*

**Keywords;** infrastructure, materials, implementation, evaluation

## Introduction

National development depends largely on educational level, quality and the extent to which the citizenry participates in the sector. It is in view of that the Federal Government of Nigeria introduced Universal Basic Education (UBE) Programme in 1999. Education has become the most powerful weapon known for reducing poverty and in-equality in modern societies. Primary education is used for laying a sound foundation for a sustainable growth and development of any nation (NPE, 2004). According to Erinsho (2012), Nigerian government introduced the UBE Programme into the country in 1999 in conformity with the education for all (EFA) and Millennium Goals (MDGS) as an integral part of poverty reduction strategy. Universal Basic Education is the transformation of fundamental knowledge to all facets of the Nigerian society from generation to generation. It is the level that develops the individual the capacity to read, write and calculate. In other words it helps eradicate literacy which is one of the strong predictor of poverty. Thus, primary education is the only level of education that is available everywhere in both developed and the developing countries as well as urban and rural areas. This explains why it is the largest subsector of any educational system that offers the unique opportunity to contribute to the transformation of the societies through the education of the young ones.

The fact is that effective implementation is very vital if primary school curriculum is to achieve its goals of inculcating permanent literacy and numeracy ability to communicate effectively. This is to lay a sound basis for scientific and reflective efforts of the federal government towards implementation of a sound curriculum for the schools. Little has been done due to inherent issues on implementation of primary school curriculum. These problems including funding of the classrooms, acute shortage of in fractures, lack of qualified teachers and neglect of mother tongue, among others. A critical look at the challenges of implementation is to be looked at.

## Curriculum Relevance

Walton et al in Yunusa (2000) defined curriculum as that content and those processes designed to bring about learning of educational values. By this definition curriculum is considered to include both what is to be taught and by what means is to be taught. Smith in Yunusa (2000) defines curriculum as the set or a sequence of potential experiences set up in the school for the purpose of disciplining children and youth in group ways of thinking and acting. To Walton, curriculum definition infers that a real understanding of the children involved in the curriculum is necessary. He further stated that the method of the teacher should be conceived within a pre-conceived framework developed as a result of answering questions as to what sort of experiences can be contributed which will both make the pupil wish to learn as problematic or what should be planned, taught and learn in school. The curriculum is centrally determined, based on the NPE guidelines of 1981 and this tends to be out dated in outlook, therefore there is the need to review the curriculum to meet the present situation.

According to Adeyemo (1979) the aims of primary education are:--

I. To develop the child morally: this means that he should have good conduct and behaviour by respecting all elderly persons.
II. To remove illiteracy: the child receives sound education so that he may be able to earn his living honestly and help the community to which he belongs.
III. To foster development of lively curiosity leading to a search for knowledge of the immediate environment and of the outside world. Education helps to develop the child's hidden talents which bring improvement in his life.

IV. To enable the child to have an understanding of the community and of what is of value for its development and of the contribution which the individual can make to the community. He must be able to know about the community in which he lives and about the world outside his community.

V. To acquire some skills of hands and to recognize the value of manual work, he must be developed to make use of his hands for a good education trains the head, heart and hands.

Issues about the relevance of the curriculum for the needs of Nigerian society have been indirectly in-effective in context. There is need for curriculum transformation in order to take into consideration the changes that are taking place in the nation as well as in the world. There is concern about the relevance of teacher training programmes for the flexibility to accommodate the changes needed in the school environment. Overall, the issue of relevance of the curriculum in meeting the needs of Nigeria has not been dealt with in a serious way. Curriculum relevance is very vital for ensuring that economic issues such as import and export, health-general hygiene and sanitation. Curriculum transformation will have to be taken into consideration and be reviewed at all levels of education in order to make sure that it meets the needs of a democratic society, economy and the Nigerian people.

The teachers can be transformed by learning about the community, gaining greater understanding of content knowledge thus enabling them to be stronger teachers and use practitioner's knowledge to assist the new. The current trend in teacher education needs to be updated, many feel that candidates display lack of training and preparation for teaching and that teacher training course do not sufficiently address how to vertical align coursework and differentiate instruction for students.

## The Role of Teacher-Education

The teachers are the key individuals for all reforms and should therefore, be placed at the centre of all educational reform Olorukoob in Sani (2013). Teachers need to learn new approaches and participate in forming educational environment. Seriousness comes from the teachers who will provide them with key to understanding of the subject in its widest sense. The growth of confidence, the elimination of fear and the binding forces of love and tenderness are the elements with which a teacher must work with.

Teachers of the 21st century are not always taught enough about students and how they learn. They often do not have sufficient background to tackle tough students' achievement issues revolving around diversity. In order to prepare teachers for the diversity of students in current public schools, many teacher education programmes would require field experience (student teaching experience) with diversity students who are of low socioeconomic status and who often speak English as a second language. A year long experience as opposed to a semester experience would facilitate future teachers in gaining valuable insight into student's cultures and histories. The education programmes will include language development processes and how to shape teaching methods that are built upon pupil's different cultural backgrounds, linguistic skills and vary academic abilities

The National Policy on Education (NPE, 2004) clearly stated that no nation can rise above the quality of its teachers. This is because teachers are the foundation of quality in the school. It is the teacher indeed who in the final analysis translates policies into practice and progress into action. We learn from high performer because evidence indicates that we are falling behind, phasing out the teacher-training colleges has been a great problem. Teacher training colleges that use to be part of secondary education program in the past was the required qualification for primary school across the country. However National Policy on Education made the National Certificate in Education (NCE) the minimum qualification for teaching in primary schools. The Grade ll teachers are the best for primary school pupils while NCE for secondary schools students because they are in position to communicate better.

The question is how adequate and qualified are the teachers?

There is general decline in quality of education in Nigeria and this has been a major problem. There is poor quality of products right from colleges of education among others. This is as a result of lowering admission requirements of the colleges and also the images of student-teachers do not find prestige in the teaching profession thereby hindering the effective implementation of the primary school curriculum. Teacher quality throughout Nigeria is un-equal. There are also in-equities in the availability of qualified teachers in different states. In addition there are disparities between rural and urban schools and between educational institutions owned and controlled by the Federal Government and those owned and controlled by the states and private agencies.

The shortage of primary school teachers need to attain the proposed 1:30 or 1: 40. The transition ratio is far from being met and is more currently operating at 1:76 in most cases. Teaching today is no longer child centred but classroom centred, due to rapid expansion in students' numbers without comparable expansion in resources, staff and facilities. The rapid growth has not been matched by substantial increase in the funding of educational institutions. Government acknowledged that as part of improving quality in educational institutions, physical facilities have to be upgraded and resources such as libraries, laboratories, modern communication have to be provided as well. Poor quality at all levels of education is compounded by lack of instructional materials for effective teaching and learning. There is shortage of textbooks in the schools due to the high cost of books. It is only then when the resources are brought that meaningful teaching and learning will take place. Efficient and effective use of resources is one of the keys of building out-standing primary schools.

## Infrastructure Provision and Rehabilitation of Existing Buildings

Moja in Sani (2015) in her analysis of performers of Nigerian education stated that infrastructure and facilities remain inadequate for copying with a system that is growing at a rapid pace. There should be better classrooms, studios and workshops. They should have well educated teachers who possess the fundamentals of liberal humanities and are diverse enough to cater for special interesting and experts in training. The government is to provide a well conducive learning atmosphere as well as playground; physical and health education (PHE) for the pupils. There is shortage of space currently existing in all the sub-sector of the educational system. This is as a result of the introduction of UBE that has put pressure on educational facilities that did not expand at the same rate as the school population. The existing buildings are in a stage of decay due to lack of maintenance and repairs. The present conditions of the buildings have a negative effect on the teachers and encourage a brain drain of teaching and administrative personnel, dilapidated school environments contributes to high dropout of learners from school.

## Raise the Prestige and Preparedness of Teachers

According to Prinsley and Johnston (2015), "once teaching becomes a high status profession, more talented people will become teachers lifting the status of the profession even higher". Great teachers are intellectually capable, passionate and knowledgeable about their subjects, rigorously prepared and well supported and resourced. They inspire students to learn and to immerse themselves in a topic. Great educational systems develop and retain these teachers by making teaching attractive:

- Appoint outstanding head teachers.
- Get the right people to become teachers.
- Develop these people into highly effective educators since the only way to improve outcomes is by improving teaching and learning.
- Excellent teaching and learning will raise the standards of every child by making him to reach the highest level of performance.

The aim of this paper is to improve educational outcomes while delivering and optimising highly efficient and cost effective provision through matching the supply of place to meet demand for years to come.

## Conclusion

It is in recognition of the importance of primary school and indeed the basic education that all governments in Nigeria both the past and present placed premium on it by making the basis education the focal point of their educational policies and programmes in Nigeria and all over the world. Educational experience and training in diverse knowledge and skills preparation is one of the challenges one faces in life. Teaching is a critical and complex task we must implement change for every school through a national approach that targets everybody's investment in primary education in line with the evidence of student's need and programme impact. The pursuit of quality in education should not only be the concern of teachers and educational institutions but also parents, students, employers of labour, government and international community.

## Recommendations

Teachers must be supported to keep pace with changes, and keep their knowledge up to date and meet the day to day pressures of the classroom.

To achieve educational goals the following suggestions are made:

To improve the quality of education is critical particularly with the prevailing educational expansion and reforms.

- Improve the educational quality by enhancing and increasing the learner-motivation as well engaging the pupils.
- Facilitate the acquisition of basic skills
- Enhance teacher training schools learning environment that will enable students achieve worthwhile learning goals as well as appropriate academic standard.
- Quality resources access as well as utilisation of it in bringing out worthwhile learning outcome.
- Interact with those resources very well.
- Develop and implement a comprehensive programme for head-teachers and principals.
- Identify, evaluate, develop and coordinate teaching practices resources as well as maintenance and management.

Finally the grade II teacher-training colleges (TTC) that were wiped out should be reconsidered and returned into the system in order to lift the status of the teachers as professionals.

# References

Adeyemo, P. O. (1979). Principles of education and practice of education. Ado-Ekiti: Omolayo standard Press and Bookshops Co (Nig.) Ltd.

Amoo, S. A. & Adewale, J. G. (2010). Access to utilisation and quality of SNNG facilities in promoting quality education in South West Nigeria. *West African Journal of Education Vol. XXX 2010*

Bandi, B. S. (2015). Evaluation of Universal Basic Education on teaching of Art at upper Basic Education in Sokoto. M.A. Unpublished Thesis, Department of Fine Art, ABU Zaria.

Erinsho, S. Y. N. E. (2012). Achieving Universal Basic education Niger: Issues of Relevance, Quality and efficiency. *Global Voice of Education: Vol. 1, No. 1.*

Federal Republic of Nigeria (2004). National Policy on Education. Lagos: NERDC.

Ngwaswu, C. C. (1997). The Environment of crises in Nigerian Educational System. *Comparative Education Vol.33 No 1*

Prinsley, R. & John, S. E. (2015). Transforming STEM teaching in Australian Primary Schools; everybody's business: Office of the Chief Scientist.

Sani, B. (2015). Evaluation of The teaching of art and crafts in special schools in Jigawa, Kaduna and Kano States, Nigeria. Unpublished Dissertation, Department of Fine Arts, ABU Zaria.

Sani, B. (2013). Transforming examination system through teacher education preparation for educational advancement. *West African Journal of Education (WAJE), Vol. XXXIII No1, June.*

Yunusa, M. B. (2000). Issues on Curriculum. ABU Press Zaria.

# 11

# Managing Adolescents in Nigerian Secondary Schools: A Panacea for Leadership and Values Re-Orientation

Ngozika A. Oleforo Ph.D, Mercy U. Ette & Anietie K. Onyenso

## Abstract

*This paper is focused on managing adolescents in Nigerian Secondary Schools as a panacea for leadership and values re-orientation. Adolescents' maladaptive/ indiscipline behaviour in Schools is on the increase and this has serious effect on the nation's educational system. One of the strategies of managing this menace is moral values, an indication that families, schools, societies and government have failed in their roles to ensure that the broad goals of secondary education, which are preparing individuals for useful living and higher education are attained. Realization of these goals is key to sustainable national development, which hinges on effective leadership skill and values re-orientation. Nigeria could be labelled an adolescent at 57 (October 1, 1960 – October 1, 2017) because, its leadership recognizes the need to follow the path of sustainable development but lacks the political will power to punish corruption cases, strengthen her institutions and combart moral bankruptsy. The paper therefore, examined the roles of the family, peer group, the school and environment in domesticating the adolescents into responsible and useful members of society, by imbibing the culture of effective leadership and values re-orientation, as against disorientation and its negative consequences on national development.*

**Keywords:** Managing Adolescents, Leadership, Values Re-Orientation, Family, School, Environment, Peer Group, and Sustainable Natural Development.

## Introduction

All over the world, the young ones (adolescents) are the foundation on which sustainable national development (SND) is laid. The adolescents are tomorrow's leaders and leadership provides direction and inspiration. Living up to the course of all full grown adult is a national challenge that must not defy and defile a peoples' collective right. McCauley and Salter in Adesegun and Michelle (2017) defined adolescence as a period of transition, in which although, no longer considered a child, the young person is not considered an adult. This universal definition of adolescence suggests that young people are fragile and critical in shaping the future of the world. Today's generation of young people (the largest in history) is approaching adulthood in a world vastly different form prevailing generations, as they contend with AIDS/HIV, globalization, urbanization, ICTs, migration, economic challenges, kidnapping, restiveness among others, which have radically transformed the landscape. These are in addition to societal context, including gender and socialization process. All these influences have transformed what it means to be young.

Worse still, the young people are not as healthy as they seem. For instance, depression, teenage pregnancy and drop out cases are gaining unmanageable proportions. When depression is not properly diagnosed produces a tragic effect. Regrettably, adolescents who experience depression at an early age often struggle with it throughout their lives (Chinawa, Manyike, Obu, Aronu, Odutola and Chinawa, 2015). The source added that ensuring that female teenagers remain in school is vital to mitigating the negative outcomes of teenage pregnancy and child-bearing. In Sub- Sahara Africa especially, in rural areas, girls are married young and pressured to start having children immediately (Population Reference Bureau, 2013). This implies that the girl-child becomes economically disadvantaged having dropped out of school. Worse still, between 23% and 57.8% of adolescence in Nigeria is under-nourished (Adinma, Umeononihu and Umeh, 2017). The source asserted that under-nourished adolescent girl and pre-pregnant women are likely to give birth to under-nourished infants, with the risk of transmitting under-nutrition to the future generation.

Hence, one of the most important commitments a country can make for future economic, social, political progress and stability is to address the health and development needs of its young people (Federal Ministry of Health, n.d). In the face of prevailing leadership failures and economic recession, adolescents' maladaptive/indiscipline behaviour in schools and society is on the rise. This is largely due to family background, socio-economic status of parents, the school, peer influence, influence of mass media among others (Ochiagha in Kwaja and Mormah, n.d). The source added that moral values enable individuals to determine whether the relationship with others is appropriate and reasonable and therefore, advocated "moral curriculum." This connotes that students need to be taught continually to imbibe the virtues of Godliness, sanctity, truth, patience, honesty, kindness, loyalty, respect, patriotism among others. If at 57, some Nigerians are still agitating for restructuring and break-up, then, the country is still an adolescent. The implication is that her leadership must get it right while values re-orientation should secure permanent seat in the homes, classrooms and society. These sets of values are meant to be imbedded in the quality of instruction at all levels of our education, as harped by Federal Republic of Nigeria (2013). Values re-orientation is the much needed tonic to re-engineering Nigerian adolescents into assets for sustainable national development. This paper therefore, is presented under the following sub-headings; Family role, Peer Group, Environmental and school variables, conclusion, and recommendations.

## The Family Factor and Adolescents

The family background under which a child is brought up largely determines the totality of the child in the society. The family, therefore, plays the most important role in the life of every individual. It is evident that parents due to the socio-economic condition of the country have failed in imparting the right type of values to their children in the past two decades, which was characterized in the alarming erosion of social and moral values in Nigerian society till date. Nevertheless, the inculcation of values in the child who will grow up through adolescence stage to become adult in the society is done primarily by the family process of child-rearing. This, therefore, means that a family that values hard work, respect for individual and authority, honesty, and discipline is sure to raise a child when, even going through this transitory phase of adolescence period will be a stable, responsible and result oriented adult. On the other hand, a family whose values are otherwise will certainly bring up a child that may constitute a problem that will extend from the family to the school and larger society. In other words, whatever the child learns or imbibes at this time of development will certainly become part of his personal values that would be closely and jealously guided when he grows older.

It is therefore, detrimental to both the child and society at large for individual family to over-look the excesses of children. This raises the issue of parenting style that is, the child rearing practices and interactive behaviours which have been developed and implemented by parents. Schwartz and scot in Akpan (2017) observed three key parenting styles (parental authoritativeness, authoritarianism and permissiveness). Authoritative parenting prioritizes the child's needs, present qualities, and sets standards for appropriate future conduct, guidance with warmth, respect, reasonable expectations as well as acceptance of the concept of bi-directionality, where both are seen as equals who influence each other's behaviours and attitude. The authoritarian parenting neglects the child's need in favour of the parents' agenda, strong demands for child's compliance, forceful-absolute standard and punishing infractions. The parents exerts excess power and control since the style assumes a unilateral interaction and restricts the child's autonomy and yet, expects high expectations, which in most cases are not reasonable. On the other hand, permissive parenting style shares equal power with child; sets no boundaries for the child, and displays no expectations from the parents who also exert no control over the child. The parent may be permissive by showing warmth and responsiveness or may be uninvolved by remaining cold and distant, depending on the nature of the parent. All this boils down to discipline and character formation.

The disciplined behaviour inculcated in the young individual within the family will see the child through any pressure of life. The end result would be a disciplined and productive individual, contributing meaningfully, to the child's life and the society he/she finds self. This position is in tandem with Awake in Ereh (2006) in the assertion that discipline is training that corrects the mind and heart and that children need it constantly. Thus, when the family plays its own role in bringing up a disciplined, positive value-oriented individual from the home into educational institutions, the management of these children becomes easier for the school. This, therefore, buttresses the need for family and values re-orientation, by continually orienting their adolescents towards basic social values through socialization process. On the basis of this, Pope John Paul 11 (1981) stressed that the family has vital and organic links with society since it is its foundation and nourishes it continually through its roles of service to life. Hence, the family is the first school of social values since what a child becomes largely depends very much upon the family and the school.

## The School Factor and Adolescents

The school is a secondary agent of socialization, which perform the task of bringing up the society's children, a function which belongs to the home. For instance, children look up to the teachers for direction, support, and protection. Since adolescents at whatever level of education spend more hours with teachers in the school, the later can contribute significantly to values re-orientation of the former, thereby complementing the much required imputes of guidance counselors. If teachers are considered as human beings by their employers (government), they would raise their academic standard to inculcate traditional and moral values to the children. Most public schools would continue to fail in the clarion call for values re-orientation largely due to flagrant violation of teachers' right. Parker in Oleforo (2014) asserted that workers must first be seen as human beings and then as workers. The humanitarian principle concepts of democracy, human relations and justice reported by Oleforo (2014) is not entrenched in the workforce especially, in schools and other educational institutions, leading to frequent strike actions annually in the country. This ugly development is a prelude to indiscipline and poor Morales in the society.

Educational managers should be keenly involved in planning the educational programmes as well as co-curricular programmes that would take adequate care of the adolescents' needs. Besides, these young ones must be seen as the raw material inputs to education. If their learning activities are planned holistically, it would embrace cognitive, psychomotor and affective domains and this will go a long way in occupying their minds and time, preventing them from idleness that may lead them to negative peer group formation. In addition, it is the responsibility of the school to provide career guidance for youth empowerment and sustainable development. The development of a nation relies to a large extent on the development capacity of available human resource to meet the needs of the nation. The school therefore is expected to make conscious effort to train and direct the focus of Nigerian adolescents to such career options that will help the country to meet her manpower needs (Oyenike, 2016). This means that adolescents should be guided to make meaningful career choice in order to be relevant in their immediate environment. This requires management practice, the kind of practice of adolescents' variables in schools that would go a long way into inculcating into the youths, certain personality traits and leadership skills that would help them to develop useful values, attitudes, consciousness and openness. For instance, such attitudes that would help the adolescents to develop internal and external locus of control, whereby they can control what happens within and around them. This will also develop in them self-esteem as well as strong sense of achievement needs and orientation to strive to work hard in their academic pursuit. It will help suppress the crisis within their minds and the urge to rebel against authority, supervision, and the idea of seeking for acceptance among peers of negative attitudes. This will further help them to focus on their school activities, leading to better performance and good result, instead of involving in examination malpractice, truancy, cultism, avoidance of people/supervision, and other social vices. School management therefore, should be mindful of these young one's level and capabilities while organizing their social learning activities, by playing effective leadership roles expected of them by education stake-holders. The need for a direction makes leadership indispensable among all social beings (Chiledo, 2016). This means that, since the highly educated and sophisticated academia as a group, subject themselves to leadership, then, the adolescents need it the most. Thus, age ranged based activities herein referred to as peer tutoring, would take adequate care of the adolescents needs, in a way that will give them equal opportunity, for the all-round development of the individual and society. The issue of children schooling is the need to inculcate the right values in the children, in order to prepare them to live at peace within their immediate environment.

## Adolescents and their Environment

The type of environment accessible to the adolescent influences his/her vulnerability to Peer Pressure. In the context of developing countries, the factors of micro-environment and macro-environment seem to have not been identified and programmed into management of adolescents. The adjustment into a child's later life tasks is a function of the environment where the child is brought up. Iloh (2005) stressed that apart from generic transfers, from parents to children, environmental factors play key roles in child outcomes. Here, Iloh's conception of environment as far as education is concerned, encompasses the neighborhood factors and other sub-systems. In the past Nigerian society, child upbringing and character formation were responsibilities of both the family and everyone around the neighborhood, when derailing children were advised, or even disciplined right away without any reappraisal from the parents. Today, it is a different ball-game as such disciplinary efforts attract reappraisals and litigations which breeds "mind your business and I don't care attitude" by the elders. Values seem to be paid lip services while wealth proliferation and monetization are the in-things. In the centre of this unfortunate template, is the erosion of the nation's moral values and sustainable development. An environment bedridden with culture of corruption and harsh economic realities will place less emphasis on values re-orientation, thereby consistently encouraging adolescents' rebellious tendencies, where peer activities (negative and positive) of all sorts go unchecked to the detriment to sustainable national development.

## Adolescents and Peer Groups' Activities

Associating with an individual's age range refers to peer group association. In adolescence, peer group association may be of positive or negative value to both the individual and the society, if they are effectively or ineffectively managed. Peer group is commonly associated with episodes of adolescents' risk-taking such as delinquency, drug abuse, sexual behaviours, alcohol, smoking, gambling, rape gangs among others, because these behaviours commonly occur in the company of peers (Okorie, 2014). Majority of the young ones exhibit these problems as a result of peer pressure which also indulges youths into loitering about in the streets, lowers academic performance and makes one do things that are anti-social (things that people frown at). Some adolescents grow hardened in these acts to adult stage thereby constituting nuisance value. However, it is widely believed that achievement and values re-orientation are measures against anti-social behaviours and their spread. Adolescents are particularly venerable to peer pressure because they are at a stage of development, when they are separating more from their parents' influences, but have not yet established their own values. In short, adolescents lack skills to make healthy choices, and this makes effective leadership and values re-orientation imperative in any nation striving for sustainable economic development.

## Conclusion

All hands should be on deck in the proper and effective management of the adolescents especially, in the face of "tempting and hard-to-ignore influences" of today's world, which is vastly different from previous generations. This is important because the young ones are not ungovernable after all, provided their adults live exemplary life-style, by doing the right thing as educators/teachers, political and religious leaders, in order to uphold values for sustainable national development.

## Recommendations

1. Parents should be encouraged to adopt effective parenting style in the up-bringing of the child. Less emphasis should be placed on disciplinary measures leading to bodily harm, as this has proven counter-productive.
2. The school (teachers) should be supported by critical stake-holders of education in carrying out their over-sight function as, curriculum implementers, loco-parentis and character-moulders of their students.
3. Security agencies should comb every nook and crannies in order to secure the environment from breeding, corrupting and contaminating good manners.
4. The society should encourage the youths to extol the virtues of positive peer influence in order to motivate one another into healthy competition.
5. Corporal punishment should be abolished in schools and a degree of freedom given to the students while closely monitoring them by consistent values re-orientation. At adult stage, such adolescent would be willing to lay down his/her life for the cause of the Nation.

## References

Adesegun F. & Michelle, J. H. (2017). Adolescents and youth in developing countries: Health and development issues in context. Journal of adolescense. 33: 499-508.

Adinma, J. I. B., Umeononihu, O. S. & Umeh, M. N. (2017). Adolescent and pregnancy nutrition in Nigeria. *Tropical journal of obstetrics and gynaecology.* Official publication of society of gynaecology and obstetrics of Nigeria. 34: 1-5.

Ajala, A, O. (2014). Factors associated with teenage pregnancy and fertility in Nigeria. *Journal of economics and sustainable development.* 5 (2) 62-70.

Akpan, A. O. (2017). Psycho-Social factors as correlates of social adjustment of primary school pupils in North-West Senatorial District of Akwa Ibom State, Nigeria. Unpublished M.Ed disertation. University of Uyo, Uyo.

Chiledo, A. C. (2016). Innovative leadership behaviour and quality management of entrepreneurial venturers in Fegeral Universities, South-West Geo- Political Zone, Nigeria. Unpublished Ph.D thesis. University of Uyo, Uyo.

Chinawa, A. T., Manyike, P. C., Obu, H. A., Aronu, A. E., Odutola, O. & Chinawa, A. T. (2015). Depression among adolescents attending secondary schools in South-East, Nigeria. Journals of annals of African medicine. 14 (1): 46-51.

Ereh, C. E. (2006). The role of the family in laying proper foundation for moral values and character in Nigeria. *Nigerian Academy of Education*

Federal Republic of Nigeria (2013). *National policy on education*. Lagos: NERDC Press.

Iloh, G. O. (2005). School, home and neighbourhood: Partnership in the education of the Nigerian child. Unpublished paper presented in the conference of Nigerian academy of education in Owerri, Imo State, Nigeria.

John Paul II (1998). *Familiaris Consortio,* Washington.

Kwaja, P. & Mormah, F. O. (n.d). Managing adolescents' maladaptive behaviours in Nigerian secondary schools.

Okorie, A. N. (2014). Relationship among peer pressures, time management and academic performance in secondary school adolescents in Umuahia Education Zone, Abia State, Nigeria. A published M.Ed. Project submitted to the Department of Educational Foundations (Guardians and Counselling), Faculty of Education, University of Nigeria, Nsukka.

Olaitan, T., Mohammed, A. N., & Ajibola, A. L. (2013). Management of disciplinary problems in secondary schools: Jalingo metropolis in focus. 13 (14): 6-9.

Oleforo, N. A. (2014). *Educational management in Nigeria: Theory and practice*. Owerri: Cel-Bez Publishing. pp.40.

Oyenike, A. O. (2016). Career guidance for youth empowerment and sustainable development. *International journal for cross-disciplinary subjects in education.* 7 (3): 1-5.

Population Reference Bureau (2013). The world's youth 2013 data sheet. Available at www. prb.org.

# ENVIRONMENTAL ISSUES

# 12

# Widowhood in Indian Society

Sudhanshu K. Sultania

## Abstract

*T*his paper is an attempt to present a picture of status of widows in Indian society from ancient Vedic era to contemporary modern India which begins with a discussion on etymology of the English term 'Widow' or Sanskrit term 'Vidhawa'. The paper also defines the term 'Widow' and 'Widowhood'. Thereafter, its present a comprehensive historical analysis of widowhood in India from Vedic period, Post Vedic era, Smriti period, Mughal period, British colonial period to contemporary India and ends with concluding remark of the researcher.

**Keywords:** Widow, Widowhood, Vedic period, Indian society, Smriti, Mughal Period, British, Patriarchal society.

## Origin of the term 'Widow' or 'Vidhawa'

The English word 'widow' originates from the Sanskrit word 'Vidhawa'. Vidhawa word is made from 'Vi' and 'Dhawa' dhatu of Sanskrit language. There are many meanings of 'Dhawa' as trembling, man, husband and thug etc. Widows were known by several terms in Vedic-Sanskrit literature and in different dictionaries as Avira, Randa, Yati, Yatni, Nishphala, Vishwasta, Katyayani, Mritbhartika, Mrit Patika and Jalika etc. In ancient India, 'Vidhawa' word is believed to have been used for two reasons, first cause is that after the death of her husband, she trembles and the other cause is that after the death of her husband, she starts running hither and thither without any control (Tiwari 1994: 4-7). There are various terms used in Hindu tradition related to widowhood. Tiwari (1994) lists the following terms:

**Avira**- The woman, who became widow at the age of 10 years.

**Randa**- The woman, after the death of her husband could not be productive. So, this word is used even today. The modified version of it, 'Rand' is used for widow.

**Yati, Yatini**- The word 'Yati, Yatini' was used for those persons, who followed an ascetic life. It was considered compulsory for a widow to live a chaste life.

**Nishphala**- This word was used for widow, who was without son.

**Vishwasta**- The 'Shwas' dhatu was used to convey breathing. According to the Indian tradition, husband is given the same importance as of breathing to the body. So, this word was used for widow.

**Katyayani**- According to Amarkosh, ' Katyayani' means the middle-aged woman, who wear maroon colour clothes.

**Mritbhartika**- It was made from words 'Mrit' and 'Bharta'. Bharta word was used for a husband.

**Mrit-Patika**- It was made from words 'Mrit' and 'Patika'. 'Patika' word was used for a husband or rakshak.

**Jalika**- This word originated from the Sanskrit word 'Jal'. As a fisherman, catches fishes. May be, this word was used for the widow of the similar character. These women were called Jalika (pp.: 2-4).

Dutt (1968) viewed that, according to Sanskrit grammarians the word 'Vidhawa' is derived from the word 'dhawa' meaning a man or a husband. Although, the word 'Vidhawa' was in general use, the basic word 'dhawa' was not mentioned in the Vedic literature. In the 'Nirukta', for the first time, the word was used to mean a man or a husband. In the 'Atharvaveda' 'Dhawa'is the name of a tree. In the Vedic times the word 'Avidhava'-a double negative word in the sense of a woman not widowed was used, instead of a positive word like 'sadhava'. Even in the European languages the word dhawa is not found (p.247). He further viewed that the word Vidhava is said to be wrongly split up by the Indian grammarians. The word 'Vi' in the word 'Vidhava' is not a prefix but part of the main root word. It must be derived from a root like Teutonic 'Wid' to lack, Latin 'Videre' to separate and Sanskrit 'Vidh'to be bereft. Yaska says that when the true derivative meaning was lost in India the word 'Dhava' in the sense of a husband came into existence in the Sanskrit language by wrongly splitting up the word Vidhava (ibid: 248). Vidhava or Widow therefore is a woman whose husband is dead and who has not married again. Silverman (1970) viewed that the very word 'Widow' has very negative connotations. Many widows feel as if it implies they are damaged as a second class Citizen. The same associations are not true for the word widower (p.175).

The term 'Vidhava' or 'Widow' is very old and can be traced beyond the Vedic language to Indo-European origin. In most Indo-European languages, there are synonyms of widow as follows:

Synonyms of Sanskrit word 'Vidhawa' in different Indo-European languages:

| Languages | Synonyms |
|---|---|
| Latin | Vidua |
| Italian | Vedava |
| Spanish | Viuda |
| French | Veuv |
| Old Slavonic | Vidava |
| Russian | Vidova |
| Old German | Wituwa |
| Gothic | Widuowo |
| Old English | Widewe/Wideuwe |
| Persian | Beva |

(Source: Dutt 1968: 247)

## Definition of the term 'widow'

The Sakanda Purana, a Hindu text, describes widow as "more inauspicious than all other inauspicious things" (National Commission for Women, 2009-10: 37). The Widow (Protection and Maintenance) Bill, 2015 (Bill No. 236 of 2015) defines the term 'Widow' as a legally married woman whose husband has expired. The bill also defines the term 'Destitute widow' as a widow stricken with infirmity due to old age, physical disability, chronic ailment, mental imbalance or who has no source of income to support herself and her dependent children, if any. The bill also defines the term 'Abandoned widow' as a widow who has been deserted or thrown out of the household by her relatives to fend for herself and who has no means to support her and her dependent children, if any.

The Destitute Women and Widows Welfare Bill, 2006 (Bill No. XC of 2006) defines the term 'Widow' as a woman whose husband has expired after her legal marriage. The bill further defines the term 'Destitute' as in relation to a woman as any female who has no independent source of livelihood or is not being looked after by any family member or relative and includes a divorced woman. On the occasion of International Widow Day 23 June, 2014, United Nation calls widow as 'Invisible women' (http://www.un.org/en/events/widowsday).

## Definition of the term 'widowhood'

Merriam Webster dictionary defines the term widowhood as a noun. The state or period of being a widow or widower is called widowhood. The term can be used for either sex. The sociological meaning of widowhood varies from society to society. It depends on culture, custom and tradition of the particular society. In every society, the term widowhood carries various types of stigma, taboo, grief and deprivation.

## Widowhood in India: A Historical Analysis

To understand the status of widow in India, it is desirable to look her changing status through a historical eye. I shall start with the status prevailing in the Vedic age because the Hindu civilization goes beyond this period and data is not available on the prehistoric phase as it is unexplored. The portrait of a widow as coming out of the study of Vedic literature is the picture as drawn by several authorities on the Vedic period.

For the Hindu woman, widowhood is more tragic and disastrous because of the superstition and the oppressive, loathsome rituals attached to it. As Abbe Dubois quotes, "The happiest death for a woman is that which overtakes her while she is still in a married state. Such a death is looked upon as a reward of goodness extending back for many generations; on the other hand, the greatest misfortune that can befall a wife is to survive her husband" (Abbe 2007: 350).

Hindus have a belief in the "Theory of Karma" and therefore the Hindu widows think that her plight is the result of her "Karmas"; it is due to her bad deeds done by her in previous births that she has to suffer widowhood. The one who has auspicious signs could not be a widow. However, it is important to note that she is not considered among the sinners (ibid: 352). In Hindu society, the husband is elevated to such a superior position as to almost enjoy the status of a God Vis-a-Vis his wife. A widow is considered as an unfortunate woman and an object of pity. Quite often she has been compared to a 'veen' without strings and to a cart without wheels. Thereby the motivation or urge for life is lost to her (ibid: 354).

Nevertheless, it may be stated that the state of widowhood is a great calamity in all societies, but it is more so in a traditional patriarchal society like India. The reason for it is that here woman is known as 'Abala' or the one without power and therefore she has to depend upon her protectors. Manu, the Hindu law maker, in fact, states that "a woman can never be a free maiden, is to be cared for by her father, brother or husband. A woman considers her husband as her greatest protector and hence his death is a great calamity to her"(ibid: 355).

## A. Vedic Period and widowhood

The Vedic era was a patriarchal society. In this age, the woman's social, religious and economic status was also not equal to man. But, in some respects, the Vedic women and widows enjoyed certain privileges of which they were deprived in latter age. Widows were permitted to remarry. This practice seems to have been accepted as normal from the Vedic period onwards (Kapadia 1958: 611). Enough references are found in the Vedas to show that widow remarriage was common though the remarried widow could not aspire to the status of wife, where she could become the mistress of the house. The use of the term "Parapurva", a woman who has had a second husband, proves that widows remarried. The word "Didhishu", used in the Rigveda, means the second husband of a woman. Atharvaveda refers to a "Punarbhu", that is, remarried widow. This shows that marriage of widows was not opposed. The custom of a widow marrying the brother of her deceased husband seemed to be common. Hence, the word "Devara" literally means a woman's brother-in-law (Dutt op.cit.: 249).

The economic condition of widows was satisfactory in this era. A widow was given her husband's share in the property. A brother less maiden was an heir to her father's property. A man was reluctant to marry such a maiden, apprehensive that her father may make her a putrika, or an appointed daughter. As it is believed that the woman's parinahya was not her absolute property. But a childless widow inherited her husband's property by right (Rigveda x, 102.11, quoted in Upadhyaya 1941). A widow who had a son by Niyoga (levirate) received her deceased husband's property as the guardian of the property during her son's minority. If a widow remarried, her financial difficulties and problems were solved, since her second husband looked after her.

## Institution of Niyoga (Levirate) in Vedic age

The institution of niyoga was in practice during the time of Dharmasutras since, in the Rigveda, we find the widow married to her brother-in-law (Rigveda X, 40.2, ibid.). But there is no reference to the necessity of his producing an heir for his dead brother and even in, Grihya Sutras there is no ritual connected with niyoga. There are differences of opinion among different Dharmasutras about its practice, as it can be assumed that the institution of niyoga came into Aryan society from some non-Aryan source. For a long period the sacred law was inclined to adopt the growing custom, although with misgiving (Sengupta1965:140).

The term 'Niyoga' is of later origin, but its implications were freely practised in the Rigvedic times. Frequent allusions are made in the Rigveda to the practice of levirate. We have several references to the wives of weaklings procuring children from agencies other than their legally married husband (Upadhyaya op.cit.). Under the system of Niyoga, a widow or a woman whose husband was not virile, was allowed to have conjugal relations with her brother-in-law, who was regarded as the most eligible person for this duty, or some other near relation, till she gave birth to offspring. It is also significant to note that there is no reference in the whole of the Rigveda to a woman marrying the elder brother of her deceased husband. Even today, a widow's marriage with her husband's elder brother is a taboo. A widow was allowed to have two sons through niyoga. Such a son had the right to perform the funeral oblations. A son by levirate was always preferred to a son by adoption in Vedic society.

## Custom of Sati in Vedic period

There are no any references to burning of widows in the whole range of the Rigveda. The vedic hymns refer to the remarriage of widows rather than their self-immolation. Widow burning was, evidently, a defunct custom at this time. It was represented only by the symbolic ritual of the widow lying beside her husband on the funeral pyre, until upon which she was asked to rise up. Both the Rigveda and Atharvaveda expected the widow to get up from the pyre and marry the husband's younger brother (Kane 1930: 618-19).

Immolation can be expected to have existed among the early Indo-Aryans in some form or the other. This Indo-European custom of widow burning came to an end when Aryans entered India and had become only a symbolic ceremony. But Sarkar observed that, "The vedic literature shows very few traces of such a custom; partly, no doubt because these texts are priestly in character, and widow burning is known to have prevailed elsewhere, mainly among non-priestly warrior families, and partly because, even amongst the ruling classes, cases of widow burning were rare and prevented throughout the vedic period as shown by authentic kshatriya dynastic traditions; while in the 'Brahman' society sex-relations seem to have been too lax to admit of the prevalence of such a practice" (Sarkar 1928: 82). The status of a woman began to decline gradually in the vedic society where importance is attached to the birth of a male child which, in turn, become responsible for the gradual rise in the status of man. The widow was given inferior position as she was unfortunate enough to lose her 'Swami' (husband).

## B. Post Vedic era (Epic Period, Sutra Period, Buddhistic Literature) and widowhood

The descriptions of the widow in the Epic period, the Sutra period and the Buddhistic literature, gives a comprehensive picture as these are the connecting links between the Vedic and the Smiriti period.

## Widowhood in Epic period

The deterioration in the status of widows commenced from the epic period. From Shantiparva of the Mahabharat, we can sense about the miserable position of widows through the words of a she-pigeon, who says, "Widows, even if mothers of many children, are still miserable. Bereft of husband, a woman becomes helpless and an object of pity with her friends. Limited are the gifts from the father or the brother or from the son to a woman. The gifts that her husband alone makes to her are unlimited. A woman has no protector, no happiness without her lord" (Shah 1995: 229). Hence, according to Ramayana, his death is a great calamity to her. Her hopes and happiness are shattered for even if she has several sons, a widow feels uprooted and her honours is destroyed. Even a woman of aristocracy is feared this calamity of widowhood. It is therefore but natural that widows are full of self-pity. They referred to themselves as 'Anatha' (orphan) and the state of widowhood as 'Paschimavastha' (Ramayana VI 32.8: III 38), which means the later state. This implies that just as sun going to the west loses its splendour and light so does the widow (Jayal 1966).

## Institution of Niyoga in Epic period

During the Vedic period the widow remarriage was in practice, whereas during the epic period Niyoga came into existence. As Jayal states, no account of a woman's life in the epics would be complete without the mention of the practice of Niyoga. The reason behind this practice might be the husband's desire for securing spiritual and family interests. Such sons were known as 'Kshetraja' i.e., born of Kshetra or field i.e., wife. He was always preferred to a son by adoption and had a legal status in the family (Jayal 1966:177). Most of the heroes of the Mahabharata were born of levirate (Niyoga). In epic era, Niyoga was practised for spiritual or dynastic interests.

## Widow Remarriage in Epic period

Remarriage was another course of life for a widow. According to Mahabharat, "a child widow can remarry and her sons by the remarriage can offer oblations to the man" (Mahabharat XIII, 55,7, quoted in Shah 1995). Hence, Mahabharat sanctions widow remarriage in positive terms and gives social as well as religious status to the children by remarriage of a widow. Child widows, therefore, remarried without fear of social astracism. In Ramayana, there is description of widow's remarriage. For instance, Tara remarried with Sugriva, brother of her deceased husband Vali. A further indication of the possibility of a widow remarriage is contained in the harsh words of Sita to Lakshman, where she refers to her position if Rama were to die (Guruge 1991: 203). During this age, niyoga was preferred to widow remarriage. Though widow remarriage was mentioned in some form in great Epics, it was not normal in practice.

## Custom of Sati in Epic period

When the Epics were composed, the custom of widow burning was known, but not prevalent. In the later parts of the Epics we find a few references to Sati. This custom came into existence by about 400 AD (Altekar 1956: 121). During this period we do have scores of instances of widows surviving their husbands and offering them funeral oblations. They also accompanied funeral processions. In cases of calamity when all the male members of a family were wiped out, the burning of the pyre (Mahabharath XI 25.19) and the watering rite (Ramayana II 76.23.) after the corpse was burnt, were performed by widows (Jayal op.cit.). On the whole, the status of widows during epic period was not as honorable as in the past.

## Widowhood in Sutra Period

It was clear from version II. 5.121 of Shankhayana Grih suta that widowhood was both undesirable as well as inauspicious in the sutra period. Hence, prayers were constantly chanted both before and after marriage for the longevity of the husband. No such prayers are said by the husband for the longevity of the wife. Polygamy was prevalent. Hence, he did not dread being a widower. From the time of sutras, the position of widows became more pitiable than before because the sutras sanctioned a widow to avoid, for the duration of a year, the use of honey, meat, spirituous liquor and salt, and to sleep on the ground. In case she had no son, she could bear a son by her brother-in-law, after the period of six months of death of her husband, with the permission of her Guru (Shankhayana Grih suta. II. 5.121, quoted in Tiwari op.cit.: 104).

Although, widow remarriage was permitted, her social status was inferior. Hence, widowhood was much dreaded by women.

## Custom of Sati in Sutra period

The custom of widow burning was not prevalent in the sutra period. Although widowhood was dreaded, the widow was not expected to immolate herself on her husband's funeral pyre. Apastambiya Grihya sutra states that the widow was brought back from the funeral pyre either by the deceased husband's brother or an old trusted servant (Apastrambiya Grihya sutra. IV. 2.18, quoted in Tiwari op.cit.: 106).

## Widowhood in Buddhist Period

During this period, a widow did not suffer any social and moral degradation due to widowhood. No stigma was attached to her by the society. There were no restrictions on her dress or food habits and she did not have to shave her head. She used to participate in socio-religious functions as in the later periods (Shankhayana Grihya Sutra I,II, 5,2,I 121). Widow enjoyed high social status and maintained the social status of pre-widowed days (Horner 1975: 58).

## Widow Remarriage in Buddhist literature

Buddhist literature reflects that, a widow had equal right to remarry as a widower. As Horner (1975) opines, "there were no religious or social obstacles to be overcome in being remarried; but as if it were a step that could quite easily be taken without raising any scandal (p.61). In practice, a widow faced difficulties in remarrying as much as any other widow anywhere else in the world owing to her greater age, look, poverty and number of children.

According to Buddhist literature, a widow's position has never been elevated. Her condition, in our society, has been the same through the track of centuries. Vasantara Jataka describes the condition of widowhood thus: "Terrible is widowhood, she eats the leaving of all, a man may do her any hurt, speak unkindly, a widow may have ten brothers yet is a nacked thing, oh terrible is widowhood" (ibid.: :74).

## Custom of Sati in Buddhist period

The custom of widow burning was not practised during this period. In Gautama's Preachings, there is no reference to this custom of sati. Hence, the custom did not exist (ibid.: 73).

## Widow's Inheritance and Succession Rights in Buddhist period

During this period husbands left their property to their widows rather than to sons and daughter in preference. There were no rules laid down against widow inheriting her husband's property. Horner (1975) states that "If the husband left any property to the widow; often she managed it all by herself" (p. 80).

## C. Smriti Period and Widowhood

During the Smriti era, Buddhism declined and Brahmanism was re-established. The Hindu law-makers of this period imposed certain duties on widows, who did not ascend the funeral pyre but opt to survive the husband. All the sages prescribed a life of severe discipline and penance on such widows for their whole life.

## Institution of Niyoga in Smriti period

The Niyoga custom was condemned by Smriti writers when chastity (celibacy) had become the main eligibility for marriage. Manu disapproved this custom of niyoga as fit for cattle. It can therefore be said that the custom of Niyoga was not in practice during the period.

## Widow Remarriage in Smriti Period

During the Smriti period, widow remarriage was prohibited. Manu mentioned that "in the sacred texts nowhere the appointment of widows is mentioned nor is the remarriage of widows prescribed in the rules concerning marriage" (Manu IX 65, quoted in Tiwari op.cit.: 105). In most of the smritis there is no passage which permits the widow's marriage. However, Manu permitted the marriage of only virgin widows. But Narada and Parashara permit widow remarriage.

## Practice of Sati in Smriti Period

The practice of sati is not sanctioned by the older smritis of Manu and Yajnavalkya. It is however alluded to and recommended by many of the later authorities such as Arti, Harita, Usanas and Parashara. The practice prevailed as early as Alexander's invasions about 325 BC. Travellers like Strabo, Megasthenes and Diodorus who accompanied Alexander, allude to this practice. The custom of sati had been well established by the end of 6th century AD. The lawgivers from smriti period forced the widows to lead a life of austerities, fasting and abstinence from pleasure.

The Manusmriti codifies the Do's and Don'ts for a widow and it spells out a deviation to result in drastic punishment in a rebirth. The following are some of the passages found in the Laws of Manu on the observance of abstinence by a widow:

[156] A virtuous wife should never do anything displeasing to the husband who took her hand in marriage, when he is alive or dead, if she longs for her husband's world (after death).

[157] When her husband is dead she may fast as much as she likes (living) on auspicious flowers, roots, and fruits, but she should not even mention the name of another man.

[158] She should be long-suffering until her death, self-restrained, and chaste, striving (to fulfil) the unsurpassed duty of women who have one husband.

[164] A woman who is unfaithful to her husband is an object of reproach in this world; (then) she is reborn in the womb of a jackal and is tormented by the diseases born of her evil (Doniger and Smith 1991: 115-16).

[166] The women who restrains her mind-and-heart, speech and body through this behaviour wins the foremost renown here on earth and her husband's world in the hereafter.

There are numerous texts prescribing the number of meals a day that a widow may take, the nature of bed she is to sleep upon and other particulars relating to her conduct. In short, she is ordered to lead a pious life for the spiritual benefit of herself as well as of her dead husband.

But Vishnu, the later smriti writer, prescribed an alternative to widows either to survive their husband or to burn themselves (Vishnu XXV 17, quoted in Tiwari op.cit.: 201).

The Manu's codes of Hindu law which are commended for a widow to lead a chaste life are not only moral precepts. Unchastity of the widow affects not only her social status but also her proprietary position. But the injunctions to emaciate her body and to live on frugal and abstemious diet, were in the nature of religious or moral injection.

## D. Age of Later Smritis Commentators and Digest Writers (C. 500 AD to c. 1800 AD) and widowhood

The customs of child marriage, sati, polygamy etc. reduced the status of women to the level of mere goods and chattel. They were regarded as nari-sudras. The status of widows were still more inferior.

## Widow Remarriage

During this period widow remarriage in general was prohibited. Altekar stated that the prohibition of widow remarriage began to be imposed from about 1000 AD even on the child widows. It was totally prohibited in Hindu society from about 1130 AD. In Hindu society, upper caste widows were prohibited from remarrying whereas lower caste widows were allowed to do so. During the last century due to Sanskritization, the lower caste began to impose upon themselves the prohibition of widow remarriage (Altekar op.cit.156).

Alberuni, the famous Muslim traveller who came to India in 11th century AD, stated that "If a wife of a Hindu loses her husband by death she cannot marry another man. She has only to choose between two things, either to remain a widow as long as she lives or to burn herself". And the latter eventually is considered preferable because as widow she is ill-treated as long as she lives (Dutt 1972: 481). Among the high castes of Rajaputs, the remarriage of women were never permitted, though, in some lower castes, such as kadoa Kunbi, a widow was eligible for nata or second marriage.

## Widow's Dress

From ancient times, widows wear white clothes. Manu smiriti asks the widow who is appointed for Niyoga to wear white (Manu IX 70, quoted in Das op.cit.: 57). The idea might probably have been borrowed from the Buddhist or Jain nuns who wore white clothes when they renounce the world, since the widow too, was supposed to have renounced the world. Later, black became the colour of mourning, since this colour depicts darkness and unhappiness. She was forbidden to wear any jewels.

## Custom of Tonsuring the Widow

The practice of widow's tonsuring was prevalent among many high castes until recently. The origin of tonsure is not definitely known. None of the Vedas or Grihya Sutras or Epics refers to the practice. Widow retained their hair but did not part it. Widows were ordained to lead a strict ascetic life and an ascetic is expected to remove the hair on the head. Hence, the custom of disfiguring the Indian widow appears to have originated from this source.

Tonsure is believed to have come into vogue in about the 8th century AD. Once widow remarriage was prohibited, society desired to make the widow as un-attractive as possible so that no man would ever want to marry her. With this idea in mind the widow was tonsured and made to wear white clothes only, sleep on the bare floor, and partake of a frugal meal only once a day. This deprived her of all her good health and good looks so that even if she wanted to marry no man came forward to do so. Veda Vyasa, in 10th century AD, stated that "If a widow does not become a sutee, she should shave her head" (Tiwari, op.cit.: 179). This is the first Smriti to mention the custom. Some Puranas and the Skanda Purana Kashikhanda advocating tonsure seem to be clearly a later interpolation. From 12 Century AD, tonsure was prevalent all over India. It prevailed more in the south than in the North of India. Foreign travellers who visited India in the 16th Century AD mentioned having seen tonsured widows.

Horner asserted that this system is believed to have been followed by the Brahmins due to the influence of Buddhism where the Buddhist nuns underwent tonsure in imitation of the Monks (Horner, op.cit.: 75). However, kane seems to suggest that a widow was tonsured, just as the son of a deceased man underwent tonsure as a matter of purification and as a symbol of bereavement (Kane, op.cit.:587). Though the cruel practice to tonsuring is dying out it is still practiced by some orthodox sects of Brahmins in southern India, but in Northern India it is generally not practiced (Kane, op.cit.:593).

## Practice of Sati

The barbaric custom of sati was widely practiced during this period. Widows had to follow strict rules and restrictions. So they frequently preferred sati to the tiresome life prescribed for them. Most widows voluntarily ascended the funeral pyres of their husbands. Sometimes, the cruel relatives of widows, burnt them forcibly because they were either afraid that they might misbehave and bring disgrace to the family or wanted to misappropriate her share in the family property. The institution of Sati came into existence from about the 700 AD. Sutee was not originally a religious practice but the supposed consequence of a widow's grief at the death of her husband. A widow was expected to prepare herself for a frightful death by burning herself on her husband's corpse. Sir Henry Maine opined that the superstitious belief, coupled with the Brahmanical dislike of the enjoyment of property by women, had led to the practice of sati, and was intended to fight the ancient rule of civil law, which made her tenant for life in respect of her husband's property (Maine 1914: 335). The rewards dangled before a sati were, as Sankha and Angiras says, that she who follows her husband in death, dwells in heaven for 3.5 crores of years (Kane op.cit.: 635).

The practice of Sati became more frequent among royal families in northern India and quite common in Kashmir during the period of 1500 to 1800 AD. The custom of sati had however, obtained the status of a well-recognized, but optional, practice in Hinduism. The practice of sati was also prevalent among the Rajputs and Marathas of central India (Altekar, op.cit.:126,130).

Several Muslim rulers discouraged sati and adopted measures to prevent it as far as possible. Traverneir, the French traveller who came to India during Aurangzeb's time, observed that "there is no woman that can burn herself along with her husband's body till she has the leave of the governor of the place where she inhabits, who being a Mohamedan and abhorring that execrable crime of self-murder is very shy to permit her" (Tavernier 1905: 407).

During the Muslim period, the status of women as well as widows was worst. Women faced a number of hardships and cruelty due to backward practices like child marriage, purdah system, sati, enforced widowhood, prostitution and devadasi system. This era led not only to the decline of women's physical, mental and social life but her rights in the educational, social, religious and economic fields were also lowered gradually.

## E. British Period and Widowhood

In the latter half of the 18th century, when the British came to India, women's status had dropped to the lowest level. It was the worst period in the history of India because of social evils, i.e. child marriage and custom of Sati etc. A.L. De'Souza writes that "Women were denied equal rights in marital, familial, social, educational, economic and political fields. They were assigned a subordinate status. The marriage ideals, power and authority exercised by the joint-family and caste system combined with illiteracy, age-old traditions, seclusion within the four walls of the house, made it difficult for them to seek full personality development. They had scant personal identity and few rights" (Ghosh, 1989:19).

Cousin (1947) pointed out that, at the end of the 19th century, the status of woman was at its lowest point of literacy, of individuality, of health, of social status, of freedom of movement, or initiative of economic status of power (p.13). This deterioration in the status of women brought about a number of consequences. The uneducated were considered equivalent to Shudras, married before their characters were fully developed, transferred from the loving and sympathetic atmosphere of the parental home to the in-law's home. Where an atmosphere of awe prevailed apprehensive of suppression, frequently forced to drag on a miserable existence in an interminable widowhood, their character suffered from forced repression in some direction and unnatural stimulation in others. They had no status in society none in their own estimation. They were more like puppets which move when someone else pulls the strings than individual human being with minds of their own (Dube 1963:196).

According to Sudha (1977), the following reasons were responsible for the decline of the women's status in India:

(1) Patriarchal joint family system, (2) Polygamy, (3) Sati system, (4) Forced widowhood, (5) Denial of the right to divorce, (6) Child marriage and (7) Purdah system. Because of child marriages with old men, there was an increase in the number of widows. Both child marriage and the purdah custom led to low literacy rate among women. Their presence to social and religious ceremonies was prohibited. They were depressed to such an extent that they could not comprehend their own freedom and independent personality. Although, we find that during British period some exceptional women like, Chand Bibi, Rani Laxmibai and Kittur Rani Channamma etc. who made the remarkable impact in the field of administration (p.90).

During the British rule, Indian society faced significant modifications by passing new social legislations. Several factors were responsible for the upliftment of women in British India. The first one was the direct influence of the British noted for their courtesy towards women; the general awakening of Asians in the 20th century and the political struggle for India's independence also gained considerable force to the feminist movement in India (Gill 1986:35).

The status of girls, women and widows was improved during the British period. British introduced modern education system in India. But the custom of child marriage came in the way of the spread of female education. Hence, in 1929 the British government passed the Child Marriage Restraint Act (Sarda Act). This Act restricted the evils of early marriages and increase in the number of girl widows. The Act not only prohibited the solemnization of child-marriages but also raised the minimum age for marriage of girls to 14 and of boys 18 years. Besides removing the evils of child marriage. It promoted female education. This led to the improvement in the position of daughter.

Datta (1972) viewed that the familial social status of the wife also improved during the British period because of rise in female education and the rise in the age of marriage. The Hindu Women's Right of Separate Residence and Maintenance Act of 1946 enabled Hindu wives to claim maintenance even without having judicial separation under certain circumstances. Women acquired a new social status because of social legislation called the Civil Indian Marriage Act, 1872. The cruel practice of 'Sati' was on increase throughout the 17th and 18th centuries, because at this time religion had become corrupt and people were governed by the priests. Hindus at this time were unenlightened and had become strict followers of customs and conventions. People firmly believed that man's sins were completely washed out if his widow was burnt alive with his dead body (p.112-24).

Datta further opined that the pitiful and pitiable plight of the widows who were forced to commit "'Sati' attracted the attention of a good number of enlightened Indians and the British under the leadership of Raja Ram Mohan Roy and Lord William Bentinck. In spite of the strong opposition, a historic resolution was passed in December, 14, 1829, by which practice of Sati was made a crime of culpable homicide punishable with fine or imprisonment or both. However, the widow was ill treated by her in-laws and kinsmen as the virtual destroyer of her husband. She was never allowed to appear cheerful or wear bright clothes or ornaments. She had to drudge along day and night and was the victim of all kinds of insolence by other women of the household including servants. In the case of child widow, the tragedy became more pitiable. Therefore, in order to improve her lot, the British passed the Hindu Widows Remarriage Act, 1856. This Act was enacted to remove all the legal barriers to remarriage of Hindu widows (Ibid.: 126).

Later, the British realized that they could stop 'Sati' by police force but they could not arrange the remarriage of widows. These widows had to suffer because they had no property of their own. To improve the economic condition of women, The Hindu Women's Right to Property Act, 1937 was passed. According to Section 3 of the Act, on the death of a Hindu male, not only his son would succeed but also his widow and the widow of the pre-deceased son. By this Act, a widow got the right to claim partition and a right of enjoyment of that property during her life-time. Though she was made a limited owner of her husband's property, she was freed from depending on other members of her husband's family for food and other necessary needs.

Besides these governmental initiatives, Mrs. Annie Besant, in 1917, tried to promote women's education through the Women's Indian Association. In 1920 the Federation of University of Women was established and in 1925 National Council of Women started. Great personalities like Raja Ram Mohan Roy, Ishwarchand Vidyasagar, Dayanand Saraswati, Keshav Chandra Sen, Gopal Krishna Gokhale, Ramkrishna Paramhansa, Swami Vivekanand, Pandita Ramabai and others tried to bring about unprecedented awakening among women who were down-trodden and had been oppressed for centuries.

The familial, social and legal status of the Hindu women as well as widows greatly improved during the British age, as compared to the Muslim period. Although a small section of women took advantage of these measures and privileges given, their initiation was indeed significant. Gill has rightly observed about the achievements with regard to the status of women during the British period that if a person who died a hundred years ago comes to life today, the first and most important change which would strike him is the revolution in the position of women (Gill, op.cit.:38).

## F. Contemporary Period (After Independence i.e. 1947 onwards) and widowhood

After independence, republic of India adopted democratic system of rule. The Constitution of India accepted the principle of social justice and equality for all citizens of the country. Article 14 of the constitution states that "the state shall not deny to any person equality before the law or equal protection of the laws within the territory of India ". It has also proclaimed the gender equality in all domains of life. In Article 15 of the constitution it is mentioned that, 'the state shall not discriminate against any citizen only on the ground of race, religion, caste, sex, place of birth or any of them. Article 16 provides that 'there shall be equality of opportunity for all citizens in matters relating to employment or appointment to any office under the state". Under Articles 325 and 326 women are not only given voting rights but also the right to contest elections. They can take part in the political life of the country and hold any office from the highest to the lowest. Even the Directive Principles of State Policy contain directives towards the emancipation of women. Article 39 provides 'equal pay for equal work irrespective of sex'. Education is also made free and compulsory for all the children of 5-14 age group. Accessibility of education and increasing opportunities for employment has brought about tremendous changes in the role of women. 73rd and 74th amendments of constitution, 1992 provides a honorable position of women in Panchyati Raj institutions and urban local governance.

Apart from the constitution, many other social legislations have improved the position of women by offering the same rights, opportunities and openings which a man already had. For example, the Hindu Succession Act, 1956 has recognized the right to property of the Hindu daughter. This Act has placed the daughter at par with the son. Now she can succeed to the undivided interest of her father in the joint property and to the separate property of the father along with other heirs specified in clause 1 of the schedule. Dowry system, an abominable social evil, which makes young woman's life miserable, has been curbed by the enactment of the Dowry Prohibition Act of 1961. After the Hindu Adoption and Maintenance Act 1956, a wife enjoys a respectable position. She can even live separately under section 18 and can claim maintenance under certain circumstances. The husband cannot adopt a child without the consent of his wife under section 7 and the wife under Section 8 can adopt a child when her husband has completely and finally renounced the world or has ceased to be a Hindu or has been declared by a court of competent jurisdiction to be of unsound mind. Under the Hindu Marriage Act 1955 both husband and wife can claim divorce.

The legality of widow remarriage is found in many provisions of the Acts in India. Section 14 of the Hindu Succession Act 1956, has made woman the absolute owner of the property. She cannot be deprived of the property, which she has inherited from her first husband even after her remarriage. Under Section 6 of the Act, she inherits the coparcenary interest of her husband along with the son and daughter. Section 6 of the Hindu Minority and Guardianship Act, 1956 recognizes her as the natural and legal guardian of her minor children after their father.

Child Marriage Restraint Act, 1929 has been replaced by the Prevention of Child Marriage Act, 2006. This new act is more effective than act of 1929.

The Maintenance and Welfare of Parents and Senior Citizens Act was passed in 2007 to provide maintenance support to elderly parents and senior citizens of India. Parents and senior citizens are entitled to claim maintenance from their children or legal heirs of the property. Section 19 of the Act also mandates the establishment of an old age home in every district by the state government and provides protection of life and property of the elderly.

To ensure that a widow is facilitated to get her entitlements after the death of her husband, Ministry of Women and Child Development of India has been working with the office of Registrar General of India as well as the state governments to ensure that the name of the widow is compulsorily mentioned in the death certificate of her husband. This is a good initiative taken by central government of India in 2017 for betterment of widows.

Ministry of Women and Child Development is running 592 Swadhar Greh in India for destitute women. These Swadhar Greh provides supportive institutional framework for women victims of difficult circumstances so that they could lead their life with dignity and conviction. But a study done by Expert Committee of National Commission for Women, New Delhi in November 2016 revealed that the status of widow/women living in these Swadhar Homes is not satisfactory. They are living in these shelter homes in very pitiable condition.

On 11 July 2017, a Group of Ministers (GoM), headed by External Affairs Minister Shushma Swaraj, approved a draft of National Policy for Women, 2017. But ironically, it is a fact that the widows are invisible in this policy document. However, according to census 2011, there are 4,32,61,478 widows population in India. India has the largest widows population in the world with 17.97% of the total widows' population of the world. According to census 2011 records of India, every fourth household has a widow in India. Census 2011 data on marital status of women and widows in India shows a huge increase in the number of widows in India since 2001. As per census 2011, 3.6% (43261478) of the total population of India and 7.4% of the total female population of India are widows.

The above stated legislations have promoted emancipation of women as well as widows to a very large extent. Besides these legislations, under the provisions of the Directive Principles of State policy each state has undertaken women's welfare and empowerment programmes. The central and state Governments have shown keen interest in betterment of the legal, social, educational and cultural status of women. There is hardly any field today wherein women have not entered. In a nutshell, it can be said that education and women's participation in all fields of economy, science and culture is helping them in achieving the real equality. But, in reality, widows are invisible in this whole picture.

Though bigamy is a criminal offence, the rate of desertion by husbands and illegal second marriage is on the increase. Hon'ble High Court of Madras observed in case entitled as "R. Malathy vs The Director-General of Police" (Writ Petition No. 21497/2009) decided on 26 September, 2011 that,"7. As she[1] belonged to the Brahmin community, she had to perform certain customary rituals after the death of her husband. Thus, she had to confine herself to lead a solitary life in her home without any connection with the outside world. The statement made by the petitioner in her revision petition really makes a sad commentary on the status of widowhood and the curse made against them even in the 21st century. For several centuries, the widows among the Hindus were isolated from the mainstream and they were despised and any deviant behavior from the traditional codes was frowned upon. The Manu smriti codifies the Do's and Don'ts for a widow and it spells out a deviation to result in drastic punishment in a rebirth. The predicament of the petitioner will have to be seen in the above context of long history of imposed isolation of the widow from the society and the customary duties to observe certain mandatory rituals".

The condition of widows is still not satisfactory. She has to earn to run the house and raise her children. If she does not earn, her condition is even worse. If the widow has no issues, she has to work hard as a maid servant in her husband's family or relations who might have taken her in and is totally dependent, for all her needs, on others. She has neither economic security nor a say in decisions concerning her. Families still believe that once a daughter is given away in marriage, she cannot be given away again to another person. Hence, widow remarriage is tough, sanctioned by Hindu Widows Remarriage Act of 1856, seldom takes place and is discouraged (Ghosh, op.cit.:19).

Recently, Hon'ble Supreme Court of India, vide judgment dated 11.08.2017, passed in a public interest litigation (PIL) bearing Writ Petition (Civil) No. 659/2007, case titled as 'Environment and Consumer Protection Foundation versus Union of India & Ors.' has observed that "It is a pity that these widows have been so unfortunately dealt with, as if they have ceased to be entitled to live a life of dignity and as if they are not entitled to the protection of Article 21 of the Constitution. They quite fall in the category of a socially disadvantaged class of our society" (Para 1, 15).

Further, Hon'ble Supreme Court has held in the aforesaid case that "It is to give voice to these hapless widows that it became necessary for this Court to intervene as a part of its constitutional duty and for reasons of social justice to issue appropriate directions" (para 18). Accordingly, Hon'ble Supreme Court of India has constituted a six members Committee to give a common working plan for empowerment of widows within a period of two months i.e. on or before 30th November, 2017. The said public interest litigation was filed by the Environment and Consumer Protection Foundation, a non-governmental organization, before the Hon'ble Supreme Court of India, in 2007, regarding the worst status of widows in India.

On the basis of above discussion, it may be concluded that the condition of Indian widows is still pathetic. The widow is still a marginalized and vulnerable section of the Indian society. There is a need of a national policy for the welfare and empowerment of widows.

# References

Abbe, Dubois & Henary K. Beauchamp (Tr.) 2007. *Hindus Manners, Customs and Ceremonies.* New York: Cosimo Inc.

Altekar, A. S. 1956. *The Position of Women in Hindu Civilization.* Varanasi: Motilal Banarasidas.

Bhattacharya, K. (1887). 'Institutes of Parasara', *Asiatic Society of Bengal*, IV(27): 30-40.

Cousin, Margret E. (1941). *Indian Womenhood Today.* Allahabad: Kitabistan.

Das, R. M. (1962). *Women in Manu and His Seven Commentators.* Varanasi: Kanchana Publications.

Datta, K. K. (1972). *Socio-Cultural Background of Modern India.* Meerut: Meenakshi Prakashan.

Doniger, W. & Smith, B. K. (1991). *The Laws of Manu.* London: Penguin books

Dube, S. C. (1963). 'Man's and Woman's Role in India: A Sociological Review' In B. Ward (ed.). *Women in the New Asia: The Changing Social Roles of Men and Women in South and South East Asia.* Paris: UNESCO.

Dutt, N. K. (1968). *Origin and Growth of Caste in India.* Vol.1. Calcutta: Firma K.L. Mukhopadhyay.

Dutt, R. C. (1972). *A History of Civilization in Ancient India,* Vol. II. Delhi: Vishal Publishers.

Ghosh, S. K. (1989). *Indian Women through the Ages.* New Delhi: Ashish Publishing House.

Gill, K. (1986). *Hindu Women's Right to Property in India.* Delhi: Deep and Deep Publication.

Guruge, W. P. A. (1991). *The Society of the Ramayana.* New Delhi: Abhinav Publication.

Horner, I. B. (1975). *Women under Primitive Buddhism.* Varanasi: Motilal Banarasidas.

Jayal, S. (1966). *The Status of Women in the Epics.* Delhi: Motilal Banarasidas.

Kane, P. V. (1930). *History of Dharmashastras,* Vol. II. Part. I. Poona: Bhandarkar Oriental Research Institute.

Kapadia, K. M. (1958). *Marriage and Family in India.* London: Oxford University Press.

Maine, H. S. (1914). *Early History Institutions.* London: John Murray.

National Commission for Women, 2009-10. *Study on Vrindavan.* Delhi: NCW

Sarkar, S. C. (1928). *Some Aspects of the Early Social History of India.* London: Humphery Milford.

Sengupta, N. (1965). *Evolution of Hindu Marriage.* London: Popular Parkashan.

Shah, S. (1995). *The Making of Womanhood: Gender Relations in the Mahabharata.* Delhi: Manohar Publishers.

Silverman, P. R. (1970). 'Widowhood and Preventive Intervention' In H.S. Zarit. (ed.), *Readings in Aging and Death: Contemporary Perspective,* New York: Harper and Row Pub.

Sudha, G. (1977). 'Changing Status of Women in Society' In Sarojini Shintri (ed.), *Women: Her Problems and Her Achievement.* Dharwad: Karnataka University.

Tiwari, D. P. (1994). *Prachin Bharat Mein Widhwas,* Lucknow: Tarun Publishers.

Tavernier, J. B. (1905). *Travels in India Book III.* Calcutta: Bangabasi Office.

Upadhyaya, B. S. (1974). *Women in Rigveda.* New Delhi: S. Chand and Co.

Vidyasagar, I. C. (1976). *Marriage of Hindu Widow.* Calcutta: K.P. Bagchi and Co.

# 13

# Impact of Environmental Factors on Students' Interest and Achievement in Physics in Bauchi, Bauchi State

Joy O. Omaga, Mangut Mankilik & Bala S. Musa

## Abstract

*The paper examined the Impact of environmental factors on students' interest and achievement in physics in Bauchi, Bauchi State. Two research questions and one null hypothesis was formulated to guide the study at P = 0.05 level of significance. The research design adopted for the study is quasi-experimental pre-test post-test control group. The instruments developed for the study are physics achievement test (PAT) and students' interest questionnaire (SIQ). The population of the study comprised of 700 physics students in Bauchi metropolis. Purposive random sampling technique was used to select two secondary schools with a total sample size of 248. The instruments used for study is physics achievement test (PAT) and students' interest questionnaire (SIQ). The instruments were validated by experts in science education and experts in measurement and evaluation. The instrument was pilot tested and a reliability coefficient of 0.85 was obtained for PAT and 0.73 for SIQ. This shows that the instrument has high reliability. After the pre-test, experimental group was taught physics using instructional materials and the treatment lasted for four weeks. The data collected for the study were analysed using mean, standard deviation and t-test. Research findings showed that (a) parents play significant role in influencing students' interest towards the learning of physics (b) Students should be encouraged to relate concepts learnt in the classroom with the environment to enable them achieve in physics.*

**Keywords:** environment, interest, achievement, physics.

# Introduction

Students' perception about a subject influence their understanding and learning of that subject (Ornek, Robinson & Haugan, 2008). Many students assume that physics is difficult and as a result of that assumption they tend to shy away from the subject and this has made it difficult for them to understand the underlying principles and concepts of physics. Research carried out by Angell, Guttersrud, Henriksen and Isnes (2004) Erinosho (2013) showed that students find physics difficult because they tend to contend with different representations such as formulas, graphs, calculations, experiments, laws, theories and explanations at the time. Adedayo as cited in Jegede and Adedayo (2013) state that the cause of negative perception of students towards Physics Include: the fear of the mathematical skills involved, harsh teacher-students' relationship, students' un-readiness to study, preconceived bad information that Physics is a difficult subject and poor method of teaching.

Physics is a natural science rather than a system of speculative constructions (Adegboye, 2009). This implies that physics is what we do every now and then either consciously or unconsciously. Uko and Utibe (2009) state that physics serves as the pivot around which the economy of the nation revolves. Physics generates fundamental knowledge needed for future technological advances that will continue to drive the economic engines of the world. Physics is an important element in the education of chemists, engineers and computer scientists as well as practitioners of other physical and biomedical sciences. It extends and enhances our understanding of other disciplines such as earth science, agricultural, chemical, biological and environmental sciences plus astrophysics and cosmology (Martinás & Tremmel, 2014). Physics also involves the physical aspect of the environment and how the forces of the universe interact with each other. There is an element of physics in the conduct of our everyday lives, from the cars we drive or bikes we ride to an airplane flying or a rocket zooming past the earth in a whiff.

Physics is a subject taught in senior secondary schools and a course that is offered in many tertiary institutions worldwide as stated in the objectives of the physics curriculum as stipulated by the Federal Ministry of Education (2008a), that the teaching and learning of physics is to provide basic literacy in physics for functional living in the society; acquire basic concepts and principles of physics as a preparation for further studies; acquire essential scientific skills and attitudes as a preparation for technological applications of physics and to stimulate and enhance creativity. It is also a discipline that requires learners to be able to translate from one concept to the other, words, tables of numbers, graphs, equations, maps, diagrams, etc. However, in spite of the importance and usefulness of physics to scientific and technological development of nations, research findings have shown that students' achievement in the subject has been poor and the enrolment figure is not encouraging (Agommuoh & Ifeanacho, 2013, Chief Examiners Report, 2009-2013;

Udoh, 2012; Akinbobola & Afolabi, 2009). Esiobu and Agwagah (as cited in Agommuoh & Ifeanacho, 2013) state that students have been exhibiting dwindling interest in the subject and achievement over the years have been consistently poor.

Interest has been identified as a motivational construct that influences students' engagement and achievement in learning (Chen, 2001; Chen & Ennis, 2004). Interest plays a key role in influencing students learning behaviour and intention to participate in future learning (Xiang, Chen & Bruene, 2005). Hidi and Anderson (as cited in Subramaniam, 2009) state that interest plays an energizing role on cognitive function and the level of a person's interest has repeatedly be found to have a powerful influence on learning. Groves (2005) states that students' intrinsic interest towards a subject motivates them to develop a full understanding of the subject and it helps them to find solution needed for any problem they encounter while learning the subject thus, leading to high achievement. This is because according to Okoye, Okongwu and Nweke (2015), students' interest relates to their achievement and interest is a major factor in academic motivation. Thus, students' interest directly influences achievement.

Interest is required for students' learning and understanding of physics concepts because when students are interested in a subject they tend to channel their energy to the learning of that subject (Subramaniam, 2009). However, the mentality and thinking of most students affect the way they approach physics and since they think that physics is of little or no use to them outside the classroom, they see physics as a subject to be passed and enable them gain admission into institutions of higher learning (Othman, Wong, Shah & Nabilah, 2009). The thinking and perception of most students about physics have greatly affected their understanding of the subject, hence they tend to show little interest in learning physics. Martinás and Tremmel (2014) state that there are quite a few students who dislike physics and have difficulty in understanding physics, however, a student's ability to solve physics problems does not necessarily mean the understanding of the underlying concepts.

Students' understanding and perception of physics can be greatly influenced by a number of environmental factors. Students' learning environment can have a great influence on their academics either positively or negatively, this is further buttressed by Tsavga (2011) who states that students' learning environment plays a vital role in determining how students perform or respond to circumstances and situations around them. The learning environment determines how a student behaves and interacts, thus learning can occur through one's interaction with the environment (Odeh, Ogwuche & Ivagher, 2015). Another external factor that affect students' interest and achievement include their learning environment, which is the school environment, this also encompasses the teachers, school administrators, leaners, fellow students and peers etc. Farrant, and Farombi as cited in Odeh et al (2015) refer to learning environment as facilities that are available to facilitate students learning outcomes, such facilities include books, audio-visual materials, soft wares and hardware of educational technology Educational environments enhance students' learning and improves academic achievement (Massachusetts Department of Education, 2006) and Tella as cited by Shamaki (2015) says that a students' environment plays a key role in shaping the quality of academic achievement of students.

A well-designed learning environment aimed at providing effective instruction enriches learning experiences as well. Students should be aware of what they really need and what they should know. Just as learning environment refers to the factors that can affect a person's learning, social environment, which includes family members and friends in a wider context, affect the learner and shapes his/her learning (Gömleksiz, 2012). Students should be provided a rich and supportive learning environment that will enrich their learning. Students' learning environment can also be stimulated to aid in their learning of a subject and the stimulation can be done through the use of devices that stimulate learning. Such devices include computers, television, games otherwise known as instructional aids etc. According to Malone and Lepper as cited in Lavonen, Bymann, Juuti, Meisalo and Uitto (2005), computer and video game research has clarified that there are some essential features for intrinsically motivating activities. Computer and video games, for example, incorporate an optimal challenge, have an appropriate goal and uncertain outcomes, provide clear, constructive, and encouraging feedback, and offer elements of curiosity, and fantasy that sustain students' interest. Other environmental influences that can help stimulate students interest when learning certain concepts perceived as difficult by students includes field trips, mechanic workshops, visits to factories, excursion, carpentry workshop and so on. These factors stated above could have great impact on learners and helps to stimulate students learning by promoting active participation in the learning process, hence arousing interest in the subject. As research conducted by Chen and Ennis (2004) stated that interest is a motivational construct that influences students' engagement and achievement in learning. This was further buttressed by Chen (2001) who states that interest shown by students in a subject is instrumental to them having high achievement in that subject.

In the light of this, the researchers intend to find out if environment can influence students' interest and achievement in physics.

## Statement of the Problem

Most instructions in physics focus on helping students amass information about scientific ideas but do not foster the development of understanding of these ideas nor does it help them learn how to apply the concepts taught them in schools to real world situations. Usually the emphasis in most physics instructions is on helping students acquire what has come to be accepted as fundamental basis of scientific knowledge. However, available research studies was conducted on the impact of environmental factors on students' choice of physics and the impact of environmental factors on students' enrolment in physics. This study investigates the impact of environmental factors on physics students' interest and achievement in physics.

## Purpose of the study

The purpose of the study is to investigate the impact of environmental factors on physics students' interest and achievement in physics. Specifically, the study seeks to achieve the purposes;

1. To find out how parents' influence account for students' interest in physics.
2. To determine if relating students' learning of physics with the environment, will influence their achievement in physics.

## Research Questions

The following research questions were asked to guide the study;

1. How will parents' influence account for students' interest in physics?
2. What is the mean achievement scores of students taught physics by relating what they learnt to the environment?

## Hypothesis

The following hypothesis was formulated at $P \geq 0.05$ level of significance

$H_{01}$: there is no significant difference in the mean achievement scores of students who were taught physics by relating what was being taught to the environment and those taught without relating what was taught to the environment.

## Research Methodology

The study made use of quasi-experimental research design. The population of the study comprised all senior secondary two and three (SS 2 and 3) physics students in all the secondary schools within Bauchi Metropolis, which is 700 students. Purposive random sampling technique was used to select two schools that are distantly located from each for the study. The study made use of intact class so as not to distort the normal school activities. The total sample size of the selected schools is 80. The selected schools were randomly assigned as experimental and control groups.

The instruments for data collection was a physics achievement test (PAT) which was adapted from past WAEC and NECO questions, this was for the purpose of standardization. Questionnaire was also structured by the researchers to collect information on students' interest in physics. The research instruments was validated by one physics teacher, one physics educator and an expert in measurement and evaluation from the University of Jos. The instruments were pilot tested at ECWA secondary school, Miango, Bassa Local Government area of Plateau State to determine the reliability of the test items and the questionnaire items. Using Pearson product correlation co-efficient, the reliability of the instruments was found to be 0.85 for the test items and 0.73 for students' interest questionnaire.

The treatment given to the experimental group involved taking the students outside the classrooms and school environment to show them how what is in the environment relates to the learning of physics. Parents of the students in the experimental group were also actively involved in students learning. At the end of each session, the experimental group usually have group discussion among themselves where they engage in active discussion about the topic taught. The aim of the discussion is to aid better understanding amongst the students. They actively discussed the topic and if they encountered any problem in the course of their learning, they researched for ways to proffer solutions to the problem encountered. The treatment was given for a period of four weeks after which a post-test was then administered to the students, which is the physics achievement test (PAT). Before the commencement of the treatment to the experimental group, both the experimental and the control groups were administered a pre-test. This was done in order to determine the comparability of the two groups in their ability and cognitive levels before the administration of the treatment. The data obtained from PAT was analysed using t-test for independent sample at $P \geq 0.05$ level of significance while descriptive mean and standard deviation was used to analyse the data collected for the questionnaire items.

## Results and Discussion

**Research question one:** How will parents' influence account for students' interest in physics?

**Table 1: Results of students' response to research question one.**

| S/No | Factors | Mean scores | Standard deviation | Remark |
|---|---|---|---|---|
| 1 | Parents when actively involved in students' academic task enhance progress. | 3.21 | 0.758 | Accepted |
| 2 | Parents support students' academic needs | 3.40 | 0.778 | Accepted |

| | | | | |
|---|---|---|---|---|
| 3 | Parents' involvement in students' academic tasks help students' academic work. | 3.26 | 0.688 | Accepted |
| 4 | Parents have good science background, thereby they encourage students in science subjects. | 2.81 | 0.994 | Accepted |

From the responses of students on research question one, the analysis showed that parents' involvement in students' academic work helped them to develop interest in physics.

**Research question two:** What is the mean achievement scores of students taught physics by relating what they learnt to the environment?

**Table 2: Results of students' response to research question two.**

| S/No | Factors | Mean scores | Standard deviation | Remark |
|---|---|---|---|---|
| 1 | Physics students are taken for field trips | 3.04 | 0.834 | Accepted |
| 2 | Physics students can relate what they learnt to other situations | 3.55 | 0.710 | Accepted |
| 3 | Physics students can relate the classroom with the outside environment | 3.24 | 0.690 | Accepted |

Result in Table 2 shows that when students' learning is related to situations or things around the environment, they show more interest in their learning thus increasing their achievement in the subject.

$H_{01}$: there is no significant difference in the mean achievement scores of students who were taught physics by relating what was being taught to the environment and those taught without relating what was taught to the environment.

**Table 3: t-test between experimental and control group on students' achievement in physics.**

| Group | N | Mean (x) | Df | $t_{cal.}$ | $t_{crit.}$ | Remark |
|---|---|---|---|---|---|---|
| Experimental | 40 | 60.8 | | | | |
| | | | 78 | 3.08 | 1.98 | Significant |
| Control | 40 | 53.1 | | | | |

The result in Table 3 shows the t-test value to be 3.08 with a degree of freedom of 78. This shows that t-cal. is greater than t-critical at $P \geq 0.05$, hence the null hypothesis which states that there is no significant difference in the mean achievement scores of students who were taught physics by relating what was being taught to the environment and those taught without relating what was taught to the environment is rejected. This implies that a significant difference exist between students taught physics by relating their learning to the environment and those that do not relate the learning of physics with the environment.

## Findings of the Study

1. Parents play significant role in students' interest and their understanding of physics concepts.
2. Students' achieve in physics when they relate what they are taught in the classroom with environment.

## Discussion of Findings

The result showed that when parents are involved in students learning of physics, students tend to develop more interest in their learning and this leads to higher achievement in physics as buttressed by Chen (2001) and Chen and Ennis (2004) who identified interest as a motivational construct that influences students' engagement and achievement in learning. Hence, interest plays a key role in influencing students learning behaviour and intention to participate in the future. Hidi and Anderson (as cited in Subramaniam, 2009) stated that interest plays an energizing role on cognitive function and the level of a person's interest has repeatedly being a powerful influence on learning. Thus, the interest of students in a learning task can result to them achieving high in that subject.

The result also shows that when students relate what they are taught in the classroom through interaction with the environment they achieve in physics, this is in agreement with the findings of Tella as cited by Shamaki (2015) who states that students' environment plays a key role in shaping the quality of academic achievement of the students and Tsavga (2011) who states that students' learning environment plays a vital role in determining how students perform or respond to circumstances and situations around them. Thus a students' learning environment is a determinant factor of students' interest and achievement.

## Conclusion

Based on the findings of the study, it was concluded that parents are very influential in influencing students' interest towards the learning of physics. That is when parents show interest in their children learning, they tend to achieve high. The environment is also a major factor that influences a students' learning, that is to say a conducive environment facilitates and sustains students' interest and enables them to achieve in physics.

## Recommendations

Based on the findings of this study, the following recommendations were given:

1. Parents should endeavour to work together with physics teachers to help students improve in their performance in physics and also to sustain their interest in physics.
2. Students should be encouraged to relate concepts learnt in the classroom with the environment and students' learning environment should be conducive to facilitate learning and enable them achieve high in physics.

## References

Adegboye, M. O. (2009). Stirring entrepreneurial skills through knowledge acquired in physics in U. A. Udofia (ed.). Developing entrepreneurial skills through science, technology and mathematics STM education. *50th annual conference proceeding of Science Teachers Association of Nigeria (STAN)*, pp299-302.

Afolabi, F., & Akinbobola, A. O. (2009). Constructivist problem based learning technique and the academic achievement of physics students with low ability level in Nigerian secondary schools. *Eurasian Journal of Physics and Chemistry Education,* 1(1), 45-51.

Agummuoh, P. C., & Ifeanacho, A. O. (2013). Secondary school students' assessment of innovative teaching strategies in enhancing achievement in physics and mathematics. *IOSR Journal of Research and Method in Education,* 3(5), 6-11. Retrieved from www. iosrjournals.org

Angell, C., Guttersrud, O., Henrisken, E. K., & Isnes, A. (2004). Physics: frightful but fun. Pupils' and teachers' views of physics and physics teaching. *Journal of Science Education,* 88, 683-706.

Chen, A. (2001). A Theoretical conceptualization for motivation research in physical education: an integrated perspective. *Quest,* 53, 35-58.

Chen, A., & Ennis, C. D. (2004). Goals, interest and learning in physical education. *The Journal of Educational Research,* 97, 329-338.

Chief Examiners' Report (2013). *Chief Examiners' Report on Physics.* Retrieved from www.examinations.ie/index.php%3FI

Cradler, R., McNabb, M., Freeman, M., & Burchett, R. (2002). How does technology influence student learning. *Learning and Leading with Technology* 29 (8), 46-56.

Erinosho, S. Y. (2013). How do students perceive the difficulty of physics in secondary school? An exploratory study in Nigeria. *International Journal for Cross-Disciplinary Subjects in Education (IJCDSE)*, 3 (3) 1510-1515.

Gömleksiz, M. N. (2012). Elementary School Students' Perceptions of the New Science and Technology Curriculum by Gender. *Educational Technology and Society*, *15* (1), 116–126.

Groves, M. (2005). Problem-based learning and learning approach: Is there a relationship? *Advanced Health Science Education,* 10 (4), 315-326.

Jegede, S. A., & Adedayo, J. O. (2013). Education in Nigeria towards enhancing a sustainable technological development. *Greener Journal of Educational Research,* 3 (2), 80-84.

Kara, I. (2008). The effect of retention on computer assisted instruction in science education. *Journal of Instructional Psychology,* 3 (1), 20-25.

Lavonen, J., Byman, R., Juuti, K., Meisalo, V., & Uitto, A. (2005). Pupils' interest in Physics: A Survey in Finland. *NORDINA*, 2 (5), 72-84.

Martinás, K., & Tremmel, B. (2014). Physics curriculum for the 21st century. *Interdisciplinary Description of Complex Systems* 12 (2), 176 - 186.

Massachusetts Department of Education (2006). *Massachusetts Science and Technology and Engineering Curriculum Framework.* Retrieved from http://www.doe.mass.edu/frameworks/scitech/1006.pdf

Odeh, R. C., Ogwuche, O. A., & Ivagher, E. D. (2015). Influence of school environment on academic achievement of students in secondary schools in zone A senatorial district of Benue State, Nigeria. *International Journal of Recent Scientific Research,* 6 (7), 4914-4922.

Okoye, C. M., Okongwu, C. J., & Nweke, S. O. (2015). Students' interest as correlate of achievement in chemistry. *56th Annual Conference Proceedings of Science Teachers' Association of Nigeria,* pp. 222-229.

Ornek, F., Robinson, W. R., & Haugan, M. P. (2008). What makes physics difficult? *International Journal of Environmental and Science Education,* 3 (1), 30-34.

Othman, T., Luan, W. S., Shah C. A., & Abdullah, N. (2009). Uncovering Malaysian students' motivation to learning science. *European Journal of Social Sciences,* 3 (2), 266-276.

Shamaki, T. A. (2015). Influence of learning environment on students' academic achievement in mathematics: a case study of some selected secondary schools in Yobe State, Nigeria. *Journal of Education and Practice, 6* (34), 40-44.

Subramaniam, P. R. (2009). Motivational effects of interest on student engagement and learning of physical education: A review. *International Journal of Physical Education* 46 (2), 11-19.

Tsavga, J. (2011). *The effect of environment on the academic performance of students in Tarka Local Government Area of Benue State.* Unpublished PGDE thesis, Makurdi: Benue State University.

Udoh, O. A. (2012). Refocusing physics education in Nigeria: issues and challenges in teacher education. *Mediterranean Journal of Social Sciences, 3* (13), 11-19.

Uko, P. J., & Utibe, U. J. (2009). Creating entrepreneurial skills through physics education. In U. A. Udofia (ed.). Developing entrepreneurial skills through science, technology and mathematics STM education. *50ᵗʰ Annual Conference Proceeding of Science Teachers Association of Nigeria (STAN),* pp 303-310.

Xiang, P., Chen, A., & Brene, A. (2005). Interactive impact of intrinsic motivators and extrinsic rewards on behaviour and motivation outcomes. *Journal of Teaching in Physical Education,* 24; 179-197.

# 14

# Domestic Violence and Female Teachers Job Performance in Secondary Schools in Ife Central of Osun State, Nigeria

Augustine A. Agbaje Ph.D

## Abstract

*The research examined the content within which domestic violence and female teachers' job performance operate. It is observed that gender-based violence has been the experience of millions of women worldwide which has affected their relationship in the homes, communities, places of work and largely their productivity in their various places of their primary assignments. Specific issues on domestic violence and female teachers' job performance such as physical abuses and economic control were identified. Psychological abuses and sexual abuse were reviewed. The major instruments used for this stud) were questionnaire tagged Domestic Violence Questionnaire(DVQ)) and Female Teachers' Job Performance(FTJP).The data collected were analyzed by using Pearson's Product Moment Correlation. Four null hypotheses used were tested at 0.05 level of significance and were also observed to be significant at the end of the exercise. The findings of the four null hypotheses were clearly spelt out and discussed in detailed showing the effects at both sides.*

**Keywords:** domestic, violence, female, teacher, performance

## Introduction

Gender-based violence has been the experience or millions of women world divide which has affected their relationship in the homes, communities, places of work and largely their productivities in their various places of primary assignments. It is a universal reality that had existed in all societies and human settlements regardless of class income, culture, or educational attainments. Hardly you will find a woman whom at one time or another in her lifetime had not experienced violence inform of wife battery, sexual assault and abuse, rape, incest, female genital mutilation and other traditional practices harmful to women and girls or discriminated against on the basis of race, language, ethnic group, culture, age, relation and membership of minority group.

The World Health Organization (WHO) also supported these claims when it estimated that at least one in every five of the world's female has been physically or sexually abused at some time (Population Reference Bureau, 2001). Amnesty International report on Nigeria submitted that on a daily basis, women are beaten and ill-treated for supposed transgressions, even murdered by members of their family and in some cases leave them with horrific disfigurements as a result of acid attacks (Amnesty International, 2015). Thus most of the cases of violence against Women are perpetrated by their partners, husbands, even fathers. For example, a woman could be beaten by her own husband or boyfriend for reasons ranging from drunkenness, financial problems, refusal to have sex, nagging, challenging the husband behavior, not preparing meals on time, being under suspicious of having a sexual relationship out of marriage, to being accused of witchcraft. Women are also subjected to multiple forms of violence in homes of which common forms which is known as wife battery includes, slapping, kicking, verbal abuse, rape and death.

Besides, three levels of gender-based violence can be identified, these are home level, the community level and the state level. This work is based on the home level which is the domestic abuse form of gender-based violence. Domestic violence includes but not limited to physical violence, sexual violence, emotional and psychological intimidation, verbal abuse, economic control, harassment or injury which take toll on the level of their productivity.

Domestic violence in the workplace is a broad concept that encompasses behavior that occurs both on and off the worksite. It also includes all behavior that interferes with an individual capability to safely and securely perform their duties at work. It includes all kinds of conduct, ranging from harassing or repeated telephone calls or taxes at work to unarmed and armed "show up" to homicide. Domestic violence in the workplace also includes conduct which occurs outside of the workplace such as sleep deprivation and physical injuries which impact on an individual's ability to perform their job. A batterer's interference in the workplace or work success of his target is one of many means by which the batterer exercises and displaces his attempt to exert power and control.

When someone is experiencing domestic violence it over shadows every aspect of his or her life including the work environment. Domestic violence does not stay at home when women go to work, therefore domestic violence often becomes workplace violence. It is imperative to see domestic abuse as a serious, recognizable and preventable problem like thousands of other workplace health and safety issue that affects a business and its bottom line. According to the Bureau of National Affairs Report (2000), the estimated cost of domestic violence to United States companies stood at 3-5 billion Dollars annually. This is due to the lost work time, increased health care cost, higher labour turnover and lower productivity.50% of the domestic violence victims who are working women miss three days of work per month as a result of the violence. Seventy-five (75%) percent of these victims used company time to deal with the violence because they could not do so at home. Sixty four percent were periodically late for work and 90% of the employed women experienced problems at work due to the abuse.

It is now a matter of concern for employers to be aware of the increasing rate of domestic violence and be prepared to make the workplace safe for all employees. It is an important business issue that cannot be ignored. The workplace is where many women facing domestic violence spend at least eight hours a day; therefore, the work place becomes an ideal place for them to get help and support. The work places have the power to save money and lives by seeing domestic violence as a workplace issue. In a business survey carried out in America fifty-seven percent senior corporate executives believe domestic violence is a major problem in the society, One third of them thought domestic violence has negative impact on their bottom lines and 40% said they were personally aware of employees and other individuals affected by domestic violence.

In Nigeria, most researches on worker's productivity had been on the impact of other aspects of economic and national issue. Scarcely do we have studies linking workers performance and productivity to the influence of domestic violence. It is against this background that this study becomes relevant in filling such missing gap by looking at the impact of domestic violence on workers' productivity performance in selected industries.

Many cultures have beliefs, norms and social institutions that legitimate and perpetrate violence against women. The same acts that would be punished if' directed at an employer, a neighbor or an acquaintance often go unchallenged when men direct them at women, especially within the family. Some studies have shown that in some countries domestic violence is to correct an erring wife (Hassan 2005). It has also been confirmed that transgression of gender norms like not obeying husband, talking back. not having food ready on time, questioning husband about money or girlfriends, going somewhere without the husband permission, refusing him sex or expressing suspicions of infidelity necessitate violence against women (Michaus, 2008).

## Concept of Job Performance

Home environment and work environment have a strong synergy in job performance of teachers especially women. To influence employees' job performance and their willingness and ability to put in their best, employers need to focus on two aspects of the work environment. First, they can provide work enablement, that is, the support that employees need to do their work efficiently and effectively. Second, employers can also create a healthy work environment, that is, one that supports employees' physical, social and emotional well-being, referred to as energy. Thus when an organization builds a workplace that actively relates high levels of employee engagement with enablement and energy, it opens the door wider to a significant performance life and enhanced job performance (Watson, 201 l).

Muchinksky (2003) remarked that job performance is the set of workers behaviors that can be monitored, measured and assessed in term of achievement at individual level. Moreover, those behaviors must also be in tandem with the organizational goals. In other words, worker's job performance is an important factor to be considered for any organization claiming to be excellent. Thus it could be inferred from this assertion that organizations success or failure depends to a large extent, on job performance of the individuals working for the organization

In industrial and organizational psychology, it is frequently expressed that job performance is a function of ability and motivation (Campell and Pritchard, 2006). In essence, it commonly refers to whether a person performs his/her job well or not. It may also involve the production of a certain number of goods or being seen as a satisfactory performer by one's boss. Wright (2006) describes job performance as behaviours that are relevant to the organizations goals and objectives and these can be measured in terms of each individual's proficiency or level of contribution, that is, it is an extremely important criterion that relates to organizational outcomes and success. This definition describes what people do, that is, behaviours and not the results of those actions.

Job performance could also be regarded as goal relevant actions that are under the control of the individual and directed towards some objectives of the organization. Campell (2000) defined job performance as only the behaviour or actions that are relevant to organizations goals. He sees it as an individual level variable which a single person does as against organizational performance. He clarifies that job performance is not the consequences or results of an action but rather, action itself. Therefore, job performance is the behaviour that contributes to the organizations goals. Motowidlo, Bovman and Schimdt, (2007) provide a similar definition, arguing that job performance is behaviour that can be evaluated in terms of the extent to which it contributes to organizational effectiveness.

Workers performance is determined by many factors, some of which are work environment. The workers' natural potentials, co-worker and personal issues, training, skills, experience and readiness to improve on the job. Ajila (2007) for example, argued that a work environment that encourages collaboration, teamwork, trust, sharing resources is more likely to foster top and high performers than one in which workers are overtly competitive and suspicious of one another. Equally important for fostering high job performance are clear and well defined job description, right skills, adequate experience and training, support and rewards whether extrinsic or intrinsic. Further personal factors such as marital and family issues, financial challenges and illness can influence job performance of any worker. For instance, coming to work after a whole night vigil with a sick child will certainly leave a worker drained and unfocused.

Performance could be high or low, keeping high-performing employees has become a top priority for today's organizations, secondary school staff inclusive (Kaye and Jordan-Evens, 2000). According to the duo, a two year study by them reveals that managers, supervisors, and team leaders play important role in employee performance, satisfaction and dissatisfaction. This is so because today's workers want challenging and meaningful work opportunities to learn and grow in the job a sense of belongingness and a good and authoritative leader as against a bad and authoritarian boss. Kaye and Jorden-Evens list the costs of losing good and high performing workers as enormous. Among the cost include time and financial cost required to recruit, interview, and hire, assess, train and integrate new employees to replace the high performing ones who have left.

To them, performance of workers in any organization is vital for the growth and development of the organization but also for the growth of an individual employee. As organizations endeavor to enhance performance of their workers so as to achieve increased output, strategies for maximizing workers contributions must be taken into cognizance. However, the success of any performance strategy depends to a large extent, on the level of performance support the employer provides (Watson, 2011). For example, organizations such as the secondary schools must also ensure that working conditions are optimal and their workers must be able to successfully surmount obstacles that may impede their optimal performance, in other words their workers must feel enabled. This translates to the fact that school management must provide at least, well-functioning tools, the necessary supplies, effective and efficient work processes and clear direction. All these will contribute positively in a direct way to workers ability to get the job done and in a proper way.

In a study conducted by Jimoh (2008) to find out whether situational judgment, emotional labour and demographic factors were predictors of job performance among university administrative workers in South-Western Nigeria, he found out that situational judgment conscientiousness, emotional labour, marital status, gender and length of service, all played major roles in determining the job performance of university administrative workers. Besides, Jimoh (2008) gives recipe for enhancing job performance of workers which includes helping employees to acquire competencies such as perception appraisal and expression of emotion, emotional facilitation of thinking, understanding and analyzing emotion as well as emotional knowledge.

Job performance is a human behavior, the result of which is an important factor for realization of the objectives of any organization. Thus, the success and failure of` any organization depends to a large extent on the job performance of the individuals working in the organization This is similar to Muchinsky (2003) who stated that job performance is a set of workers behaviours that can be monitored, measured and assessed. More over these behaviours are also in agreement with the organizational goals in that job performance of workers is an important factor for any set up to be labeled an excellent organization. Shahu and Sole (2008) in their empirical study found out that the relationship between job stress, job satisfaction, and job performance among 100 managers of private manufacturing firms found out that higher stress levels are related to lower job performance whereas higher job satisfaction indicated higher performance. When these and many more are done, they are likely to enjoy higher job performance from their workforce which may eventually contribute in no small measure in helping to realize the vision and mission of their various organizations.

## Physical Assault and Female Teachers Job Performance

Physical assaults may occur in domestic violence, the abuser is also very likely to use non-assertive types of abuse, such as verbal abuse or economic control. Not only that, women are also subjected to multiple forms of violence in homes of which common forms which is known as wife battery includes kicking, slapping, verbal abuse, rape and death. Physical abuse may lead to a number of physical ailments including irritable bowel syndrome, gastrointestinal disorders and various chronic pain syndromes. According to Gilbert (2006), domestic abuse can affect the ability of the victims to maintain employment or effectively perform their jobs. Research has estimated that 24% to 30% of the abused female workers lose their work partly because they are being abused. Domestic violence causes employees to miss work, where 62% of victims report being late for work or leaving early as a result of the abuse. Violence affects the workplace in a number of ways. Absenteeism, impaired job performance and loss of experienced employees are only some of the costs that organizations bear as a direct result of violence.

The following behaviours and actions have been identified as those used by perpetrators to interfere with their victims work. Attempts to prevent the victims from getting to work or looking for work, such as interfering with transportation by hiding or stealing the victim's car keys or transportation money, hiding or stealing the victim's identification cards, threatening; deportation if the victim was sponsored, failing to show up to care for children and physical restraining the victim, interfering with victim at work by repeatedly phoning or e-mailing him or her, stalking and or watching the victim, showing up at the workplace and pestering co-workers with questions about the victim (where is he/she. who is he/she with. when will he/she be back and so on), lying to co-workers (he/she is sick today. he/she is out of town, he/'she is home with a sick child and so on) threatening the co-workers (it you don`t tell. l would report you to the permanent secretary in different patterns), verbally abusing the victim or co-workers, displaying jealous and controlling behaviours, destroying the victims or organizations properly and physically harming the victim and/or co-workers (Swanberg, Macka and Logan, 2006). The victim may try to cover bruises, be sad, lonely, withdrawn and afraid, have trouble concentrating on a task, apologizing for the perpetrator behavior, be nervous about speaking in the perpetrator's presence, making last-minute excuses/cancellation, using drug or alcohol to cope, and missing work frequently or more often than usual.

## Economic Control and Female Teachers Job Performance

Economic control can occur when the abuser prevents the victim from getting to work by taking her car keys away, controls all the household income or denies her money for her day-to-day needs (Jejeebhoy, 2008). For above expressions, it is glaring that abuse behaviour is a tactic used with the intention of maintaining power and control over another individual that results in causing that individual harm. The power and control can be in form of using coercion and threats, intimidation, emotional abuse, isolation economic abuse, male privilege, using children, denying and blaming,. Economic abuse is a form of abuse when one's intimate partner has control over the other partner`s access to economic resources, which diminishes the victims' capacity to support herself and forces her to depend on the perpetrator financially (Adams, Sulhvian, Bybee and Greeson, 2008).

It is related or also known as financial abuse which is the illegal or unauthorized use of a person's property, money, pension book or other valuables, (including changing the persons will to name the abuser as heir), often fraudulently obtaining power of attorney, followed by deprivation of money or other property or by eviction from own home. Financial abuse applies to both elder abuse and domestic violence (Carrot, 2003).

Economic abuse in domestic situation may involve:

- Preventing a spouse from resource acquisition, such as restricting their ability to find employment, maintain or advance their career and acquire assets.
- Preventing the victim from obtaining education.
- Spending victim's money without his or her consent and creating debt, or completely spending victim's savings to limit available resources.
- Exploiting economic resources of the victim.

Brewster (2003) stated that in its extreme form, this involves putting the victim on a strict "allowance" withholding money at will and forcing the victim to beg for the money until the abuser gives the victim some money. It is common for the victim to receive less and less money as the abuse continues. This also includes, (but is not limited to) preventing the victim from finishing education or obtaining employment or intentionally squandering or misusing communal resources, economic abuse is often used as a controlling mechanism as put of a larger pattern of domestic abuse, which may include verbal, emotional, physical and sexual abuse.

The following are the ways that abusers may use economic abuse with other forms of domestic violence:

- Using physical force or threat of violence to get money
- Providing money for sexual activity
- Controlling access to telephone, vehicle or ability to go shopping, other forms of isolation.
- Threatening to evict the spouse and children from the house without financial support.
- Exploiting the victims economic disadvantage
- Destroying or taking resources from the spouse or children.
- Blaming the victim for an inability to manage money or instigating other forms of economic abuse such as destruction of property.

There are several ways that abusers may impacts victims' economic resources. The abuser can prevent the victim from working or make it very difficult to maintain a job. They may likewise impede their ability to obtain educational frequent phone calls, surprise visits and other harassing activities interfere with the spouse work performance. In couples where the spouse is lesbian, gay, bisexual, transgender or questioning of their sexuality, the abuser may threaten to "out them" with their employer (Economic Abuse Wheel, 2011). By denying the victim access to money, such as forbidding the victim from maintaining bank accounts so that he or she is totally financially dependent upon the abuser for shelter, food, clothing and other necessities. In some cases, the abuser may withhold those necessities, also including medicine and personal hygiene products. They also greatly limit their ability to leave the abusive situation by refusing to pay court-ordered spousal or child support (Economic Abuse Wheel. 2011).

## Economic abuse include

- Deprivation of all or any economic or financial resources to which the aggrieved person is entitled under any law or custom whether payable under an order of a court or otherwise or which the aggrieved person requires out of necessities including, but not limited to, household necessities for the aggrieved person and her children if any, stridhan, property jointly or separately owned by the aggrieved person, payment of rental related to the shared household and maintenance.

- Disposal of household effects, any alienation of assets whether movable or immovable, valuables, shares, securities bonds and the like or other property in which the aggrieved person has an interest or is entitled to use by virtue of the domestic relation or which may be reasonably required by the aggrieved person or her children or her stridhan or any other property jointly or separately held by the aggrieved person.

- Prohibition or restriction to continued access to resources or facilities which the aggrieved person is entitled to rise or enjoy by virtue of the domestic relationship including access to the shared household. Explanation II - for the purpose of determining whether any act, omission, commission or conduct of the respondent constitutes "domestic violence" under this section the facts and circumstances of the cases shall be taken into consideration.

## Psychological Abusive and Female Teachers Job Performance

Psychological abuse is defined as the sustained and repetitive inappropriate behaviour that damages or substantially reduces the creative and developmental potential of mental faculties and mental processes. Domestic violence as an act saps women's energy, undermines their confidence compromises their health and deprives the society women's full participation. Carrillo (2002) observed that women cannot lend their labour or creative idea fully if they are burdened with the physical and psychological sears of abuse. It is a major cause of injury to women, ranging from relatively minor cuts and bruises to permanent disability and death Studies have shown that 40%-75% of women who are physically abused by a partner are injured by this abused by a partner are injured by this abuse at some point in life (Nelson and Zimmerman, 2006).

Further domestic violence is among the most common causes of post-traumatic stress disorder (PTSD) (Briggs and Joyce (2007). Post-traumatic stress disorder causes difficulties in sleeping and concentration. The sufferer is easily alarmed or startled. This is a sign of mental health erosion. Many women consider the psychological consequences of abuse to be even more serious than it physical effects. The experience of abuse often erodes women's self-esteem and puts them at greater risk of a variety of mental health problem, including depression, post-traumatic stress disorder suicide and alcohol and drug abuse. For some women the burden of abuse is so great that they take their own lives or try to do so. Studies from Nicaragua, Sweden and the United States have shown that domestic violence is closely associated with depression and subsequent suicide (Kaslor and Joyce, 2008).

## Sexual Abuse and Female Teachers Job Performance

Sexual abuse or sexual coercion exists along a continuum, from forcible rape to non-physical forms of pressure that compel women to engage in sex against their will. The touchstone of coercion that a woman lacks choice and faces severe physical or social consequences if she resists sexual advances. It should be noted that most non-consensual sex takes places among people who know one another spouses, family members, courtship partners, or acquaintances (Heixe, Agbaje and Adeyemo, 2005). Non-consensual sex takes place within consensus unions and become just another medium tor male control. Researchers have shown that some married women gave in to sex out of tear of the consequences of refusal, such as physical abuse, loss of economic support or accusation of infidelity (David and Chin, 2008).

Sexual harassment is abusive, unlimited and unwelcome behaviour of a sexual nature typically in the work/studying places which may include intimidation bullying or coercion of a sexual nature or the inappropriate promise of rewards in exchange for sexual favours. It can be verbal or physical and it is often perpetrated by a person in a position of authority against it subordinate (Jejeebhoy, 2008). In the United States sexual harassment is a term of discrimination which violates title II of the Civil Rights Act of 2004. The council of Europe Convention on preventing and combating violence against women and domestic violence defines sexual harassment as "any form of unwanted verbal, non-verbal or physical conduct ofa sexual nature with the purpose or effect of violating the dignity of a person in particular when creating an intimidating hostile, degrading, humiliating or offensive environment (Council of Europe Convention on preventing and combating violence against women and domestic violence, 2006).

Sexual abuse and violence are serious problems that transcend racial, economic, social and regional lines. Violence is frequently directed towards females and youth who lack the economic and social status to resist or avoid it. Adolescents and young women in particular may experience abuses in the form of domestic violence, rape and sexual assault sexual exploitation and/or female genital Mutilation. Accurately estimating the prevalence of sexual abuse and violence in the developing world is difficult due to the limited amount of research done on the subject. Cultural mores against reporting abuse makes it difficult to assess accurately and few adolescent health programmes in sub-Saharan African countries addresses these critical issues.

Domestic violence is not going unnoticed, for example more than one in three Americans has witnessed an incident of domestic violence (EDK Associates, (2003).four out of five American survey says that, domestic violence is an extremely or very important issue to them personally, Lieberman, 2006. it is against this background that domestic violence became a work place issue because it affects the workplace in terms of bottom-line economics. productivity and employees safety and wellbeing. Nearly five million women are working women (Commonwealth Fund Commission, 2003). Domestic violence can result in reduced productivity, increased medical expenses, absenteeism and increased risk of violence at the workplace. Domestic violence affects not only the person directly experiencing the abuse but it canal so have a profound effect on the personal and professional lives and productivity of co-workers.

Therefore, this research delves into the various types of gender-based violence, level of gender-based violence, the forms and prevalence of domestic violence and effect of domestic violence on job performance of female teachers in secondary schools.

## Statement of the Problem

Female Teachers are expected to perform optimally in their job, that is, the main reason they were employed and paid. Many factors have engendered the performance of female teachers such as poor motivation, late and non-payment of salary for months in Nigeria, delayed promotion for years, poor school environment, administrative style, lack of facilities and instructional materials, incompetency of teachers in terms of quality, qualification and experience. It may be possible that domestic violence such as physical abuse, domestic control, psychological abuse and sexual abuse may predict female teachers' job performance.

Due to the stigma associated with domestic violence, many victims are not willing to disclose the facts. The reason may be but not limited to lack of trust in employer, fear or losing their job, cultural taboo and invasion of privacy, seen as a personal or private matter, fear of humiliation by the perpetrator, too ashamed to speak about it, co-worker, supervisor or union representative might be a friend of the perpetrator tear of being held responsible for the domestic violence fear of perpetrator being harmed, fear that perpetrator will seek, revenge belief that the employer neither cares nor has time for domestic violence problems. A plan to prevent domestic violence from entering the workplace has a better chance of success if the employer is well informed of all the risk factors, Open disclosure therefore decreases the risk for everyone at the workplace since the most effective prevention strategies can be implemented when the employer is aware of the actual threats.

The victim may be willing to disclose her plight if she perceives to have the sympathy of the supervisor, co-workers or union representatives who are willing to listen. She therefore feels safe in the work environment. Other reasons are that she needs someone to confide in and talk to, wants to explain decreased work performance increased absences or tardiness to avoid losing her job, and needs time off from work for court appearances,wants to confirm supervisor co-worker or union representative suspicious, wants to explain reasons for calling in sick or appearing upset at work, physical injuries and bruises wants to explain past or future phone calls or visits from the perpetrator, wants to warn the workplace that the perpetrator may show up there, is afraid for her safety wants support to call the police or other helpers, knows her rights and wants justice, supply a photograph und physical description of the perpetrator and his vehicle, develop a personal safety plan for work and non-work times. Therefore this research is designed to investigate the relationship between domestic violence and female teachers' job performance in Ife Central Local Government of Osun State, Nigeria.

## Objectives of the Study

The main purpose of this research was to investigate the relationship between domestic violence and female teachers' job performance in Ife Central of Osun State. Specifically this research was to determine the relationship between:-

1. Physical abuses and female teachers' job performance
2. Economic control and female teachers' job performance
3. Psychological abuses and female teachers job performance
4. 4. Sexual abuse and female teachers' job performance

## Research hypothesis

1. There is no significant relationship between physical abuses and female teachers' job performance.
2. There is no significant relationship between economic control and female teachers' job performance.
3. There is no significant relationship between psychological abuses and female teachers' job performance.
4. There is no significant relationship between sexual abuse and female teachers' performance.

## Significance of the Study

A cursory look at the literature in the area of domestic violence and female teachers' job performance, particularly in the aspect of physical abuse, economic control, psychological abuses and sexual abuses and their job performance reveals that not much has been done. Besides, there is a dearth of literature and empirical research on the relationship between physical abuses, economic control, psychological abuses and sexual abuse and job performance in Nigeria with special reference to secondary school teachers. Thus, this study will contribute to the study of literature in human resource management, school administration as well as four construct of domestic violence as seen above. The study will help female teachers to use legal means to protect themselves against violence by their intimate partners' as well as enlighten their spouse on the need to live harmoniously. It is also believed that this study will contribute positively to the body of literature in counseling psychology.

The findings of this research would be of tremendous assistance to the school management in Nigeria as well as other corporate organizations to put in place strategies that may eventually lead to curbing the stress of domestic violence coupled with appropriate motivational strategies to enhance job performance of female teachers. It would serve as a blueprint for the management of various schools to formulate appropriate action plans aimed at boosting the morale of their workers consequently resulting in increased and improved job performances as this would eventually translate to better and enhances performance. The findings of this research would help government to put in place adequate measures to address violence against women so that they can be efficient in their work environment and thereby develop self-confidence.

## Research Method

### Research Design

The study is an ex-post facto type which does not involve manipulation of any variable. The event has already occurred and the researcher only investigated what was already there.

### Area of the Study

The study was conducted in public secondary schools in Osun Ife Central. Ife Central has fifty two (52) public secondary schools with four hundred and eighty six female teachers (State Secondary Education Board, SSEB, 2015).

### Participants

A total of two hundred and forty-seven (247) participants were involved in the study, made up of two hundred and seventeen (217) female teachers and thirty (30) principals. The participants were drawn from the population of tour hundred and eighty six (486) female teachers and fifty two (52) principals. Krejice and Morgan's (2010) model was used to determine the sample size of female teachers while 96%of the principals were used. Thereafter, a simple random sampling technique was used to select the respondents. All the respondents were literate and could understand the questionnaire clearly and properly.

## Instrumentation

The major instruments used for the study were the questionnaire tagged 'Domestic violence questionnaire (DVQ) and female teachers' job performance questionnaire (FTJPQ). The questionnaire DVQ and FTJPQ were structured with a-4 point rating scale. DVQ has 24 items while FTJPQ has 16 items. It is a forty (40) item scale with response format ranging from strongly agreed (4) and strongly disagreed (1) for DVQ and very good (4) and poor (1) for (FTJPQ). The instruments were validated by four experts in the department of educational foundations guidance and counseling, University of Uyo, Uyo. The reliability value of the instrument DVQ was 0.85 while FTJPQ was 0.87 using split-half test.

## Data Analysis

The data collected was analyzed by using Pearson's Product moment correlation to answer the research question. The four (4) null hypotheses were tested at 0.05 level of significance using Pearson's product moment correlation.

# Testing of null hypotheses

**Hypothesis 1**

There is no significant relationship between physical abuses and female teacher's job performance.

**Table 1: Pearson's Product Moment Correlation coefficient (PPMC) of the relationship between physical abuses and female teachers job performance, N= 247**

| Variables: | $\sum x$ | $\sum x^2$ | $\sum xy$ | r-cal | df | r-crit | Decision at P< 0.05 Alpha |
|---|---|---|---|---|---|---|---|
| | $\sum y$ | $\sum y^2$ | | | | | |
| Physical Abuses (x) | 4952 | 100310 | | | | | |
| | | | 270603 | .621* | 245 | .139 | S |
| Job Performance (y) | 13427 | 734901 | | | | | |

Data as presented in Table 1 shows that the calculated correlation index, r-cal for the relationship between physical abuses and female Teachers job performance is 0.621 while its corresponding critical value at df 245 is 0.139. The critical r-value is less than calculated r-value at 0.05 alpha in which the decision is based. This simply implies that the r-cal is statistically significant. This means that there is a significant positive relationship between physical abuses and female teachers' job performance. With this observation, the null hypothesis, which assumes that there is no significant relationship between physical abuses and female teachers' job performance, is rejected.

**Hypothesis 2**

There is no significant relationship between economic control and female teachers' job performance.

**Table 2: Pearson's Product Moment Correlation coefficient (PPMC) of the relationship between economic control and female teachers job performance.**

| Variables | $\Sigma x$ | $\Sigma x^2$ | $\Sigma xy$ | r-cal | df | r-crit | Decision at P< 0.05 Alpha |
|---|---|---|---|---|---|---|---|
| | $\Sigma y$ | $\Sigma y^2$ | | | | | |
| Economic control (x) | 5002 | 102218 | | | | | |
| | | | 272335 | .642* | 245 | .139 | S |
| Job Performance (y) | 13427 | 734901 | | | | | |

Data as presented in Table 2 shows that the calculated correlated index, r-cal for the relationship between economic control and female teachers' job performance is .642, while its corresponding critical value at df 245 is .139. The critical r-value is less than calculated r-value at 0.05 alpha in which decision is based. This implies that the r-cal is statistically significant, that is, there is significant positive relationship between economic control and female teacher's job performance. Thus, the null hypothesis which assumed that there is no significant relationship between economic control and female teachers' job performance is rejected.

**Hypothesis 3**

There is no significant relationship between psychological abuses and female teachers' job performance.

**Table 3: Pearson's Product Moment Correlation coefficient (PPMC) of the relationship between psychological abuses and female teachers' job performance.**

| Variables | $\Sigma x$ | $\Sigma x$ | $\Sigma xy$ | r-cal | df | r-crit | Decision at P< 0.05 Alpha |
|---|---|---|---|---|---|---|---|
| | $\Sigma y$ | $\Sigma y^2$ | | | | | |
| Psychological abuses(x) | 4983 | 101703 | | | | | |
| | | | 272335 | .601* | 245 | .139 | S |
| Job Performance (y) | 13427 | 7349013 | | | | | |

Data in this Table 3 shows that the calculated correlated index, r-cal for the relationship between psychological abuses and female teachers' job performance is .601, while its corresponding critical value at df 245 is .139. The critical r-value is less than calculated r-value at 0.05 alpha in which decision is based. This implies that the r-cal is statistically significant, that is, there is a significant positive relationship between psychological abuses and female teachers' job performance. Therefore, the null hypothesis which assumed that there is no significant relationship between psychological abuses and female teachers' job performance is rejected.

**Hypothesis 4**

There is no significant relationship between sexual abuse and female teachers' job performance.

**Table 4: Pearson's Product Moment Correlation coefficient (PPMC) of the relationship between sexual abuse and female teachers' job performance.**

| Variables | $\Sigma x$ | $\Sigma x^2$ | $\Sigma xy$ | r-cal | df | r-crit | Decision at P< 0.05 Alpha |
|---|---|---|---|---|---|---|---|
| | $\Sigma y$ | $\Sigma y^2$ | | | | | |
| Economic control (x) | 4990 | 101786 | | | | | |
| | | | 272501 | .562* | 245 | .139 | S |
| Job Performance (y) | 13427 | 734901 | | | | | |

Data in Table 4 show that the calculated correlated index, r-cal for the relationship between sexual abuse and female teachers' job performance is .562 while its corresponding critical value at df 245 is .139. The critical r-value is less that calculated r-value at 0.05 alpha in which decision is based. This implies that the r-cal is statistically significant; this indicates that there is a significant positive relationship between sexual abuse and female teachers' job performance. Thus the null hypothesis which assumed that there is no significant relationship between sexual abuse and female teachers' job performance is rejected.

## Discussion of the findings

### Physical Abuse and Female Teachers' Performance

The findings of the study would be discussed in accordance with the four hypothesis formulated to guide the study. Physical abuses and female teachers hob performance as seen in hypothesis 1 sows that the calculated correlated index r-cal for the relationship of the variables indicated that the data .621 while its corresponding critical value at df 245 is .039. The critical r-value is less than calculated r-value at 0.05 alpha in which the decision is based. This implies that the r-cal is statistically significant, with this observation, the null hypothesis which assumes that there is no significant relationship between physical abuse and female teachers' job performance is rejected. The finding of this study agrees with the report Gilbert (2006) who opined that domestic abuse can affect the ability of victims to maintain employment or effectively perform their jobs. Research has estimated that 24% to 30% of the abused female workers lose their jobs partly because they are abused. Domestic violence causes employees to miss work, 62% of victims report late to for work or learning early as a result of the abuse. Violence affects workplace in a number of ways. Absenteeism, impaired job performance and loss of experienced employees are only some of the costs that organizations bear as a direct result of violence.

## Economic Control and Female Teachers' Performance

The findings of the second hypothesis which emphasized economic control and female teachers job performance indicated that the calculated correlated index, r-cal for the relationship between the two variables (economic control and female teachers job performance is begged to .621 while its corresponding critical value at df 245 is .139. the critical r-value is less than calculated r-value at 0.05 alpha in which the decision is based. This shows that the r-cal is statistically significant, that is, there is significant positive relationship between economic control and female teachers' job performance. Thus the null hypothesis which assumed that there is no significant relationship between economic control and female teachers' job performance is rejected. The findings of this study agree with the report of Jejeebhoy that said economic control can occur when the abuser prevents the victim from getting to work by taking her car keys away, controls all the household income or denies her money for her day-to-day needs. From the above aggressions it is glaring that abusive behaviour is a tactic used with the intention of maintaining power and control over another person that results in causing that individual harm. The power and control can be in form of using coercion and threats, intimidation, emotional abuse, isolation, economic abuse, male privilege, using children (2008) posited that economic abuse is a form of abuse when one intimate partners has control over the other partner's access to economic resources which diminishes the victim's capacity to support herself and forces her to depend on the perpetrator financially.

## Psychological abuses and Female Teachers Job Performance

Data presented in hypothesis 3 showed that the calculated correlated index, r-cal for the relationship between time goal setting and student academic achievement is .601 while corresponding critical value at df 245 is .139. The critical r-value is less than calculated r-value at 0.05 alpha in which the decision is based. This indicates that the r-cal is statistically significant, that is, there is a significant positive relationship between psychological buses and female teachers' job performance. With this observation the null hypothesis which assumed that there is no significant relationship between psychological abuses and female teachers' job performance is thus rejected. This findings agrees with the report of Carrillo (2002) who observed that women cannot end their labour or creative idea fully if they are burdened with the psychological cases of abuse. This drastically reduces their concentration and productivity. It is a major cause of injury to women, ranging from relatively minor cuts and bruises to permanent disability and death. Studies have shown that 40% -70% of women who are physically abused by a partner are injured by this abuse at some point in life, Helson and Zimmerman, (2006).

**Sexual abuse and Female Teachers' Job Performance**

Data as presented in hypothesis 4 shows that the calculated correlated index, r-cal for the relationship between sexual abuse and female teachers' job performance is .562 while its corresponding critical value at df 245 is .139. The critical r-value is less than calculated r-value at 0.05 alpha in which the decision is based. This implies that r-cal is statically significant, that is, there is a significant positive relationship between sexual abuse and female teachers' job performance. Thus the null hypothesis which assumed that there is no significant relationship between sexual abuse and female teachers' job performance is rejected. The findings of this study agrees with the report of Lieberman (2006) who opined that domestic violence became a workplace issue because it affects the workplace in terms of button-line economics, productivity and employees safety and wellbeing. Nearly four million women are battered in America every year and most of these women are working class-ladies. Domestic violence can result in reduces productivity, increased medical expenses, absenteeism and increased risk of violence at the workplace. Domestic violence affects not only the person directly experiencing the abuse, but it can also have a profound effect on the personal and professional lives and productivity of co-workers.

## Conclusion

Based on the findings of this study, the following conclusions are drawn: Domestic violence has negative implication on female teachers' job performance. The most outstanding of this violence includes physical abuses, economic control, psychological abuse and sexual abuse that plays significant role in enhancing ineffectiveness among female teachers in secondary schools.

## Recommendation

Based on the findings of the study and discussions the following recommendations are made:

- government should make a legislation to protect the rights of female workers
- perpetrators of violence against female workers should face the full wrath of the law.

# References

Adams, J. A. (2003). Toward and understanding of equity. *Journal of Abraham and social psychology,* 67, 422-36.

Adam, A., Sullivan. Bybee, & Greeson, T. (2008). "Development of the Scale of Economic Abuse", violence against women 14(5):563-588 doi: (0) *1177/177801208315529 PMID 18408173,* Cite uses deprecated parameter/co-authors= (help).

Ajala, E. M. (2008). Impact of domestic violence on the workplace and workers productivity in selected industries in Nigeria, *Anthropologist* 10(4) 257-264.

Ajila, C. & Abiola. A. (2004). Influence of rewards on workers performance in an organization. *Journal of Social Science* 8(1) 7-12.

Ajila, O. C. (2007). Job motivation and attitude to work as correlates of productivity among workers in manufacturing companies in Lagos State. Nigeria OlafemiAwolowo University unpublished Ph.D Thesis.

Alshallah, S. (2004). Job satisfaction and motivation: how do we inspire employees? Radiol manage, 2004, 26Pubmed Abstract. Accessed 19/12/2011 from http/www.nehialm nichgov. Amnesty International Nigeria Unheard Voice (2005), available at http// webamnesty.org/library/index/engfr440042005.

Armstrong, M. (2003). A Landbook of Human Resource Management Practice, 9th Edition London KoganPage

Brewster, M. P, (2003). "Power and Control Dynamics in pre-stalking and stalking situations". Journal of family violence 18(4) 207-217.

Brief, A. P., & Weiss, H. M. (2002). Organizational Behaviour: Affect in the workplace, Annual Review of Psychology 53, 279-307.

Brief, A. P., & Robertson, L. (2006). Job Attitude Organization: An exploratory study. Journal of Applied Social Psychology 19:717-724.

Briggs, I., & Joyce. P. R. (2007). What determines post-traumatic stress disorder symptomatology for survivors of childhood sexual abuse? Child Abuse and Neglect 21(6) 575-582.

Cambridge Public Health Report retrieved fromwww.cambridgepublichealth.org. Accessed on May, 2014.

Campbell, J. P. (2000). Modeling the performance prediction problem in industrial and organizational psychology. In M. D. Danrrette and L. M. Hough (Eds), Handbook of industrial and organizational psychology. Vol. 1 2nd Ed. Palo Alto. C. A. Consulting Psychologists Press.

Campbell, J. P. & Pritchard, R. D. (2006). "Motivation Theory in Industrial and Organizational Psychology" in M. D. Dunnette Ed. 1976. Handbook of Industrial and Organizational Psychology, Chicago: Rand McNally College Publishing Co.

Campbell, L., Simpson, J. A., Stewart, M. & Manning, .J (2003). Putting Personality in Social context: Extraverson, emergent leadership and the availability reward.

Cawillo, R. (2002). Battered Dreams: Violence against women as an obstacle to development. United Nations Development Fund for Women. New York.

Carnot, E. J. (2003). Your Parents in Good Hand? Protecting your aging parent from financial abuse and neglect (capital books).

Council of Europe (2003). Economic and Psychological influences of family planning on the lives of women in Western Visayas. Central Philippines University and Family Health International. IIoiloCity Philippines.

Economic Abuse Wheel. Women domestic abuse helpline. Retrieved November 20. 201 l.

EDK Associates (2007). The many faces of domestic violence and its impact on the workplace. EDK Associates. New York.

Gilbert, L. (2006). Urban violence and Health - South Africa (2005). Social Science and Medicine 43 (5)873-886.

Hassan, Y. (2005). The haven becomes hell: A study of domestic violence in Pakistan: 72 in women living under Muslim laws. Cantt,L. Pakistain. August (2005).

Heize, A. & Agbaje, A. (2005). Nigeria literacy educators and their technological needs in a digital age. Education focus l(l) 27-30.

Jejeehboy. S. J. (2008). "Wife Battering in Rural India. A Husbands' Right".

Jimoh, A. M. (2008). Situational judgment. emotional labour. conscientiousness and demographic factors as predictors of job performance among university administrative workers in south western Nigeria. University of Ibadan unpublished Ph.D Thesis.

Judge, T. A., Locke, E. A., & Durham C. C. (2006). The dispositional causes of Job satisfaction: A core evaluation approach, Research in Oganizational Behaviour 19,151-188.

Kaye, B. S. (2003). How to retain high performance employees. The 2003 annual, Vol. 2. 291-298 http.//www goggle.com. Accessed 11/09/2012.

Locke, E. A. (2006). "The nature and causes of job satisfaction in Duunette", M. D. (Ed) Handbook of Industrial and organizational psychological. Chicago. RanMcNally

Michau, L. (2008). Community based research for social change in Mwanza, Tansania Centre for health and gender equity (CHANGE) proceeding of the third Annual Meeting of the International Research Network on violence against women. Washington Dc. Jan. 9-11-2008.

Moorman, R. H. (2003). The influence of cognitive and effective based job satisfaction measures on the relationship between satisfaction and organizational citizenship behaviour. Human Relations 6, 759-776.

Motowido, S. J,. Borman, W. C. & Schmit, M. J. (2007). A theory of individual differences in task and contextual performance. Human performance 10.71-83.

Muehinsky, P. M. (2003). Psychology applied to work (7th Ed.) Behmont. CA: Wadsworth.

Ottu, I. F. A. & lnyang. W. C. (2003). Perceived self-efficacy, domestic violence and ability to break industrial glass ceiling, advancing women in leadership. 33. 177-187.

Penasylvania, Blue, Shield Institute (2002). Social problems and rising health care costs in Pennsylvania, Pennsylvania.

Population Reference Bureau (2000). MEASURE Communication, Washington.

Rotland, J. P. & Defraet, F. (2003). The validity of FFM personality dimension and maladaptive traits to predict negative affects at work. A six month prospective study in a military sample. *European Journal of Personality,* 17:5101-5121.

Schultz, D. P., & Schultz, S. E. (2010). Psychology and Work today: An introduction to industrial and organizational psychology. 10th Edition.

Shahu, R & Cole. S. V. (2008). Effect of the job stress and job satisfaction on performance an empirical study. *AIMS International Journal of Management,* vol. 2 No. 3. 237-246.

Spector, P. E. (2007). Job satisfaction: Application Assessment causes and consequences, Thousand Oaks, CA; SAGE.

Survey Data, Economic and Political Weekly, 33 (15) 855-862 (2015).

Thomson, E. R. & Phua. F. T. T (2012). A brief index _job satisfaction, organization management. 37(3)275307.

Viswesvaran C. & Ones, D. S. (2000). Perspectives on Models of job.

Performance International Journal of Selection and Assessment 8(4) 216-226. (2014).

Waster, E. E., Berscheid, G. A. & Waster. G. W. (2003). "New Dimensions in equity research. Journal of Personality and social Psychology, 151 – 176.

Weiss. H. M. & Cropanzano, R. (2006). Affective events theory: a theoretical discussion of structural causes and consequences.

Wright, P. M. & Noe, R. A. (2006). Management of Organization, Chicago: Irwin publishers 289-332.

# 15

# Potentials of Peace Education on the Nigerian Educational System

Agbegbedia O. Anthony

## Abstract

*The paper examined the potentials of peace education on the Nigerian educational system. The paper identified types of peace education and the theories that support the inclusion of peace education in the curriculum. In the end, the paper categorically made justifications for the potentials of peace education, while showcasing the skills that are derivable from the curriculum when peace education is included. The paper concludes that peace education and peace culture should as a matter of urgency be included in the curriculum of Nigerian educational system in order to promote peace in the society.*

**Keywords:** potentials, peace education, educational, system

## Introduction

Peace together with freedom, equality and justice is one of the most desirable values in almost every society. It has become a universal symbol; a master concept that connotes a general positive state including all the positive qualities that are valued, cherished and inspired by all human beings (Bar-Tal, 2002). Oppenheimer (2002) noted that Peace Education is mainly a matter of changing mind-sets; the general purpose is to promote understanding, respect and tolerance towards yesterday's enemies. It is the process of promoting the knowledge and skills needed to bring about behavioural changes that will directly and positively impact on the general society thereby aiding in the prevention of conflict and violence generally. It is an education on social relationships that should mould the interaction between various strata of the society which involves preventive mechanisms which thereby aid in creating a conducive environment for the sustenance of peace.

Peace education enhances the purpose of education, which is to reveal and tap into those energies that make possible the enjoyment of a meaningful and productive existence (Morrison, 2013). Morrison further maintained that peace education is meant to help humans tap into their full potential beyond the regular lessons learnt from other disciplines. Peace education involves students and educators in a commitment to create a more just and peaceful world order; it begins with the individual's quest for inner peace and moves outward to embrace family, community and the world. Nevo (2002) concurred with the idea when he stated that, peace education is not Pacificism Education; the goal is not to make students and citizens quiet, complacent, and content; peace educators try to point out the problems of violence that exists in a society and then instruct their pupils about strategies that can be used to address those problems, hence empowering them to redress the circumstances that lead to violence.

Peace Education being a concept that aims to change the mind-set of humans globally has its own objectives just like every other concept or ideology. However, these objectives vary in relation to nationalities, ethnicities, social groups and other large groups humans identify with. In Australia, Peace education is concerned with challenging ethno-centricism, cultural chauvinism and violence on the one hand, and promoting cultural diversity, nuclear disarmament and conflict resolution on the other. In Japan, peace education is concerned with nuclear disarmament, militarism and nature of responsibility for violent acts performed in the past. In South America, it is preoccupied with structural violence, human rights and economic inequality (Bar-Tal, 2002). In the United States, Peace education programs often concern prejudice, violence and environmental issues (Harris, 2008). In Africa, peace education programs offer one the knowledge about the spirit of *ubuntu* (I am because you are), oneness, unity and identification. The objectives of these various countries which are aimed at achieving sustainable peace can only be achieved by implementing specific values, skills, and attitudes that correspond with the objectives. Thus, this work discusses the important of the potentials of peace education with relation to African in general and Nigerian educational environment in particular.

## Definition of Peace Education

Education is the process by which teaching and learning take place with a view to effecting a change in people's behaviour. Peace Education, therefore, refers to a deliberate attempt to educate children and adults alike in the dynamics of conflict and the promotion of peace-building and peacemaking skills through both formal and informal instruments of socialisation (Gumut, 2006). Children and adults of varying age grades across cultures have to appreciate the inevitable character of conflicts and embrace non-coercive means for managing them with a view to promoting positive peace and downplaying violent acts in all areas of life.

Over the ages, people across various cultures have been exposed to aggressive behaviour, inclined towards coercive approaches to conflict management, and presumed that violence and injustice are a fact of life. Hence, their minds are prone towards developing the theories of war and violence at the expense of commitment to the valued aspects of cultural heritage that propagate peace tradition (Fisher *et al.*, 2000). It is this imbalance that peace education is set out to redress by emphasizing the fact that we can build a better world and live in harmony with one another through self-respect, tolerance, empathy, justice and fairness, irrespective of differences in colours and cultures. Moreover, the United Nations chapter states that "since wars originate in the 'minds of men', it is in the minds of men that the defences of peace must be constructed" (Fisher *et al.*, 2000:142). Hence, peace education attempts to shed light on the reality of nonviolent, peaceful co-existence, and equips people to become active participants in their world, rather than mere passive bystanders.

## History of Peace Education

According to Harris (2008:15), peace education can be defined simply as "the process of teaching people about the threats of violence and strategies for peace," whether this teaching happens inside or outside a classroom. With this broad definition, peace education's history is arguably as old as human history, as cultures throughout the world have learned and then taught the next generation how to live peacefully with others. For example, diverse religious and philosophical traditions have been a rich and influential source of peace learning, even though people have also promoted violence in the names of these traditions.

Peace education in its modern form, however, stems primarily from specialized written traditions and formal schooling. Peace education scholar, Ian Harris described this modern peace movement as beginning in nineteenth century Europe with many intellectual efforts to learn about violent conflict, evolving in socialist political thought, and spreading to the United States and elsewhere before World War I. Scholars began to study war and started trying to educate the public about its dangers. More and more people tried to persuade each other and their governments to use mediation instead of war to solve international conflicts. For example, with educational theorist John Dewey, many teachers across the United States began using progressive education to teach their students about our common humanity in order to promote peaceful social progress (Harris, 2008:16-17).

In the early 1900s, women became especially active participants of this modern peace education movement. Peace educators at this early date, often led by women, began campaigning for social justice, arguing that poverty and inequality were causes of war. Maria Montessori is one example of an influential mid-20th century theorist who found new connections between peace and education. She linked teaching methodology to peace-building, hoping to help the next generation avoid the violence of authoritarianism.

Other peace educators at that time, such as Herbert Read, began encouraging the use of art and students' creativity to promote peace, while others such as Paulo Freire focused on training students for critical analysis and reform of society. Curle and Lederach acknowledged the influence of Freire whose pedagogy of the oppressed was published in 1970, in the development of their ideas (Ramsbotham *et al,* 2012:238). Freire (1970 cited in Ramsbotham *et al,* 2012: 202) working with the poor in Brazil and Chile in the 1960s argued against the banking or teacher-directed nature of education as a form of oppression and in favour of education as liberation. On the other hand, according to Ramsbotham *et al* (2012:238), Curle's education for liberation was published in 1973 with strong influences from Freire and his 'Making Peace', published in 1971 represented his attempt to integrate his idea on education and peacemaking in the broader project of liberating human potential and transcending violence. More recently, critical thinking by some scholars, activists and theorists have suggested that the field has lost contact with its radical core values, making it implicated in the technocratic and blueprint dominated version of the liberal peace noted above.

International organizations, from the League of Nations to United Nations bodies, as well as non-governmental organizations have been growing in influence and importance since the end of World War I; where the League of Nations failed, the establishment of the United Nations achieved new levels of global cooperation, norms and ideals. The Charter of the United Nations has since served as inspiration for the development of peace education, as educators aspired to help in the global effort to "save succeeding generations from the scourge of war," "to reaffirm faith in the… dignity and worth of the human person (and) in the equal rights of men and women," "to establish conditions under which justice and respect for the obligations arising from treaties and other sources of international law can be maintained," and "to promote social progress and better standards of life in larger freedom…." (Preamble of the UN Charter, 1945 cited in Agbegbedia, 2014). With this mandate, the study of sustainable peace and education in promotion of it began to take on new urgency and sophistication to achieve these universal ideals.

Peace studies became a more serious academic subject soon after World War II, and the threat of nuclear war throughout the Cold War encouraged many scholars to devote their studies to creating a sustainable peace. From the 1980s in particular, peace education scholarship has developed in many directions. Some have emphasized minimizing masculine aggression, domestic violence, and militarism; others have sought to foster empathy and care in students; and many have argued that critical thinking and democratic pedagogy are vital. With the Convention on the Rights of the Child (CRC) in 1989, peace education and human rights education took on new importance, as this type of education came to be seen as a fundamental right that all children should have. As UNICEF scholar Susan Fountain writes, "It is significant that the framers of the CRC viewed the promotion of understanding, peace and tolerance through education as a fundamental right of all children, not an optional extra-curricular activity" International organizations of all types, along with local teachers and communities, felt renewed pressure to provide peace education to all students as part of their core studies; this provision became an explicit duty for everyone in society, and especially for those involved in formal education (Fountain, 1999 in Agbegbedia, 2014).

Since the 1990s, peace education scholarship from around the world has provided an even greater variety of perspectives on the practice and its goals. In documenting peace education's implementation, scholars have found varying degrees of emphasis on positive or negative peace, on local or global peace, and subordinate or dominant status of students. Scholars have argued that the context of the peace education program has become one of the most important factors in shaping the form it takes. Thus, peace education has been shown to use local peace potentials and local traditions of conflict transformation (Agbegbedia, 2014). Teachers and others have shaped their programs to address their communities' needs and goals. For example, some scholars like Murithi (2009) have suggested *ubuntu* - an ethical philosophy of Southern Africa that roughly translates to "I am because you are" - as a helpful component of peace education in parts of Africa. The history of peace education, therefore, has various roots and has developed on various paths; nonetheless, every instance of peace education can be seen as part of a larger movement toward the creation of a more peaceful world.

Moreover, despite their differences in particular areas, these teachers have much in common. Many peace educators since the 1980s especially have come to seek to promote some combination of the following ideals: human rights and the right of the child, social justice and the minimisation of structural violence, critical analysis and transformation of violent concepts and institutions non-violent interpersonal and inter-communal conflict resolution, universal empathy, global familiarity and peaceful coexistence with the environment (Salomon, 2002). Around the world, teachers have drawn upon the work and research of international activists, scholars, and each other for ideas. At the same time, these peace educators' work continues to inspire further work and study concerning new possibilities for peace education (Agbegbedia, 2014).

The development of peace education as a central component of peace-building provides an opportunity both to fix the main values of conflict resolution around non-violence and emancipation in order to define a transformative cosmopolitan model which seeks to apply these values in peace-building. In 2000, the World Education Forum was held in Dakar, Senegal and at this forum, the problems of the effect of war and humanitarian emergencies on children's education were highlighted. Besides, suggestions were made for the educational programmes that address the need to promote mutual understanding, peace and tolerance which will help to prevent violence (World Education Forum, 2000 cited in Agbegbedia,

2014). At this forum, education for all goals were agreed upon but a study by Marc Sommers has shown that the majority of primary school children in war affected areas have no realistic hope of attending school and that, even in those conditions where some schooling exists, girls are much more likely to be excluded than the boys. More so, beyond the primary level, programmes for youth are poorly encouraged and the pressure or coercion to join aggressive militias is unavoidable. Sommer's conclusion makes a persuasive case for a major investment in education as an important component of post-conflict peace-building: lack of investment in creative art, participatory work on education for children and youth at risk makes a return to peace extremely difficult if not impossible (Sommer, 2002:1 cited in Agbegbedia, 2014).

It is also the case that a provision for the development of education and educational resources is increasingly a component of peace agreements. According to Dupuy (2008:155), of a total of one hundred and five (105) peace agreements signed between 1989 and 2005, fifty-seven (57) had some provision for education as a component of post-war reconstruction. Four main themes emerged in these agreements which include respecting and implementing the right to education; resuming education services; responding to conflict-created issues within the education sector and actively reforming the education system as a way of addressing the issues at the heart of the incompatibility between the warring parties.

In this context, investment in education for peace provides a strategically effective driver for the transformative cosmopolitan model (Ramsbotham *et al*, 2012:240). Harris (2004) on his part identified five main assumptions that characterise contemporary peace education. They include the following (i) it explains the roots of violence; (ii) it teaches alternatives to violence; (iii) it adjusts to cover different forms of violence; (iv) peace itself is a process that varies according to context and (v) conflict is omnipresent. Affirming this definition, Audra Degesys noted the potential of new pedagogies of peace education to address the goals of education as liberation. He noted thus:

> As education systems can sustain conflict within schools, they can also liberate it. Just as racism, sexism and xenophobia were mentioned earlier as embedded and learned through the curriculum, these same power structures can be 'unlearned' and replaced with humanism, tolerance, diversity, democracy and critical thinking. Schools can play an important role in promoting alternative understandings of racism, xenophobia and what it means to be tolerant or democratic. To participate in this world as conscientious citizens or peacemakers, students need to be educated so that they might bring with them their own worldviews to respond to conflict... the pedagogy which engages students as participatory learners and visionaries of alternate possibilities of social reality is called transformative learning. Reflections, active learning

and transformative methods are necessary for the content of peace education to change attitudes towards conflict (Degesys, 2008).

Peace education, defined in this way, provides a space for exploring the via media called for by Richmond in the negotiation of context-sensitive and hybrid values of peace and peacemaking. It also carries within it the core values of resistance to war and violence (Ramsbotham *et al*, 2012:240). Thus, the trend in recent history appears to be one of moving toward an expanding informal network of activists, scholars, teachers, and others that draw on each other's work to improve their understanding and promotion of peace. New participants join the movement every day, and peace education continues to evolve in its theory and in its practice.

## Types of Peace Education

Agbegbedia (2014) identified two types of peace education: formal and informal peace education.

### The Formal Peace Education

According to Agbegbedia (2014), the formal peace education is the one that could be incorporated into the school curriculum and taught within the school subjects such as in history, peace and conflict studies, music drama to mention but a few. Some of the programmes in formal education include but are not limited to the following:

i. **Knowledge:** it is a fact that knowledge is power and so, students should know certain things about themselves and others, the poor and the rich, about peace and conflict, the environment and the world tomorrow.

ii. **Attitudes:** positive attitudes are important for the attainment of peace. Such attitudes affect our responses to conflict and the ways we deal with the things and people around us. Some of these attitudes affect our responses to conflict and the ways we deal with the things and people around us. Some of these attitudes include the human dignity, curiosity and appreciation of others' culture, empathy, justice and fairness.

iii. **Skills:** overtime, peace is built through the processes of encounter and reflection that address not only practical issues of conflict but also deeper issues of relationships, human development and structural realities. In essence, it is a basic requirement for students to acquire skills which will equip them to be peace builders in every society they found themselves. Such skills include but not limited to the following: enquiry, communication skills and tools, grasping concepts, critical thinking and political skills.

**The Informal Peace Education**

Agbegbedia (2014) opined that it is the type of education and knowledge which is acquired outside the schools and colleges. This concurred with Gumut (2006) ideas that informal peace education takes place in informal settings where people gather for work or leisure, through socialisation and initiation processes within the community, in family settings, as age-groups to mention but a few. Like in schools, informal peace education mainly addresses attitudes and focuses on how to develop a direct impact on personal behaviour. Thus, peace education in both formal and informal settings, require a more relaxed environment than the known lecture/pupil relationship need to be credited, a more open and welcoming arrangement where people can be encouraged to embark on the herculean task of looking at issues that are vital to them, reflecting on their own behaviour and generating alternatives for the future. An important way of informal peace education is the use of folk language, proverbs, old poems, and anecdotes for promoting peace in the immediate environment. This raises peoples' awareness of how language can shape attitudes and behaviours and even create room for languages to be more peace sensitive (Agbegbedia, 2014).

## Theories of Peace Education

The following are theories of peace education:

**Human Capital Theory**

Human capital theory rests on the assumption that formal education is highly instrumental and even necessary to improve the production capacity of a population. This implies that an educated population is a productive population. The economic prosperity and functioning of a nation depend on its physical and human capital stock. Whereas, the former has traditionally been the focus of economic research, factors affecting the enhancement of human skills and talent are increasingly figuring in the research of social and behavioural sciences. In general terms, human capital represents the investment people make in themselves that enhance their economic productivity.

Human capital theory emphasizes how education increases the productivity and efficiency of workers by increasing the level of cognitive stock of economically productive human capability which is a product of innate abilities and investment in human beings. The provision of formal education is seen as a productive investment in human capital, which the proponents of the theory have considered as equally or even more equally worthwhile than that of physical capital.

Furthermore, the rationality behind investment in human capital could be based on three arguments which are:

1. The new generation must be given the appropriate parts of the knowledge which has already been accumulated by previous generations.
2. New generations should be taught how existing knowledge should be used to develop new products, to introduce new processes and production methods and social services.
3. People must be encouraged to develop entirely new ideas, products, processes and methods through creative approaches.

This theory therefore provides a basic justification for large public expenditure on education both in developing and developed nations. The theory was consistent with the ideologies of democracy and liberal progression found in most western societies. Its appeal was based upon the presumed economic return of investment in education both at the macro and micro levels. Efforts to promote investment were seen to provide returns in the form of individual economic success and achievement. Most economists agree that it is human resources of a nation, not its capital nor its material resources that ultimately determine the character and pace of its economic and social development. Psacharopoulos and Woodhall (1997) concluded that, human resources constitute the ultimate basis of wealth of nations. Capital and natural resources are passive factors of production, human beings are the active agencies who accumulate capital, exploit natural resources, build social, economic and political organization and carry forward national development.

This theory thus brings to the limelight the importance of peace education and education as a whole to a society, whereby it emphasizes that if a society is educated, at the same time taught a peace culture, the future generations will be able to maximize their full potential through skills they have learnt which will also lead to proper management of both human and natural resources and further prevent conflicts.

## The Integrative Theory of Peace

A theory relevant to the field of multicultural education is the Integrative Theory of Peace (ITP), which is based on the concept that peace is, at once, a psychological, social, political, ethical and spiritual state with its expressions in intrapersonal, interpersonal, intergroup, international, and global areas of human life (Danesh, 2008: 55). The integrative theory of Peace includes four tenets:

1. Peace is a psychosocial and political as well as a moral and spiritual condition.
2. Peace is the main expression of a unity-based worldview.

3. The unity-based worldview is the prerequisite for creating both a culture of peace and a culture of healing.

4. A comprehensive, integrated and lifelong education within the framework of peace is the most effective approach for a transformation from the conflict-based meta-categories of survival-based and identity-based worldviews to the meta-category of unity-based worldview (Danesh, 2008).

Furthermore, Danesh (2008) described three different kinds of worldviews: survival-based, identity-based, and unity-based. The survival-based worldview according to him is normal during infancy and childhood and corresponds to agrarian and pre-industrial periods of development. Unequal power relations and use of force are common manifestations of this worldview, and it requires conformity, blind obedience, and passive resignation. This worldview is not conducive to peace, as it tends to concentrate wealth and power, and results in disadvantage for large segments of the population.

The identity-based worldview corresponds to the coming-of-age of an individual or society, and is typically characterized by increased democracy. However, this phase is also characterized by extreme competition and power struggle, and an individualistic survival of the fittest mentality. Both the survival-based and identity-based worldviews are conflict-based worldviews, in which conflict is seen as an inevitable part of human existence.

With the unity-based worldview, a new level of consciousness is reached and humanity becomes aware of its fundamental oneness. In this worldview, society operates according to the principle of unity in diversity (Danesh, 2008:68). The unity-based worldview supports the equality of all members of society through a cooperative power structure. The unity worldview encompasses a different view of conflict. While other worldviews hold that conflict is an inherent part of being human, the unity worldview proposes that once unity is established, conflicts are often prevented or easily resolved. Also, the unity worldview would be a process of creating health, rather than trying to eliminate the symptoms of a disease. Thus, within the unity worldview, conflict is not inevitable; it is preventable.

Ultimately, peace is achieved when both the oneness and the diversity of humanity are safeguarded and celebrated (Danesh, 2008:69). The celebration of unity through diversity is precisely the goal of multicultural education. This theory thereby brings to the limelight the importance of peace education and education as a whole to a society, whereby it emphasizes that if a society is educated on the unity-based world view, will develop a peace culture that will not only resolve conflict but ultimately prevent it. The future generations will be able to inter-relate based on the unity-based worldview which would foster a sense of unity and strength in diversity thereby preventing conflict based on identity or survival of the fittest.

# The Potentials of Peace Education on the Nigerian Educational System

As the aim of peace education is to help individuals to become good citizens and to respect diversity, it is non-sectarian and non-religious in its nature. Peace education constitutes one of the key means to reach peace. However, the absence of war does not mean peace in itself. Indeed, peace is a virtue, a state of mind, and a disposition for benevolence, non-violence, justice and confidence (Morrison 2013). Peace education is of very high importance, as it enables people to adopt a positive attitude regarding the different issues they can face throughout their life and to develop the necessary skills to peacefully resolve conflict. This, in turn, will impact positively on the society.

The peace education curriculum in Nigeria is designed to empower students with knowledge, attitudes, values and behaviours to live in line with themselves, others and their environment. Moreover, the programme will enhance the development of the necessary skills to resolve situations of injustice, conflict and will disseminate the culture of peace. This curriculum has been designed to meet the needs of the situation in Nigeria in particular and Africa in general, where most of the conflicts occur between members of different tribes. Through its implementation in educational institutions, it will focus on constructive elements that will enhance the students' confidence and will make them aware of their responsibility to avoid using violence. The curriculum will assist teachers in setting up peace education classes specific to the Nigerian context. The peace education curriculum is made of different parts: teaching, participative activities and interactive sessions. The focus of the curriculum will be the relationships between the knowledge, behaviours, skills and attitudes that are crucial to peace education. The Possible impacts of peace education in Nigeria therefore include;

1. Through Peace education programme, students will learn how to predict, resolve or prevent issues that can lead to conflict.
2. Through the activities of the curriculum, students will be empowered with the necessary skills to become agents of peace and change.
3. Through peace education, students will learn how to create a peaceful environment by respecting the equality of human rights. The equality between individuals is crucial as inequality can generate structural violence. By avoiding structural violence, it will be possible to prevent the acts of direct violence to happen, as Galtung (1996) suggested. Students will be taught that equality is very important, not only in school but also in their daily lives.
4. The peace education classes will act as platforms for the expression of opinions regarding peace and will give occasions to practice non-violent approaches. They will also provide support for the students to bring about social change.
5. During their classes, teachers will try to create a safe and unbiased environment where students can freely ask questions and discuss controversial public issues

that often lead to violence. Through these discussions, the students will develop constructive elements that can contribute to positive impact on the development of the nation.

6. Through peace education programme, students are expected to improve their knowledge, skills and attitudes by participating in activities and cooperate with others for the realization of projects. By creating an environment filled with care, tolerance and respect, teachers will encourage the students to explore and exchange ideas and to respect others' opinions. As students will be asked to actively participate in the classes, they will be encouraged to take responsibility for their own learning process and personal achievement of peace.

7. The activities organized during the classes will allow the students to put in practice the acquired skills. Through mediation exercises, they will discover the benefits they can get when adopting a peaceful approach to resolve conflicts. Thus, students will enhance their skills, knowledge and attitudes.

8. During the peace education classes, the constructive elements required to achieve peace will be presented to the students, which will then be expected to put them in practice in their daily activities.

9. As the concepts will be gradually built on one another, this curriculum will be able to meet the specific needs of the students.

10. The peace education programme will act as a tool to develop the capacities of the future leaders to have a positive impact on the development of the society. It will not teach students what they must think but will rather encourage them to think critically in order to avoid repetition of past mistakes

## The Skills Derivable From the Curriculum

i. **Empathy and Compassion:** Students will be encouraged to emotionally identify with the issues. This will enable them to have positive feelings of compassion for those who have been struck by misfortune and not to be hard-hearted. Thus, this will promote the development and expression of positive thoughts and feelings. Through this empathic attitude, students will be able to become good citizens that show compassion for their fellows and act in order to have a positive impact on the society.

ii. **Mediation, Negotiation and Conflict Resolution:** As mediation, negotiation and conflict resolution are parts of the peace process, students need to be aware of them. After having presented notions and concepts related to mediation which combine elements of communication and cooperation, the teacher will organize practical exercises through which students will have opportunity to put in practice what they have been taught and improve their mediation skills. Students will study what is the role of a third-party and how it can facilitate the resolution of a conflict. After having presented the skills of mediation, teachers will encourage the students to apply these methods when they are experiencing a conflict situation. For example, in case of a conflict between two students, one of the senior students will be asked to act as a mediator to peacefully resolve the conflict without involving any teacher in the matter. Thus, students will be able to understand what positive outcomes they can expect when they choose to resolve a conflict with the assistance of a mediator rather than resorting to violence.

iii. **Critical Thinking and Problem Solving**: During the classes, students will be asked to think individually and to imagine solutions to resolve a particular issue presented by the teacher. Teachers will encourage them to use their creativity when designing approach to peacefully overcome challenges. Then, each student will explain his/her approach to the rest of the class. By comparing and contrasting their ideas, students will improve their problem-solving skills and think critically. This exercise will help to increase the students' confidence in their ability to resolve problems. In so doing, they will be confident enough in designing ways to resolve the issues.

## Conclusion

This paper focused on how peace education could be introduced into the Nigeria's education system as potentials for managing conflict and for promotion of peaceful co-existence. Peace education tends to promote preventive diplomacy and peace-building processes by reducing hostile perceptions through educational exchanges and curriculum reform, thereby forestalling a re-emergence of cultural and national tensions which could spark renewed hostilities. The work examined the possibility of peace education in preventing conflict in the sense that, peace education being mainly a matter of changing mindsets, promoting understanding, respect and tolerance changes people's view on conflict in general. They begin to see conflict in a constructive manner and thus, will employ the skills learnt from peace education in managing situations of conflicts.

It is imperative to note that both formal and informal models of peace education do collaborate to promote peace culture and non-violent tradition. Besides, having examined the impacts of peace education, it is safe to say that peace education will have a positive impact on conflicts. These positive impacts of peace education should not just be historical records but should serve as the starting point for trusting in the power of peace education in influencing conflicts either in its total prevention or limiting its negative effects. Thus, peace education and peace culture should as a matter of urgency, be included in the education curriculum by the Nigeria government in particular and Africa in general in order to promote peace in the society.

# References

Agbegbedia, A. (2014). Integrating Peace Education/Culture as conflict Management Strategies into Nigeria's Educational System for Peaceful Co-existence. *International Journal of Peace Education and Development*, 76.

Bar-Tal, D. (2002). *The Elusive Nature Of Peace Education. Tel- Aviv University, School of Education.*

Danesh, H. B. (2008). *Unity based peace education, Encyclopaedia of peace education.* North Carolina: Information Age Pub.

Degesys, A. (2008). Transformative pedagogy in conflict resolution as an alternative route to peace-building-road less explored in T. Woodhouse (ed) *Peace-building and security in the 21$^{st}$ century.* Evanston: Rotary Canters for International Studies.

Dupuy, K. (2008). Education in peace agreements, 1989-2005. *Conflict resolution quarterly,* 26(2): 149-66.

Fisher, S., Abdi, D., Ludi, J., Smith, R., & Williams, S. (2000). *Working with conflict skills and strategies for action.* London: Zed Books.

Fisher, S., Abdi, D., Ludi, J., Smith, R., & Williams, S. (2000). *Working with conflict skills and strategies for action.* London: Zed Books.

Galtung, J. (1996). Peace by peaceful means. London: Sage

Gumut, V. (2006). Peace education and peer mediation in Shedrack G, B (ed) *Introduction to peace and conflict studies in West Africa.* Ibadan: Spectrum Books limited.

Harris, I. (2004). Peace education theory. *Journal of peace education,* 1(1):5-20.

Harris, I. (2008). *History of Peace Education.* Wisconsin: Univerisity of Wisconsin Press.

Morrison, I. M. (2013). *Peace Education.* Mcfarland and company, inc, Publishers.

Murithi, T. (2009). "An African Perspective on Peace Education: Ubuntu Lessons in Reconciliation," *International Review of Education* (55), p. 221-233.

Nevo, G. S. (2002). *Peace Education: the Concept, principles and practices around the world.* Lawrence Erbaum associates.

Oppenheimer. (2002). *Peace education: The concept principles and practices around the world.* Gavriel Salomon.

Psacharopoulos, G. & Woodhall, M. (1997). *Education for development: An analysis of investment choices.* U.S.A: Oxford University Press.

Ramsbotham, D., Woodhouse, T & Miall, H. (2012). *Contemporary conflict resolution. Cambridge:* Polity press.

Salomon, G. (2002). "The Nature of Peace Education: Not All Programs Are Created Equal" in Nevo & Salomon, eds., *Peace Education: the concept principles, and practices around the world,* New Jersey: Lawrence Earlbaum Associates, p. 3-13.

# 16

# Play Activities and Performance of Specific Vocabulary Development Tasks in English Language

Thelma Ekukinam Ph.D

## Abstract

*T*he study examined the frequency of play activities and the opportunities pupils' have to perform specific vocabulary development tasks. The study adopted a survey research design with the area of study in Akwa Ibom State. The population of the study stands at thirteen public primary schools in Uyo Metropolis, out of which six primary schools were randomly drawn for the study. Within each school, the intact classes of the first stream of primary six were used for the study were the school had more than one stream and this brought the sample size to 154 primary six pupils. Two research questions and one hypothesis were set to guide the study. A researcher designed questionnaire tagged: 'Play Activities for Vocabulary Development in English Language'(PAVDEL) was used to gather data from the respondents. Through test of Cronbach Alpha the reliability Coefficient of 0.84 was realized for the instrument thus making it fit for the study. Independent t-test analysis was used to analyze collated data at 0.05 level of significance. The results revealed that the frequency at which pupils engage in various play activities were high for non-computer games but low for computer games. The results further showed that there was significant difference in the specific tasks performed by pupils who played computer games and those who played non-computer games. The mean score rating indicated that the resulted tilted to players of non-computer games who had more opportunity to perform vocabulary development related tasks. It was therefore recommended that computer games with educational value should be made available and accessible to children in order to create a proper blend of the benefits the children derive from play activities. Thus, there should be a conscious effort by school authorities, parents and other to stakeholders place computer games within the reach of pupils in public schools.

**Keywords**: Play Activities, Computer Games, Non-Computer Games, Vocabulary Development, Specific Instructional Task.

# Introduction

Children's preoccupation with various activities would be incomplete without play as the major aspect of their engagements. From birth children keep themselves occupied with anything they can lay their hands on. During the pre-school years as toddlers children engage in different forms self-centered play activities as they try to discover more of the world around them. In some cases parents and guardians try to provide the children with toys and safe environments like play pens for the children to play in. In some other cases too, where parents cannot afford such luxury, the children make do with anything at their disposal which might expose the child to dangerous objects and environments. In any case the child fills every unoccupied time with some form of play activity.

During the early school years the child starts interacting more with other children as they run around and share fun activities. Throughout the lower basic, to the middle basic and upper basic primary years the child joins different play groups where various forms of games and play activities are created for fun and peer association. There are outdoor and indoor games for children in school and at home. At home, the former could be more or less restricted depending on parental control for security reasons and socio-economic background of the parents. In school, outdoor games are a part of school routine for children during break periods as children leave their classrooms to exercise themselves after sitting in for two or three hours stretch. Outdoor games might involve a lot of physical movements and group activities. Indoor games often allow the children to play with their toys and different kinds of games. These range from computer, video, board and card games, hand held game devices and local games that children derive from their cultural and traditional settings which are mostly passed on from generation to generation. In addition, children design their own games which are mostly characterized by clapping, jumping, skipping, singing, repeating rhyme pattern, and question/answer drills, guessing, hide and seek (Ekukinam, 2003; Adura, 2015) There are also some ground games where children draw the frame for the game on the ground outside or on the floor using charcoal or chalk if available. Here stones, leaves, flowers and dry seeds of fruits can be used as the chips. The wordings and lyrics of most the play activities exhibit useful information for learning in specific subject areas. Ekpo and Ekukinam (1998) in a study on adaptation of local play into useful instructional packages for primary school pupils in Akwa Ibom, it was discovered that most of local plays had instructional values relevant to one subject area or the other. These local plays could be adapted to teach language and numerical structures and forms. They are suitable for quick word development among children as they unconsciously engage in some meaningful drills (Ekukinam, 2003).

Video Games are electronic games that involve the players interaction with an interface to produce visual feedback on platforms such as television screen, a computer monitor, a video console or a handheld game device. The computer game, video game and handheld device are basically the same as the provide fun and opportunity for players interaction with the game procedure, character, or object. The only difference lies in the hardware used to display, control and also provide feedback. The video console or machine is purposely designed with the game in the system. The computer on the other hand which serves other purposes, the game software has to be downloaded and installed as a program. The handheld device is a small portable self-contained video game console with built in screen, game controls, and speakers. These handheld devices are miniature forms of video games with input and output components are in-built into the console (Stuart, 2015, Prensky, 2006).

Researchers have shown that video games have learning benefits for children ranging from fun, social interaction with peers, gaining speed and quick decision making skills. Oblinger (2006) for instance, puts it clear that generally games motivate children to learn how to learn in a conducive environment of fun and enjoyment, passionate involvement, ego gratification, problem solving, creativity and social interaction. Prensky(2006) says that "play has a deep biological, evolutionary important function, opportunity to practice knowledge gained from formal teaching and learning. Noemi,(2014) after assessing the game TIKTAK HITZAK for specific objectives in vocabulary development in a learning environment asserted that the game equips the players with skills for persistent and individual skills for real time learning. Adura, (2015) argues that the problem is not the question of whether there are educational games for acquiring literacy skills but the fact that the games might be available but not accessible to the pupils. She further adds that the ones that are accessible could be the ones with no other instructional values apart from combat and sports games for defeating an opponent and competing for high scores. The more detailed games show relevance to specific subject areas and objectives and may likely be more expensive (Edith, 2014). It is common to see children with simple hand held game devices which only expose the children to knock out and combat games. Some of these could be powered by small batteries or just manually operated. The negative aspects of computer games should not be over looked because without proper limitations and guidance the children can be exposed to violent games (Adenaiye, 2006; Edith 2014)

Board games are designed to be placed flat on a table, floor or any convenient flat surface. Players get involved in solving one problem or the other by way of taking turns to outdo one another or to beat each other to a certain goal or mark. Players gain experience from constant interaction with other players on the game. Board games such as Ludo, Snake and ladder and Checkers are more games of chance with no special skills required but designers of educational board games now include aspects of cognitive development

(Scrabble). Players manipulate objects which come in different forms following the rules and procedure of a game. These objects could be wood, metal, plastic paper chips or objects that represent the visual or verbal cues or characters required to play the game. Yao (2018) calls these chips position markers. The boards have certain graphics printed on the surface as a basis for players' interaction.

Card games are hand held portable packs of flash-like cards that are played in pairs or more players depending on the type. These were also initially only games of chance but designers have added some educational values that demand for the players' knowledge and skills. The commonest ones that that are available for children are WHOT and HEARTS. Card games are easily learnt and played within short durations unlike board games which can last for hours and require the players' full concentration. The rules of card games are flexible and can be adapted to suit the players' fun and pleasure (Stuart, 2015).

A choice of the kind of game to purchase could be a mirage as games company have flooded the market with all kinds of games probably because they have seen opportunity for quick financial turnover. Even though all kinds of games can be adapted to suit the educational environment, but there are specifically designed educational games that enhance and help children learn about certain subjects, reduce abstraction of concepts, reinforce learning, follow historical events and help players learn certain skills (Prensky, 2006). On the basis of this fact, how much of the games children engage in do enrich their word power and vocabulary development.

Vocabulary development can be placed as the second most important aspect of language acquisition. After children recognize the phonics of a language which comes naturally for the mother tongue but has to be leant for the second language, they start building their vocabulary. In Nigeria, English language is not only the second language but language of communication, and other businesses especially education. The National Policy of Nigeria requires that every child should be taught in his native language at the onset of education, specifically during the ECCD years with English taught as a subject. Then during the lower basic primary years, the pupils start learning through English Language as medium of instruction (FGN, 2013). Thus from then on apart from being a compulsory subject, it remains as the medium of instruction at primary and secondary school. It is thus expedient that children should be exposed to various learning experiences that will enhance their vocabulary development.

A child in primary six is a twelve year old child who according to Nyere (2009) should have learnt enough words in preparation for college which is only a year away. In The child is gradually moving away from objective and subjective type questions and answer requirements to longer essay type requirements in the formal teaching and learning examination setting. She adds that the child also needs more vocabulary to be able to cope with the demands of assessing and providing information for a functional life in the world of knowledge and the society at large The National Policy on Education stipulates as one of its major goals to train and equip the child to be able to develop self and also contribute meaningfully to the growth of the Nigerian society. In Loraine's analysis, a primary six child at this stage should have a vocabulary of at least 50,000 words.

This study derives its theoretical framework from Situated learning theory of Lave and Wenger (1991). It argues that learning should not be regarded as a simple process of transmission of abstract and decontextualized knowledge from one person to another, but a social process whereby knowledge is co-constructed. Situated Learning Theory states that learners should enter learning scenarios to acquire knowledge. As pupil engage in different forms of games and play activities, their cognitive processes are provoked and learning experiences gained at such times leave a permanent impression on them. Play activities provide the learners with an interactive and collaborative situation in which they have both the means and opportunity to acquire new ideas, knowledge and understanding of English language vocabulary. Crawford (2004:15) notes that "play as an activity is considered to be the exclusive preserve of children. Children are expected to play games because we recognize (perhaps unconsciously) the fundamental utility of games as an educational tool." Empirical studies confirm that one recalls more easily, things they were involved in or experiences acted in real-life forms, than they were merely fed with (Sarasin, 1999; Heinich, Mollenda, Russel and Smaldine, 2002; Ajuzie, 2013).

The development of vocabulary thus means building a good stock of words that one can appropriately draw from to ease both written and oral expressions. This implies that one needs to understand the meaning of a word, be able to spell it correctly, use it correctly in terms of tense and number, and if possible know its antonyms and synonyms. Amanda (2013) adds that vocabulary development requires constant exposure to right forms of usage and expression in formal and non-formal situations. This means that the child's preoccupation away from the classroom situation is also essential for the development of vocabulary. It is based on this backdrop that the researcher studies games and play activities as a major preoccupation of the child's normal activities. The question is after spending long periods in play activities, do children have opportunity of being exposed to tasks that have specific relevance to specific vocabulary development in English Language?

## Purpose and Significance of the Study

This study surveys descriptively the pupils' frequency of playing various kinds of games. It further assesses the relevance of these games to the performance of specific vocabulary development tasks in English language.

The findings of this study will greatly inform instructors, parents and other education resource providers on how to guide and control children's engagement in playing games for meaningful instructional gains.

Curriculum designers will also be concerned about the need to incorporate specific games for specific vocabulary development tasks.

## Research Questions

The following research questions were answered in the study.

1. What is the frequency of primary six pupils' involvement in playing various kinds of games?
2. Do games played by primary six pupils show relevance to specific vocabulary development task.

### Hypothesis

One hypothesis was formulated for the study:

Primary six pupils do not significantly differ in their mean score ratings for relevance of computer games and non-computer games to their performance of specific vocabulary development task.

### Method

The study used the expost factor research design... The sample consisted of primary six pupils from Uyo Local Government Area (LGA) of Akwa Ibom State, Nigeria. The sample was selected through random sampling technique whereby six schools were selected out of thirteen public schools in Uyo. From each of the schools, the intact class of one stream of primary six was used where there was more than one. This resulted in a sample of 154 pupils.

### Instrumentation

A researcher developed instrument tagged: 'Play Activities for Vocabulary Development in English Language'(PAVDEL) The questionnaire PAVDEL had two sections A and B. Section A elicited information from pupils on their frequency of playing various game on a four point likert scale of very often (4) often (3) not often (2) never (1). Section B listed the different games coded with different numerical values: Computer games (6), video games (5) hand held device games (4) Board games (3) card games (2) local games (1). The pupils had to tick for each specific task, a game that enabled them to perform that task, which were twenty in number.

The instrument was assessed for content validity by the researcher's colleagues from the disciplines of Test and Measurement, Instructional Design and English Language Education in the Faculty of Education, University of Uyo. The reliability test for the instrument was established using Cronbach Alpha consistency estimate. An appropriate reliability coefficient of 0.84 was obtained.

**Data Analysis**

The data gathered using PAVDEL was collated and mean scores; standard deviation and independent t-test were used to answer the research questions and hypothesis. The mean scores of the pupils' responses to the frequencies of how often they played various games (section A) were computed and a decision rule established. Accordingly, a mean score of 2.50 and above indicated high frequency and 2.49 and below indicated low frequency. In section B a mean score of 3.50 above indicated high performance of specific took for development of vocabulary and 3.49 and below indicated low performance of specific tasks for vocabulary development. The t-test statistic was used to determine the significant difference in specific vocabulary development tasks in the course of playing various games. The games for this study are categorized as computer games (computer games, video games and hand held device games) and non-computer games (board games, card games and local games).

# Results

**Research Question One:** What is the frequency of primary six pupils' involvement in various play activities?

**Table 1: Mean and standard deviation on the frequency of how often primary six pupils play various games.**

| S/N | Types of Games | Mean | SD | Frequency of playing various games |
|-----|----------------|------|------|------------------------------------|
| 1 | Computer Games | 2.36 | 0.85 | LOW |
| 2 | Video Games | 3.32 | 0.95 | LOW |
| 3 | Other Hand Held Devices | 3.48 | 0.78 | HIGH |
| 4 | Board Games | 2.42 | 0.51 | HIGH |
| 5 | Cord Games | 3.38 | 0.80 | HIGH |
| 6 | Local Games | 3.64 | 0.48 | HIGH |

Table 1 presents mean scores and standard deviation of the pupils' responses to their frequency rate of playing various games. The table shows that the pupils highest levels of frequencies were non-computer games followed by hand held game devices (3.64, SD 0.48;

3.48, SD 0.78; 3.38, SD-0.80); while they exhibited low frequencies to computer games (2.42, SD 0.51) and video games (2.36, SD -0.85).

**Table 2: Mean and standard Deviation Data on Relevance of Games played by primary six pupils to specific vocabulary development task in English Language**

| S/No | Vocabulary Development Task | Mean | SD | Mean | SD | t-cal |
|---|---|---|---|---|---|---|
| 1. | Spell words | 4.57 | 0.57 | 4.56 | 0.57 | 0.14 |
| 2. | Mention names of objects | 3.50 | 0.67 | 3.04 | 0.98 | 2.82 |
| 3. | Fill in missing words | 4.43 | 0.65 | 4.35 | 0.68 | 0.41 |
| 4. | Cancel misspelt words | 4.42 | 0.70 | 4.03 | 0.79 | 1.46 |
| 5. | Rearrange letters to form words | 4.53 | 0.58 | 4.41 | 0.76 | 0.99 |
| 6. | Connect objects to their sounds | 4.43 | 0.71 | 4.24 | 0.71 | 1.04 |
| 7. | Resound words in games | 4.82 | 0.70 | 4.31 | 0.72 | 2.08 |
| 8. | Make word chains | 4.29 | 0.59 | 3.22 | 0.85 | 2.49 |
| 9. | Say names of birds | 3.26 | 1.08 | 4.21 | 0.65 | 2.74 |
| 10. | Say names of animals | 4.00 | 0.77 | 3.28 | 1.01 | 3.22 |
| 11. | Say names of fishes | 4.05 | 0.68 | 3.19 | 0.88 | 3.40 |
| 12. | Say different ways of greetings | 4.41 | 0.66 | 3.96 | 0.81 | 2.65 |
| 13 | Perform actions on words | 3.19 | 1.04 | 2.96 | 0.88 | 2.91 |
| 14. | Write shopping list | 2.28 | 0.90 | 2.21 | 1.04 | 0.29 |
| 15. | Group words by families | 4.62 | 1.03 | 3.77 | 0.83 | 2.62 |
| 16. | Follow directions in games | 4.25 | 0.78 | 4.22 | 0.70 | 0.22 |
| 17. | Sing rhymes | 4.06 | 0.59 | 3.20 | 0.88 | 3.40 |
| 18. | Say names of fruits | 4.08 | 1.01 | 4.13 | 0.78 | 0.19 |
| 19. | Tell stories | 2.42 | 0.72 | 2.23 | 0.71 | 1.05 |
| 20. | Form syllable, prefix and suffix | 3.29 | 0.90 | 3.21 | 1.03 | 0.28 |

Overall cal t-score =2.71; $P< 0.05$, Degree of freedom = 152, critical t score = 2.60

**Research Question Two**: Do games played by primary six pupils show relevance to specific vocabulary development task.

The finding on Table 2 indicate that many of the items show high mean scores above the cut-of-point of 3.50 for specific vocabulary tasks derived from both computer games and non-computer games. For non-computer games, only five items fell below cut-of-point. These include task such as; mention names of birds, perform actions of words, write shopping list, tell stories and form syllables, suffices and prefixes (3.26, 3.19, 2.28, 2.42,

3.29) respectively. Then for tasks pupils perform through computer games, nine items fell below 3.50. these include; mention names of objects, make word chains, mention names of animals, mention names of fishes, perform actions of words, write shopping list, sing rhymes, tell stories and form syllables, suffixes and prefixes. The results here indicate that tasks relevant to vocabulary development are performed more by pupils who play non-computer games than those who play computer games.

**Hypothesis**: Primary six pupils do not differ significantly in their mean score ratings of their performance of specific vocabulary development tasks based on computer games and non-computer games.

On the table two, the calculated t-values of items that show significant difference are 2.82, 2.68, 2.74, 3.22, 3.40, 2.65, 2.91, 2.62 and 3.40 accordingly for the following items: mention names of objects; resound words, mention names of birds, mention names of animals; mention names of fishes, say different ways of greetings, perform actions of words; group words into families and sing rhymes. The null hypothesis of no significant difference in mean score rating was therefore rejected for the nine items listed above. However, it was retained for the remaining eleven items on specific tasks for vocabulary development.

On the whole, the overall calculated t-value was 2.71 which exceeded the critical value of 2.60. Thus the hypothesis of no significant difference in means score ratings of specific tasks on vocabulary development based on various games was rejected. This implies that pupils perform more specific tasks on vocabulary development in non-computer games than computer games considering the mean score ratings.

## Discussion

The findings of this study on games children play and specific vocabulary development tasks they can perform through the games point back to the facts expressed in relevant literature. Children play games that are at their disposal and the ones they can create for the fun they derive from the game with little or no considerations for educational benefits not to talk of specific instructional tasks. Generally the fun the children derive from the game is primary while other benefits are secondary.

The findings that pupils indicated high frequency for non-computer games and low frequency for computer games is in line with Adura (2014) who argued that children will naturally create fun activities with what is readily available and accessible. The games categorized as computer games could be out of the reach of the pupils and as such children will fall back on non-computer games to fill the gap for their play activities. This will also affect the frequency at which they engage in the computer games. Nyere (2004) supports the fact that there are educationally designed computer games with knowledge base in all subject areas but the cost of these games could deter children from benefitting from its instructional value.

The null hypothesis which stated that there was no significant difference between the mean scores of specific vocabulary development tasks performed by pupils who play computer games and those who played non-compute games was rejected. This implies that one group has more exposure to games that expose them to specific vocabulary development tasks. This is in line with Ekukinam (2003) who confirmed that local play activities have instructional values that can enhance learning in various subject areas. Adura (2015) adds that children turn what they learn in the classroom into play activities. This may come in form of rhymes, listing and naming various objects, outdoing each other in spelling competitions, telling stories, role playing various characters which at times requires using the exact words of the character being imitated. These non-computer play activities motivate and challenge the players into better performance in the classroom. Thus, apart from the formal method of learning new vocabulary through reading and comprehension, children have the opportunity of gaining new words and reinforcing already learnt words in their field of play.

## Conclusion

The twenty specific tasks considered in this study are important behavioral task that can enhance pupils' vocabulary development in English Language. The findings reveal that pupils play activities especially the computer games do not offer them exposure to these tasks. This is a pointer to the fact that the hand held game devices that children can afford may not have the required instructional value in the area of vocabulary development. The educational video and computer games are not accessible. The children fall back on their local play activities and the ones they can create which still points to the gap created by an imbalance of the types of games the pupils assess.

## Recommendations

It is therefore recommended that a conscious effort should be made to provide a proper blend of both computer games and non-computer games which are rich in experiences that can help children build up their vocabulary. Parents, teachers and other stakeholders of education should guide children on the kinds of games to play for practice and reinforcement of knowledge and skills acquired during the formal learning situation. Teachers should not shy away from incorporating play activities in the teaching learning session.

# References

Adenaiye, A. (2016). Nigeria: The Negative Impact of Video Games on Children. *Daily Trust* (Abuja) 10th October, 2014.

Adura, B. A. (2015). Informal play Activities and Development of Literacy Skills. *Proceedings of 2015 Conference for Child Care and Development.* Accra, Ghana

Amaka, I. C. (2013). Computer technology in Nigerian Secondary School Education: Problems and Prospects. *Journal of Resourcefulness and Distinction.* Vol. 6, No. 1, Dec. 2013

Baid, H. & Lambert, N.(2010). Enjoy Learning: The Role of Humour, Games and Fun Activities in Nursing and Midwifery Education Today, 30(6): 548-552

Crawford, C. (2004). Art of Computer Game Design. Available at: http//www.vancouver. wsu.edu/fac/pabody/game-book.Date accessed 27th January, 2017

Edith, M. O. (2014). Setting goals and placing limits on children's preoccupation with computer games. *Newsletter on Literacy resources enhancement Tips. Global Education Network.*

Elder, J. (n.d). How much do you know about vocabulary? In; *Entry ways into College Reading and learning.* Chapter 3.

Ekpo, C. M. & Ekukinam, T. U. (1998). Adapting local plays as valuable resource materials for junior primary school pupils: Implications for the Nigerian educational system. *Journal of Curriculum and Instruction (NACT),* 7(3) Nov.

Ekukinam, T. U. (2010). Figure-out game: Medium for integrating Nigerian youths into emerging national innovations. *Proceedings of 31st Annual Conference and Convention of Nigeria Association for Educational Media and Technology* held at College of Education, Minna, Niger State.

Ekukinam, T. U. (2003). Using local games for the acquisition of science skills by junior primary school pupils in Akwa Ibom State. A Book of Readings: Strategies for Effective Teaching and Learning of Science, Technology and Mathematics (STM) Education.

Federal Government of Nigeria (2013). *National Policy on Education.* 6th ed., Abuja: NERDC Press

Gee, J. P. (2004). *What Video Games have to teach us about Learning and Literacy.* New York: Palgrave, Macmillan.

Glenberg, A. M., Guiterrz, T., Levin, J. R. Japuntic, S., & Kaschak, M. P. (2004). Activity and Imagined Activity Can Enhance Young Children's Reading Comprehension. *Journal of Educational Psychology,* 96, 424-436.

Heinich, R., Molenda, M. Russel, J. D., & Smaldino, S. E. (2000). *Media and Technology for Learning.* New Jersey: Pearson Education, Inc.

Lave, J. & Wenger, E. (1991). *Situated Learning, Legitimate Peripheral Participation.* Cambridge: University of Cambridge Press.

Loraine, S. (2008) Vocabulary Development. *Super Duper publications,* No. 149. Retrieved from: www.superduperinc.com. 27th January, 2017.

Nagle, R. (2001). Enrichment games and instructional design: can game based learning transfer to other domains? Retrieved at: http//www.imaginary planet.net/essays/literary/games/games6.php. Assessed 27th January, 2017

Noemi, P. and Maximo, S. H. (2014).Educational Games for Learning. *Universal Journal of Educational Research* 2(3), 230-238, Bilbao, Spain.

Nyere, S. J. (2016). Strategies for Improving Vocabulary Development at the Primary School Level. *Journal of Educational Research and Development.* 67-73, Ethiopia. U-TEP publications.

Oblinger, D. (2006) Simulations, Games, and Learning. http://www.cameron.edu/~lindas/DianaOblingerSimsGamesLearning.pdf

Prensky, M. (2006) presentation at the 2006 EDUCAUSE Learning Initiative (ELI) Annual Meeting, Retrieved January, 27th, 2017 http://www.educause.edu/upload/presentations/ELI061

Yao, A. (2018). Board Games. Retrieved from https://www.pcgamer.com>board games

Zigler, E. F., Singer, D.G. and Bishop-Joset, S. J. (2004). Children's play, the Roots of Reading. Washington, DC, USA. Zero to Three National Center for Infants, Toddlers and Families.

Printed in the United States
By Bookmasters